The New Human in Literature

Also available from Bloomsbury

Mapping World Literature: International Canonization and Transnational Literatures by Mads Rosendahl Thomsen
The Transformative Humanities: A Manifesto by Mikhail Epstein
Beyond Human: From Animality to Transhumanism edited by Charlie Blake
How Literature Changes the Way We Think by Michael Mack

The New Human in Literature

Posthuman Visions of Changes in Body, Mind and Society after 1900

Mads Rosendahl Thomsen

B L O O M S B U R Y

LONDON • NEW DELHI • NEW YORK • SYDNEY

Bloomsbury Academic

An imprint of Bloomsbury Publishing Plc

50 Bedford Square	1385 Broadway
London	New York
WC1B 3DP	NY 10018
UK	USA

www.bloomsbury.com

Bloomsbury is a registered trade mark of Bloomsbury Publishing Plc

First published 2013

British Library Cataloguing-in-Publication Data
A catalogue record for this book is available from the British Library.

ISBN: HB: 978-1-4411-8319-4
ePub: 978-1-4411-1406-8
ePDF: 978-1-4725-3125-4

Library of Congress Cataloging-in-Publication Data
A catalog record for this book is available from the Library of Congress.

Typeset by Fakenham Prepress Solutions, Fakenham, Norfolk NR21 8NN
Printed and bound by CPI Group (UK) Ltd, Croydon, CR0 4YY

Contents

Acknowledgements

I would like to thank Hans Ulrich Gumbrecht for once again being there; Tore Rye Andersen and Peter Simonsen for carefully crafted responses; Jørn Erslev Andersen and Svend Erik Larsen for being great readers and colleagues; Christian Borch, Johanne Helbo Bøndergaard, Sébastien Doubinsky and Marie Hastrup Sørensen for putting their skills and knowledge into their readings; David Damrosch, Francis Fukuyama and Stelarc for stimulating and vital critique on the book's framework; Henning Goldbæk, Peter C. Kjærgaard, Verner Møller and Martin Puchner for good directions; Michaela Scioscia for working with my words as well as my ideas. Thanks also to my co-editors of *The Posthuman Condition: Ethics, Aesthetics and Politics of Biotechnological Challenges*, based on the 2010 conference with the same title, Kasper Lippert-Rasmussen and Jacob Wamberg; the participants in the conference and contributors to the conference volume; Michael Bøss for creating opportunities, Hans Henrik Plauborg for getting me into gear; The Aarhus University Research Foundation for financial support; colleagues and students at Aarhus University for providing a splendid *millieu*; and the students in class in the fall of 2011 for bearing with my interests. A special thanks to the Bloomsbury Academic staff for support in all aspects of the process, in particular to David Avital, Colleen Coalter, Laura Murray and Mark Richardson. Most of all thanks to my parents, my wife Lene and our sons Marcus and Jonathan for giving me all a human can hope for.

Introduction

If our world survives, the next great challenge to watch out for will come
– you heard it here first – when the curves of research and development in
artificial intelligence, molecular biology and robotics all converge. Oboy.
It will be amazing and unpredictable, and even the biggest of brass, let us
devoutly hope, are going to be caught flat-footed.

Thomas Pynchon: 'Is It O.K. To Be A Luddite?'

There are manifold and diverse reasons for writing a book on the new human in literature since 1900, but one of them should be very obvious: that is, the horizon of the possible, radical changes to the human species made possible by biotechnology. This is the result of the constantly accelerating invention of techniques that may be able to influence and change the genetic makeup of plants, animals and humanity itself. The technological developments have also increasingly integrated interactions between humans and machines, in another open-ended and potentially accelerating process. Furthermore, speculation regarding whether artificial intelligence could become superior to human intelligence is becoming less and less a topic of science fiction, and increasingly part of a realistic scenario for the future.

These developments have also placed the idea of posthuman and transhuman[1] beings on the research agenda, across a number of disciplines. This is a theme loaded with ethical questions, and the topic appears in disciplines such as medicine, law, philosophy, sociology and the arts, because the idea of the posthuman foregrounds questions regarding what constitutes the human. It also makes it clear that a definition of 'the human' is by no means easy to derive or to do without.[2]

It is not difficult to see a sharpened conflict between regarding the human as the being which is the most valued, as is overwhelmingly reflected by cultural structures, religion, laws, and philosophy, and the values of progress supported by the imperfection and sufferings of humanity as it is now constituted. At the same time, it is important to keep in mind that any idea of a first 'new' human entails the idea that some will be the last humans. A field of tension is created, where all the positive and negative traits of two conditions may be brought to light: imperfect, but familiar and slowly evolved humanity, versus a not-yet-extant, 'improved', and perhaps frightening posthumanity.

Until the mid–1990s, the term 'posthuman' was rarely used,[3] but it has since established itself across a number of disciplines.[4] The posthuman horizon is not likely to go away, and this book, like many others, is written *in media res* of a process that many would prefer to have avoided. However, these developments can hardly be ignored, but it is not certain whether they can be controlled.[5] Ethics and emotions propelled by visions of the future collide in this field, and some technologies even facilitate what Jürgen Habermas, in *The Future of Human Nature*, has called 'liberal eugenics', understood as the opportunity for people to make decisions regarding the genetics of their offspring by utilizing a number of new technologies for selecting and manipulating the fetus (Habermas 2003, 19).

The rapidity of the developments that affect us is illustrated by something that had not yet happened when this book was initially researched, nor was it part of imagined future discussions; namely, the imminent possibility of birth of children who technically have three parents (Hanlon 2012). By substituting small parts of the human genome with portions of DNA from a third person, three-parent humans are on the verge of becoming a reality, and the idea that our genetic codes are solely the combination of what two individuals have brought together (and a few mutations) no longer holds. Its practical conse-quences may be unnoticeable – apart from the prevention of disease, such children will mostly carry the traits of two persons – but the very idea of three parents makes a significant difference, philosophically.

The object of this book is to demonstrate how literature, particularly fiction, contributes to creating a richer and more complex idea of the contexts and issues arising from the idea of a posthuman or new human, and that the idea of the new human is not just something that relates to technology, but has a long history of fascinating humanity. I use the term 'the new human' in a wider sense than 'the posthuman'. Whereas the latter refers to a break with the human species at a genetic level, the new human also covers idea of changes in human mindset and culture. I discuss the typology of human change in greater detail in chapters two and three.

The many political, ethical, and legal debates surrounding this field are not the primary focus of this study, but they are an inevitable part of the subject, just as the concrete developments of technology are shaping the horizon of thought at any given moment, by both constraining some visions of the future, and creating the opportunity for others.

In science fiction, as well as in other genres, it is evident that there are many engaging, uncanny, imaginative, impossible, but also realistic ideas concerning the new human and the posthuman. While these are certainly worth examining in the context of this theme, as has been done by a number of scholars,[6] there are less obvious works of twentieth century literature that may be of even greater interest. The readings of works that do not present a clear vision of a transformed humanity risk stretching the argument of human transformation, and over-interpreting vague signs, but apart from their broader circulation, compared to that of much of science fiction, they offer the opportunity to examine more subtle links between 'old human' identity and visions of change, and to see how a number of related questions concerning the relationships between individual and collective, normality and improvement, and memory and future, find different expressions in ways that perhaps only literature can articulate.

An eerily far-seeing Mary Shelley contributed to the embodiment of visions of both a new and a last human, in two novels. She wrote at another time in history, when imaginings about the creation of life could be invoked without many of the constraints set on us by modern science, and when numerous technical achievements that we now take for granted were unimaginable. Her most renowned work, *Frankenstein, or the Modern Prometheus*, is known by many more people than those who have read the novel about the creation of a new being by assembling parts from other humans. This is accomplished by a method Victor Frankenstein does not reveal in detail, and which in popular adaptations happens through the force of lightning. Shelley was of course not obligated to scientific realism in this creation of new life, but recounted events as they might take place.

Today, several aspects of the novel stand out clearly: it is remarkable how the technical capacity to manipulate cells, genes and body parts far exceeds what is suggested in Shelley's fiction, although the creation of life in the fashion Shelley describes exceeds what is currently possible. Even more important and worth examining than the technical details are the surroundings in which Shelley sets her new being. The nameless being is a new human that cannot be integrated into society, but has been deemed – also by the public discourse that comprises a considerable portion of the extended life of the book and by himself – a monster. This again draws attention to the limits of normality, of what distinguishes a human from other beings, and of what a society is willing to tolerate. All this plays out in a nuanced way in Shelley's book, to which I will return in a later chapter.

The end of *Frankenstein* does not suggest a continuation of Frankenstein's experiments, but expresses hope for a return to normality, where the world can continue almost undisturbed. The illusion of such an undisturbed continuation is probably something that few today consider, faced with the developments of biotechnology and its influence on the future. As Shelley's work also demonstrates, the question of the evolution of humanity must be viewed in a larger social context. This stance is also central to another literary classic involving a radical change in humanity, Aldous Huxley's *Brave New World*, which chronicles a future in which humanity is divided into clearly distinct groups, some of which are clearly deprived of what might be considered human dignity.

A relatively less known novel by Shelley, *The Last Man*, describes a twenty-first-century apocalypse caused by epidemics and natural disasters. The protagonist, Lionel Verney, becomes the last human being, without any hints of a possible posthuman future, and thus the end is more like a whimper than a violent devastation of humanity. Variations on this sort of thinking about the end of humankind have dominated human imagination and cultural history, and are not without a basis in other developments. Since the middle of the twentieth century, toward the end of the Cold War, the possibility of a nuclear Armageddon was a real threat to the continued existence of humanity. Lately, ecological catastrophes and long-term scenarios of an Earth without humans have become parts of the collective imagination (Weisman 2007), but the posthuman remains a problematic and usually unnerving figure.

Ever since the second half of the nineteenth century, when Charles Darwin's theories established a new agenda for discussions about the order of nature, there has been a scientific basis for discussing future human evolution, but it is a discussion that, interestingly enough, has been taken up neither broadly nor intensely; understandably, as human evolution by natural means is too slow to be really significant, but even so, a logical consequence of Darwin's theory would be to envision an ongoing evolution of the human into more categories of humanoids than the one we know today. While Darwin did not describe humanity as the endpoint of natural history, his speculation did not extend beyond it either, and, given the broad public awareness of the kinship of Homo sapiens to now-extinct members of hominid family, it is remarkable how much public debate has, for a number of reasons, shied away from imagining what Homo sapiens could become.[7]

Technology has changed the idea of reliance on natural selection, and, for better or worse, promises much more rapid changes. The idea of a Homo evolutis, put forward in the book of the same title by Juan Enriquez and Steve Gullans, is a provocative, yet in many ways well-founded vision of how humanity might change because of its technical ability to influence selection, incorporate advanced technology, and ultimately change its genetic base through gene manipulation. In *Before the Dawn*, Nicholas Wade presents a similar argument, first by pointing out how strange it would be if humans ceased to evolve as they have done for millennia (Wade 2006, 276). Second, he tries to sum up the pathways of humanity, according to two related choices. One is between natural and directed evolution, which may take on many forms. The other choice is in many ways much more troubling, namely, whether speciation should be allowed, or even promoted (Wade 2006, 278). Enriquez and Gullans argue that the existence of a single humanoid species is not a given, and like them, Wade points out that humanity most likely killed off their kindred species in prehistoric times (Wade 2006, 279; Enriquez and Gullans 2010, Chapter 1). Biologist Richard Dawkins seeks some sort of re-enchantment in the theory of evolution, an aspect to which I will return, but he is also a humanist who balances the joy of the possible occurrence of the unexpected with a pronounced discomfort with interference with the essential aspects of humanity. He envisions chimeras, hybrids between humans and chimpanzees, or even the discovery of a branch of hominids that might profoundly change our world view, while hoping that these particular examples will not materialize (Dawkins 2009b, 19).

While Dawkins, Wade, Enriquez and Gullans' conjectures are informed by recent technical developments, the idea of the new human is by no means new, but has taken quite different forms, historically. During the great explorations of the late fifteenth century, 'the new human' was used to designate those encountered by the Europeans, who, owing to their real or alleged practice of cannibalism, for example, presented a radical otherness to the Europeans, and thus were the objects of extensive myth making. Eventually, this myth making declined through increased interaction between cultures, more complex descriptions emerged, and this rhetoric of the new human lost its meaning in a wider perspective, but it has been evoked at various time for political reasons (Palencia-Roth 1985, 22). The idea of a united humanity with equal rights was, in practice, far from being realized, considering the extent of the violence perpetrated from the age of imperialism through the genocides of the twentieth century.

Humanity's development of a new self-understanding has been thematized as the creation of a new human since the Renaissance, when the anthropocentric view yielded a series of attempts to define the human in new ways. With reference to the writers of the period, Andy Mousley has collected a series of attempts at a definition of the human from the Renaissance, comprising the following elements: a sense of superiority with regard to other species, the capacity for self-development, having an inner life, individuality, the will to create societies, an interest in all things human, as opposed to all things divine, the ability to use literature to give life to moral truths, and finally, possessing an epistemology that relies on human and natural causes, rather than divine ones. All these elements are interconnected in various ways, and one should also consider that the human has never been defined simply and monolithically. Mousley's argument goes on to point out that, no humanism has ever been able to cease redescribing humans, in defiance of the restrictions on what humans can be or become (Mousley 2010, 250; Badmington 2010, 374).[8] This view of humanity as evolving is at the heart of posthumanist thought.

While Shelley's new human has a short life on Earth, and her last man really is the last man without successors, Friedrich Nietzsche envisions something after Homo sapiens (Nietzsche 2006, 6; Nietzsche 1968, 519). His widely misunderstood concept of the superman primarily refers to a progression of moral norms, where many of the self-inflicted restrictions on humanity have been discarded. A much more cautious rhetoric was brought forth by George Orwell, for example, who, in an early draft of *Nineteen Eighty-Four*, had entitled the work *The Last Man in Europe*, with reference to the possibility of changing society so radically that human dignity would be lost. As much as anything, the last man is the bearer of the values produced by cultures over centuries.

In recent years, more pressure is being brought to bear on the idea of the human from a different perspective. Whereas 'posthuman' suggests a transcendence toward a new mode of being, the idea of 'posthumanism' signals a shift in the mode of thinking about humankind's place in the universe, particularly its place among other species on the planet. The concept of posthumanism further adds to the complexity of the field, as the discourses of the posthuman and posthumanism may be at odds with one another, and in some respects bring together humanism and the posthuman, in an advocacy for solidarity among people, and the advancement of the species.[9]

It is not difficult to present humans as imperfect beings with many vices, and to compose a long history of more than questionable acts. Humans have also demonstrated a remarkable ability to repeatedly justify their morals and habits, even though human beings may themselves judge former eras harshly.[10] One could hold that it makes no sense to put humanity on a pedestal and regard it as a collection of beings with an absolute or special worth. This perspective on humanity may be perceived as controversial, both with regard to religious convictions, and to the humanism that has shaped progressive thinking for the past few centuries.

Positive and negative views of humanity are not irreconcilable, but will always remain parts of the complex descriptions of past, present and future, when uneven time-frames may muddle discussions by introducing long-term perspectives on what humans have been and could become, when debating political issues with short-term consequences. But it is also unsatisfactory and escapist to not reflect on the history of humankind, and the changes that have taken place, most notably in knowledge, technology and morality, over the past two centuries.

In 'Ecce Homo, Ain't (Ar'n't) I a Woman, and Inappropriate/d Others: The Human in the Post-Humanist Landscape', Donna Haraway mentions notable attempts in the twentieth century to define the human. One is the 'Declaration of Human Rights' of 1948, which, from a legal point of view, assigns all humans a series of fundamental rights, not least of which the right to dignity (Haraway 2004, 48f.). This is also a declaration written at a time when the atrocities of war signaled one of the all-time lows, in terms of respect for human life. More interestingly, it is a declaration written during a time when the idea of human evolution was not influenced by new technologies, and when religious under-pinnings were not an essential part of the argument.

A second large-scale attempt to define humanity took place through the mapping of the human genome, which was completed in 2003, and has a biological point of view, rather than a legal one. The consequences and interpretations of this project are manifold. Humanity's close relationship to (other) great apes has become even more evident, but despite a 98.4 per cent similarity between the genetic codes between the species, the differences in intelligence and humanity's ability to produce an advanced culture remain significant and obvious. The human genome project has also given rise to ideas of finding genes of central importance to the development of both biological and social traits, even though there is a rising awareness of the complex interplay among different genes, which makes it very difficult to make conclusive statements about individuals. The task of defining humanity may seem like an endless task of defining borders, as Eileen Joy and Craig Dionne have argued:

The human *self* may be an increasingly indefensible subject, both because of its ethno- and phallogocentrism, but also because it lacks any kind of real 'center' or 'unity' and only really becomes legible when it is mapped as a kind of embodied, yet also *distributed* cognition that is always part-human, part-something else; nevertheless, how different *singular persons* in different times and places manage, and have managed, to compose a sense of self (or 'I') in the face of struggles over agency, expression, embodiment, identity, well-being, resources, community and the like still matters a great deal and likely always will […] (Joy and Dionne 2010, 3)

Part of the fascinating and troubling aspect of devising a definition of a human is that it is not a problem of everyday life. We can easily recognize a human when we see one, and we should be able to do so far into the future.[11] But this strong kernel of everyday knowledge about what constitutes humanity is challenged by borderline cases that may increase in number. The difference between fetus and human is accepted widely in law, but particularly in the United States, remains at the heart of heated debates about when something becomes a human being. The cyborg, the genetically modified human being, the chimera, are expressions of a number of scenarios that may be foreseen, if not as existing in real life, then as possibilities that might force humanity to decide whether or not it will tolerate such beings. Some of the issues are distant and some are imminent, but they are, at any rate, interlinked.

Objects and theses

The motifs of the new and the last human have a limited range in art and literature. Most art, literature and philosophy do not address these topics at all, and the literary works that I will be analyzing could also be contextualized and interpreted according to different guiding interests. However, the ideas of the new human and the posthuman are themes in art, literature and philosophy that enable us to confront central questions concerning human identity and history, at a time when technological development has revealed a new horizon that will come closer over time. As this development sheds new light on older ideas of human nature, humankind's ability to transcend itself and its need for history and society become apparent. The new human is a motif that entails both positive and negative elements, and grounds for optimism and pessimism, as it is connected to ideas of development, progress and enhancement, as well as loss of identity, uncontrollable situations and a looming dystopian future.

The current relevance of the topic is reflected in mainstream and popular culture. Movies such as *Blade Runner, Limitless, The Matrix* trilogy and *Immortal* present visions of improvement on, and unlimited, human capacities. It is also striking that James Cameron's *Avatar*, set in 2154, was able to capture an audience large enough to make it the highest grossing movie ever. Cameron's film is no masterpiece, although it pushes the technical possibilities of cinematography, yet in its thematization of the new human, it is exemplary. On the one hand, it explores the technical possibilities of changing humankind in a future scenario that may be regarded as dystopian, and which, according to Daniel Mendelsohn, is also an expression of how, in this film, Cameron apparently values the idea of resistance among cyborgs and robots more than humanity itself (Mendelsohn 2010, 12). At the same time, it is remarkable how the film's fascination with technology and the ability to produce chimeras are countered by references to older human cultures, thereby carrying an anti-colonial and ecological message (Mendelsohn 2010, 13).

Both the creation and expression of the movie are influenced by the erosion of the distinction between real and virtual, which is one of the characteristics of the digital age, and the technical aspects of the movie itself are a part of its message that is almost certainly familiar to every moviegoer. But the world view presented by the Na'vi people of the planet Pandora is akin to Jean-Jacques Rousseau's call for a return to nature (Theweleit 2010). It is very likely that this duality between ecological thinking and technological potential, spun around a materialization of the limits of humanity, accounts for a significant part of the movie's appeal to a broad audience. *Avatar* provides characters that provoke fundamental questions regarding what a human being is, what its relation to nature should be, what a culture is, how the past should be made accessible and tangible, and above all, what to hope and fear for the future.

This study explores literature's response to some of the many complex questions that have been presented above, and which will be addressed more extensively on the following pages. I believe that there are a number of ways in which literature and other arts make valuable contributions to the debates surrounding the posthuman, of which modes of reflection are not, or are less capable. Central are literature's capacity to 1) scrutinize the potential for re-enchantment and risk of alienation, 2) connect individuality and collectivity in a coherent artistic rendition, 3) connect ethical questions and aesthetic expression, and 4) include cultural or collective memory in a presentation of the complexities of human existence. Hopefully, the analyses along these lines will also have the side-effect of revealing how a constellation of literary works present fresh nuances, and gain new actuality after being seen in the light of other visions of human change.

While each of the foregoing points resonated throughout the twentieth century, a central thesis of this study is that the subject of the new human must be divided into three principal phases in the twentieth century. At the beginning the twentieth century, following Nietzsche, the idea of a spiritual modernization or a shift in consciousness was a widely held ambition, hope, or observation of how humanity had changed. This was followed by a political use of this idea in the middle of the twentieth century, often directly using the rhetoric of the new human in a number of societies, in ways that frequently had catastrophic outcomes. Finally, toward the end of the twentieth century, a new horizon appeared, where the human biological heritage was seen as an instrument for the creation of a new human, and within this horizon, the significance of earlier visions of the new human also changed. That is not to say that there have not been visionaries who broke with this tripartite division – as I will make clear later – yet I hold that these have been the dominant positions in the thinking about human change that match the division suggested by this study. The three main lines of the visions of human change determine the chronology of the readings of the works in this study. Different lines could have been drawn; for example, one based on the subjects of aesthetics and ethics, individuality and collectivity, and cultural memory and human transformation, but the structure chosen here will give the clearest possible presentation of a subject that addresses the interests of both cultural and literary history.

It is possible to question whether the three perspectives on mind, society and body fit together as one unit, given their historically and technologically complex and differing standing. The vision of a biologically altered transhuman is far easier to define and present than breaks with the past, in the form of changes in consciousness and culture. A cyborg with an unimaginably large memory or a human who does not undergo the natural process of aging is different from, and more tangible than a new organization of society and its influence on humans. I will argue that, at any given point in time, the intertwining of consciousness, sociality, and biology is crucial to the historical view of change, to literature's descriptions of effected and envisioned change, and ultimately, to how humanity views itself and its future. Humanity's desire to transcend itself, and its equally great desire to remain itself, form a fundamental conflict that unfolds in all three modes of envisioning human change, and gives relevance to the consideration of the subject of human change as a united field with different perspectives and historical conditions from which to consider the kinds of changes that could occur or be avoided.

Returning to the points sketched out above, this study's goal is to demonstrate how literature, based on its rootedness in cultural history, contributes to specific ways of thinking about transcendence, by probing these five theses:

1 *Both alienation and the possibility of a re-enchantment of the world are important reactions to the visions of a change in human identity.* One of the most forceful aspects of the idea of the posthuman is that it entails radical alienation, owing to a possible future scenario wherein life as it is lived today will diminish in value, and elements that define human dignity may be jeopardized. On the other hand, both the arts and theories dominating the visions of a future where humankind can interact proactively with the world at large, explore new vistas for further unfolding human potential. The contributions of literature have a long and ongoing history of cultural influence on visions of both alienation and re-enchantment.

2 *Literature has an extraordinary capacity to link the individual with the collective, in a transformation of the past and a vision of the future.* Human dependence on social interaction inevitably forms a part of any definition of humanity, while at the same time, the difference between individual and collective remains a division rife with conflict. This, both in terms of the influence and pressure that social systems impose on individuals, and ultimately, owing to the inevitability of the death of the individual, while society persists. Art and literature explore this conflict in numerous ways, with the genre of the *Bildungsroman* as a pertinent example, but with even greater relevance with regard to visions of a new human.

3 *Aesthetics possesses an ethical dimension, when it connects imperfection and beauty.* Many of the questions concerning human change, and the use of biotechnology, in particular, have been studied from the viewpoint of their ethical implications. Ideas for improvement entail questions about the essence of beauty, or how the good life may be lived, drawing on values and expressions that constitute a parallel to philosophy and religion, and are profoundly shaped by art, literature and other forms of aesthetic expression. In particular, modernist aesthetic values remain a dominant frame of reference, and provide unexplored arguments for a concept of beauty that does not entail perfection, but instead equates perfection with more mundane and complex aspects of human life, thereby leading the way for a more inclusive, and ultimately more ethical conception of aesthetics, which also embraces real complexities, rather than idealized perfection.

4 *Cultural memory is essential to making continuation and discontinuation work in the creation of a future-oriented identity.* There is evident potential in exploring how the use of cultural memory influences the shaping of visions of the future, with art and literature being the most complex media that provide configurations of such perspectives. The production of, and reflection on the continuity and discontinuity of the many aspects of human existence and history are vitally important to the creation of new visions of the future.

5 *The theme of the posthuman can reinvigorate the status and use of canonical works of art and literature.* Finally, the study of human change and the posthuman offers an approach to art and literature that may elicit new understandings of classical works. I will explore the works of a number of authors, and add new dimensions to our understanding of several seminal works. There is a need to reconsider how certain nodes of cultural memory shed light on the complex issues of human change, individuality and collective organization, sources of enchantment and the use of the past, and so demonstrate the advantages of an aesthetic approach encompassing past, present, and future.

In Part one, the first four points will be elaborated, while the demonstration of the fifth point depends on the persuasive power of the readings along the lines of the first four theses in parts two to four.

Exposition

This book is divided into four parts. Part one presents the historical and theoretical foundations of the subsequent three parts' analyses of representations of visions of the new human in literature since 1900.

Part one, 'The Triune Human', establishes a historical framework for the representation of the new human in the twentieth century, based on the shifting focuses on changes in mind, society and bodies. The division draws on Niklas Luhmann's theory, which is further discussed in order to provide one of many existing perspectives in the debates on human identity, and to emphasize the central role played by communication and societal systems in human evolution. This is followed by a historical overview of visions of human change and the methods for bringing about enhancement, even if the value of such enhancements may often be questioned. Both imagined and technically possible forms of change are addressed, which in many ways mirrors humanity's current situation, between immediate and applicable, incremental changes, and potential (if improbable), radical changes over a longer timescale. The chapter also discusses the role of literature and its capacity to deal with questions of change, in its critical role and limited capacity to affirm changes. Finally, the guiding theses that were sketched out above, and which are central to the analyses in parts two to four, will be elaborated.

Part two, 'Self-modernization', is a reading of seminal works from the first part of the twentieth century, with a focus on the conception of a changed state of mind, as evident in works by Virginia Woolf, William Carlos Williams and Louis-Ferdinand Céline. Here too, the works were chosen not so much for their full commitment to the idea of a new human, but for their complex and mixed emotions about the changes they envision, and the works' capacity to present these emotions in such a way that the literary form becomes part of the argument. This combination of literary strategies and an ambiguous stance on the relations between cultural memory and visions of the future is central to these works.

Part three, 'The Grand Projects', opens with an overview of the historical attempts to convert the rhetoric of the new human into profound and often radical efforts to change culture and society. Although the use of the rhetoric of the new human was not applied in all instances of twentieth century totalitarian catastrophes, it plays a more or less explicit role in various ideas of shaping society, and thereby changing human nature. However, the ambitions and promises were mostly countered by humanitarian disasters. Moreover, the ideas of cult-like, isolated creations of a new human species or significantly different cultures also played a prominent role in popular culture, and thus are part of a worldwide fascination with the new human created through societal change. The literature analyzed in this part addresses changes in society after the fact of having obtained a perspective on the gains and losses attributable to radical changes. Three influential authors address three different kinds of changes. In *Things Fall Apart*, Chinua Achebe portrays the intrusion of colonizers and missionaries into a traditional African culture, which, in less than a generation, changes everything in a process that is not planned, but instead leaves behind change as a side-effect of the influence of powerful interests. In contrast, Mo Yan describes the planned and forced changes to traditional Chinese communities and their dire consequences, particularly through the Great Leap Forward and the Cultural Revolution. Finally, there is the politically motivated, but not totalitarian Westernization of Turkey that took place after the First World

War and Kemal Atatürk's rise to power. The effect of the unfinished project of Westernization is a central issue in the works of Orhan Pamuk, particularly his autobiography, *Istanbul.*

Part four, 'The Final Frontier', concerns literature's responses to the horizon created by biotechnology, and visions of various changes directed at the human body, either in terms of genetic modification, as in cloning, or in terms of seamless interactions between humans and machines. The first chapter presents an overview of the ideas of human change in modern literature, including science fiction, in particular the works of Olaf Stapledon, Philip K. Dick, Octavia Butler and other authors of science fiction classics, as well as mainstream authors writing on the borders of the genre, such as Thomas Pynchon and Kazuo Ishiguro. Following this, two bodies of work will be analyzed: first, Don DeLillo and his range of future fantasies, which include annihilation in cyberspace, leaps of the human species into something more advanced, the use of biochemical products to mitigate the fear of death, and a fundamental skepticism regarding the future of human consciousness; second, Michel Houellebecq's combination of a critique of contemporary society, and visions of either a posthuman world created through genetic engineering, or the extensive use of cloning.

While in some respects the motif of the new human in literature is limited, in other respects it is extremely broad, and exceeds the scope of any single monograph. This book both presents a framework that might inspire analyses of other works, and explores specific works that are analyzed and understood in their own right. The selection of works and authorship is motivated by their relevance to the overarching topic of the representation of the new human in literature, but it must also be emphasized that they have not been selected on a merely thematic basis, but as works that problematize the ideas of change and the rise of a new human in ways that are most challenging, both as literature and as documents of cultural history. There are works that, for the purposes of this study, could have been substituted by others as it will be evident from a number of references.

The selection of works also reflects a gradual expansion of the world view in the international canons, about which I have written elsewhere (Thomsen 2008). While the early works dealing with changed human consciousness are bound to a European and American context, the works concerning the societal changes are from Africa, Asia, and the Middle East. The final section is dominated by European and American writers, but their works are embedded in a globalizing world, where information and bodies move faster than ever.

Science fiction is not at the centre of this study, not so much because of its marginal position in literature, and its general lack of recognition as a literary genre, but because it is my view that the most stimulating representations of the new human are not found in the most explicit and manifest descriptions of the new human, which are often constructed with a certain sensationalism and hyperbole. It is rather in the subtle demarcations of changes and desires that a substantial dialogue with our present occurs.

This study, like any other, builds on the work of a number of other contributions to the field of the new human and the posthuman. Some of these are studies of specific historical instances, such as Jochen Hellbeck's history of Soviet ideology, and Yinghong Cheng's analyses of the idea of new humans in communist societies. Other works are concerned with the ethical problems of the posthuman, such as those of Francis Fukuyama and Julian Savulescu. A third group of works are more direct precursors to this book, such as Elaine Graham's *Representations of the Post/Human*, N. Katherine Hayles's *How We Became Posthuman*, and Donna Haraway's work on the limits of the human, *vis-à-vis* both animals and cyborgs, although none of these works addresses the various modes of change to body, mind, and society, as this study does. Finally, Niklas Luhmann's work is important for its theory of identity and communication in societies.

Technological developments have created a new horizon that art and literature cannot and should not ignore. Cécile Alduy has put this into perspective by emphasizing the change from the days of high modernism to now, and asks what happens when what was thought of as impossible in the Surrealists' world, or in the world of Brueghel, becomes part of contemporary reality.[12] In literature, the situation is different from that of the other arts, but this new situation still alters the perspectives on the ideas of the *Doppelgänger* or a chimera, when such phenomena are no longer wild ideas conceived without any expectation of being brought into existence.

As I wrote at the outset, there are many dimensions to the field of posthuman visions and ideas of human evolution, and there are both short-term and long-term perspectives that influence our imaginations in various ways, and challenge societies to develop answers to the ethical questions that are raised. This book is written out of the conviction that even though not all developments can be controlled, their actual development is highly dependent on the level of reflection that occurs in societies. The capacity of individuals and societies alike to describe and imagine their past, present and future provides them with a greater capacity to adapt to and handle change. In this way, Hans Ulrich

Gumbrecht has described the interest in the past as providing a repertoire for thinking of the future in a more complex way (Gumbrecht 1997, 420ff.), and that is one of the key reasons that literature and others arts play significant roles in imagining the new human.

It is significant that Charles Darwin's theory of evolution established a world view that was non-deterministic, yet included a strong sense of aesthetic values (Darwin 1985, 459). Writing contemporaneously with Darwin, in *Notes from the Underground*, Fyodor Dostoyevsky wrote with great irony about the positivist ideas of being able to foresee the future and one day compile all the calculations of events to come in a great almanac (Dostoyevsky 1992, 19). That is not how things developed, and with the great discoveries in physics at the beginning of the twentieth century, most notably Albert Einstein's theory of relativity, and Niels Bohr's theory of quantum mechanics, the world proved to be much more complicated and, on a micro level, less mechanical than hitherto supposed. But in contrast to the situation a century and a half ago, technology plays a much larger role, and foregrounds the question of what humanity can become, between past and future, mind, body and society, and individual and collective. These are issues that literature continues to address without finding clear answers, but which are valuable in creating fiction in which sense and sensibility can meet.

Part One

The Triune Human

Definitions of what a human is have abounded at least as far back as the
ancient Greek philosophers, who established traditions for reflecting on and
systematizing thinking that remain valid today. As then, current definitions of
the human are bundled with different agendas related to metaphysics, belief
systems, ethics, politics and science. In everyday life, it is not difficult to distinguish humans from the rest of the world. In Philip K. Dick's fiction, filled with
replicas, discerning machines from humans is a problem, but that point has
not yet been reached, and may never be. However, contexts such as those Dick
presents give rise to very different ideas of what humans are, and what they
need. Definitions of the beginning and the end of human existence are central
to both ethics and religion, and the rights of humans are a constant theme in
politics. The hope of being able to scientifically specify what separates humans
from other species is challenged by the idea of ongoing human evolution, and
the long history of speciation that led to the unity of humankind we observe
today, which is at the heart of humanism.

There are many ways to approach the central question of what a human
is, and what might constitute a new human. As my starting point, I have
chosen the description of humans constituted by the juncture of the physical
body, linguistic awareness and social communication, which is central to the
work of the German sociologist Niklas Luhmann. This description provides a
foundation for the approach of the following analyses, and to my argument for
historicizing the new human since 1900, according to three dominant ideas of
change, namely those of the body, mind and society.

This chapter will introduce and discuss how Luhmann's theory relates to a
changing idea of identity, and how societal systems produce their ideas of what
a human is, which will also draw on the work of Francis Fukuyama, before

making the case, in Chapter 2, for how the shifting focus on body, mind and society structures a cultural history of human change since 1900, which in turn is fundamental to the division of the subsequent three parts of literary analysis. Chapter 3 addresses historical visions of human change and the practical possibilities for change, and the fourth chapter makes the case for areas in which literature makes a distinct contribution to the representation of, and thinking about the new human.

1

A Systemic View of the Human

Niklas Luhmann developed his systems theory into a wide-ranging and ambitious theory of sociology that continued to evolve until his death in 1998. Luhmann's theory is 'cold', in the sense that it primarily attempts to describe the world of human interaction and communication, rather than to bring about suggestions for improving the world. He was very open about this, for example, in his article 'The Individuality of the Individual', where he reminds the reader to be careful, that this is not an edifying theory that lauds human individuality, but merely states the conditions under which individuality may be described, while simultaneously doing away with all ideas of a privileged human reason or subjectivity (Luhmann 1990, 119).

In *What is Posthumanism?*, Cary Wolfe draws significantly on Luhmann's work, noting that systems theory has not been received warmly in the USA, particularly in the field of sociology, and he ascribes this to the seemingly disinterested descriptions of the world, which are often misunderstood. When Luhmann writes that people cannot communicate, only communication can, it really means that humans always interact via social systems (Wolfe 2010, 6). Luhmann's work has been much more influential in Germany and other European countries than in the English-speaking world, even though the original impulse that led Luhmann to systems theory came from American sociologist Talcott Parsons. However, it is also noteworthy that new works, such as W. J. T. Mitchell's and Mark B. N. Hansen's *Critical Terms for Media Studies* rely heavily on Luhmann's work, and that a leading scholar of cybernetics and posthuman theory, N. Katherine Hayles, has been greatly influenced by his theory of autopoietic systems.[13]

Luhmann's central work, his *Social Systems*, of 1984, was written in an attempt to reformulate the vocabulary of sociology, to align it with the world view, or rather, the analytical approach to the world for which Luhmann argues. The ability to recognize the existence of different kinds of dynamic communicative systems, and to be able to differentiate among them, is fundamental to this approach. Objects are not systems, because there is no processing of information in a stone or a book, in and of itself. A thermostat on a radiator is part of a system that can process information, but it is of a lower order than the systems in which Luhmann is interested, because even though a thermostat can react to its surroundings, it does not have the capacity to alter the way it reacts, and it has no conception of the difference between itself and its environment. This contrasts with autopoietic systems, which are aware of their own unity, even if the material that comprises it is gradually replaced. A well-known example of this is that the human organism replaces most of its cells over seven year cycles, while maintaining the ability to identity itself as a unity.[14]

The theory of autopoiesis was originally developed by biologists Humberto Maturana and Francisco Varela as a way of defining life, and to better describe how self-identity may be maintained over time in a system that changes its elements over time. This conception is also reminiscent of the way humans describe themselves as being the same, although they are changing. Luhmann's decisive step in his adaption of the biological theory of autopoiesis, and which is crucial in determining how far one can follow Luhmann, is his claim that human consciousness and human societies are also autopoietic systems that do not produce life as biological system do, but instead operate in terms of meaning, whether this is part of communication, or internally, in a mind. Meaning should not be confused with 'making sense' or similar versions of meaningfulness, but is merely a description of information that enables more information to be generated (Luhmann 1995, 59ff.).

Luhmann is not a Cartesian dualist in the sense that he believes there is a realm of meaning that is independent of material conditions, but he leaves it to others to solve what consciousness is, and treats it as an empirical reality and an emergent phenomenon that cannot be understood by claiming that the mind is part of the body.[15] For Luhmann, the human consists of two systems that are mutually dependent, but operate at different levels. The body creates life, whereas the mind creates meaning. This dualism in the description of human beings is not necessarily widely acceptable, and the separation of body and mind is not as central as Luhmann's model suggests, just as his theory fully acknowledges what he calls 'interpenetrations' between unlike systems. It is probable that few would seriously claim that they experience no difference between their mind and body, even if the human is one biological entity. Scholars drawing on the work of Maurice Merleau-Ponty might also stress the interrelatedness of body and mind, and criticize the persistent distinction between them (Carman 2012, xv).

The opening and central claim in *Social Systems* is controversial, difficult to verify or refute, but intuitively appealing, namely, that there are social systems, and they are empirical (Luhmann 1995, 12). It would be fair to claim that social systems, like bodies and minds, exist over time in a way that combines stability and transformation in an evolving structure. If this argument is countered by claims that communication is something that takes place among people, and that social structures or systems only exist because of people, it would also be fair to claim that consciousness only is a function of the body, which is true, but is not a satisfactory description. But Luhmann expresses the strong conviction that humans should not identify with the situations in which various social phenomena place them, and that the forces of the vast complex of more or less codified systems that they encounter during their lives are separate from themselves. On the other hand, it is also evident that the social realm exerts a substantial influence.

By describing humans as two systems brought together in an environment of other systems, and by insisting that psychic and social systems operate in terms of meaning that is central to communication, Luhmann distances his theory from theories of subjectivity and reason, or other ways of describing a certain quality of the human capacity to produce information. This distancing should be seen in connection with the tendency to render reason and subjectivity indistinguishable from a metaphysics that assigns humans a privileged role in the world. In this respect, his theory is on the same page as that of pragmatist philosopher Richard Rorty, who does not accept the idea of a primacy of certain linguistic descriptions of the world (Rorty 1989, 15; Luhmann 1993, 169).

Luhmann does not claim that systems theory is the only theory that is useful in describing the world, but ultimately returns to a social constructivist stance, which weakens the ontological status of his theory, but is also a blunt recognition of the fact that there is no privileged point from which the complexity of the world may be understood without having any blind spot. Ultimately, systems theory is dependent on being useful and plausible.

Overall, Luhmann is not a theorist who draws much attention to existence, but one who primarily describes how social systems regulate communication and action. However, there is a significant passage in *Social Systems*, where Luhmann emphatically identifies the death of the individual human being as the event in which the difference between individual consciousness and social systems is seen very clearly as systems theory:

[...] postulates a distinctive converse relationship between individualization and the semantics of death: the more individual a psychic system conceives itself to be and the more it reflects that in its own autopoiesis, the less it can imagine living after death and, in conjunction, the less imaginable becomes the final moment of death. Even communication does not help with the unimaginable. It leaves consciousness to itself. The difference between psychic and social systems cannot be made any more brutally. The social system can guarantee or deny the psychic system neither constant self-continuation nor the companying implicit possibility of an ever-present end, neither the positive nor the negative unity of the psychic system's own autopoiesis. (Luhmann 1995, 277)

Luhmann describes both a very common experience, namely the individual's uncomfortable knowledge that the world will continue after his or her death, and a more specific idea concerning the ability of a system to comprehend its own termination. Psychic systems operate with meaning, and they can only produce an idea of the end of meaning production by generating more meaning. Minds operate as though they were immortal, but they can produce ideas that thematize the fact that they are not. It is no wonder that some of the world views that have been most influential in the history of humankind, religions, have laid claim to solutions to the problem of the end of the mind.

Changing concepts of identity and human nature

Two related questions concerning the new human and the posthuman are those of human nature and of identity. Both have been problematized, without being replaced by a new set of concepts that might radically change the debate. Just as 'culture' is a vague and inclusive term, questions of identity and of human nature may be defined and used in many ways, because the complexity of the perspectives always allows for the inclusion of new dimensions.[16] It is also difficult to merely claim that there is no such thing as human nature, or some 'essence' that distinguishes human life from other life, just as in sociology it is difficult to not make use of some idea of a relationship between individuals and 'cultures' that resembles identification.[17]

One aspect of Luhmann's theory is his skepticism concerning the idea of identification with one system or another. Since humans can be never a part of a social system, but only interact with it, any higher symbiosis between individual and collective will ultimately be illusory. That does not mean that social systems are bad; on the contrary, they are necessary for the evolution of the human species, but in modern society they also possess both more positive and negative feature than they did in early societies that were organized as feudal or tribal orders.

While Luhmann's theory of the human and his or her identity does not speculate about what makes people happy, but leaves such questions to the individuals, in another sense it is a positive and optimistic theory. Partly, this is so because it is not based on a normative principle, but emphasizes the ability to reflect on systems' relations to their environments, and to use that reflection to change the system as a central feature of systems, and following that, Luhmann sees the acceptance of contingency, which has increased in modern societies, as a good thing, rather than as the loss of meaning, as it is often described.

Systems theory is complex, and focuses on the mutual interdependence of different systems, which may be useful for establishing grounds for a critique of analytical approaches or political projects that are biased toward one kind of system as part of a fundamental description of what humans are and need, whether the body, mind or the social realm is the grounding category. One particular case of a shift in focus from one aspect of human existence to another is particularly relevant to this book: In the introduction to *Our Posthuman Future*, Francis Fukuyama concedes that his focus on societal orders in *The End of History* led him to overlook how biotechnological changes to humankind might change the premises of his thesis, both by undermining the political stability that liberal democracies might ensure, and by providing a different set of goals for history that would not be centreed around the societal order, but the capabilities of the human body and mind (Fukuyama 2003, xii).

Fukuyama has constructed a balanced defense of his original thesis on the end of history, claiming that the general trend still holds, while also challenging arguments that reject any ideas of essentially human features or ideas of human nature. Fukuyama does not dismiss the idea of evolution as central to the understanding of human existence, but tries to demonstrate that certain evolutionary features are not easily identified as part of something uniquely human. He promotes an idea of human nature that is dynamic, but that still defines significant differences between humans and other animal life (Fukuyama 2012, 14).

One of Fukuyama's key examples of this way of defining a non-static human nature is the ability to learn language, an ability that by no other primate has developed past the abilities of a four-year-old human child. This language-learning ability is far superior to that of other animals, as Norbert Wiener also has pointed out (Wiener 1954, 82), and it is understandable that it may be regarded as a defining human trait (Fukuyama 2003, 140). Human language acquisition has its own evolutionary history, and it will most likely continue to develop, but this does not change the fact that the capacity for learning language is part of a definition of something that defines human nature.[18]

Fukuyama's point is that this ability to learn language, like many other evolutionary traits, is so complex that one must be very careful when thinking about changing traits – particularly through biotechnology – that have developed over a long period of time, not only because of the potential for harm to individuals, but also because of the potential effect greater coherence of societies, which extends beyond personal fantasies of enhancement. Fukuyama seeks to position his argument between an ahistorical idea of human nature, and the equally ahistorical idea that there are no constitutive traits. But counterarguments are not scarce in this situation. Are people with brain damage, who have lost their capacity to use language no longer human? If a machine passes a Turing test and handles communicative situations as well as any human, what is the status of that entity? The lure of the language argument is that is easily observable, and is so obviously part of a shared, normal cognitive capacity across cultures, whereas consciousness, for example, is a far more complex phenomenon to explain and define. In this respect, one strength of Luhmann's theory is that it employs a clear distinction between the difficult to explain, but universally acknowledged importance of consciousness, with the observable use of language and communication.

The role of literature in human culture only enhances the probability of the formation of complex symbolic systems of communication that allow humans to alternate between concrete and abstract references, between past, present and future, between fiction and reality, and to do so in such a manner that arguments may be tied together through a series of conditions and qualifications, as well as making pronouncements that shift between self-reference and collective references. But while this use of language may be regarded as privileging humans, it will be seen that a great deal of literature displays an ambiguous attitude toward those things language enables people to do.[19] The role of language in the changing of societies is also central to the persuasive reflection in George Orwell's *Nineteen Eighty-Four*, regarding Newspeak's ability to control people's minds (Orwell 1989, 312).

Fukuyama notes that while arguments about language may be used to give humans an exceptional status among life on Earth, this position thrives better in Western monotheistic cultures, whereas the religions and cultures of the East emphasize a greater degree of continuity among humans and other life, and therefore have less clear-cut ideas of human nature and the value of such a term (Fukuyama 2003, 190). Humanism becomes a choice that has consequences for other life, and large segments of humanity subscribe to it, without having philosophically solid grounds for arguing for its naturalness or rightness. However, Fukuyama believes humanism is worth fighting for, arguing that having no other values, such as compassion, equality or human dignity, is the 'Nietzschean dead end from which Western philosophy has still not emerged' (Fukuyama 2010).

Fukuyama clearly wants to preserve values that cannot be taken for granted in a post-Nietzschean description of the world. It is striking how seldom it has been noticed that the optimism that defines *The End of History* is countered by *Our Posthuman Future*, which explicitly acknowledges that technology and science will continue to develop the potential to alter the idea of what a human is, and heavily influence the order of cultures and societies. What makes this correction even more interesting is that, while *The End of History* finds some empirical backing for developments of which Fukuyama was a proponent, to a large extent that is not the case with *Our Posthuman Future*, which instead poses a series of complex and often frightening scenarios that threaten the idea of what it means to be human, and the development of a humane society. Thus, Fukuyama is confronted by a series of likely developments that may possibly be avoided, but only by delicately balancing the implementation of technologies, and not through a pervasive Hegelian logic (Fukuyama 2012, 163). Essentially, his argument is that one must be careful in a situation where uncompromising thinkers are able to declare the absence of human nature, by countering it with a historicization of the human condition and underlining the complexity of human existence.

In an approach akin to Luhmann's, Fukuyama draws attention to the complex relationship between individual and collective, which renders the isolation of single elements of human existence untenable. With regard to extended life expectancy, one of the most frequently raised issues, Fukuyama emphasizes the societal consequences of individual changes and enhancements, and uses these to shed light on how they might influence the lives of humans. For example, prolonged life would change family structures, job markets and economic opportunities in ways that at least constitute a risk, and furthermore, longer lives, the final years of which might still be lived with diseases such as Alzheimer's, are not necessarily preferable (Fukuyama 2003, 64ff.). Incidentally, this was a scenario already conjured up by Jonathan Swift in *Gulliver's Travels*, where the immortal Struldbrugs would disturb the social order, if transplanted into another society (Swift 2011, 198f.).

Fukuyama points out that values that shape societies and make it possible for individuals to imagine a good life are not universal or ahistorical, but evolutionary, and difficult to fully comprehend, which leads to the essentially conservative argument that rash and accelerated visions of change should be countered with a fair amount of skepticism. Finally, Fukuyama takes on one dream of transhumanism that recurs, namely that of immortality, which makes some of the posthuman visions indistinguishable from religions, by promising an absolute gain in a world of otherwise relative gains (Fukuyama 2003, 58; Mehlman 2012, 46).[20] This rendering of Fukuyama's critique is just one example of how the perspectives from different kinds of systems may be used to criticize arguments rooted in a certain conception of the world. The strategy of presenting the complexities of change is also central to the readings in this book about literary works.

Luhmann's theory does not have much to say about biological systems, but takes them for granted as conditions for other systems. In one of Luhmann's more engaged pieces, he recalls an experience from a Brazilian *favela*, where he noted that the people seemed to be reduced to bodies, and not parts of communication among individuals (Luhmann 1995, 147). Luhmann's theory includes asymmetries that have developed over time; for example, his growing interest, during the last ten years of his life, in developing the theory built on paradoxes and the self-referentiality of distinctions, which opened up a very different set of analytical insights than those generated by his original conceptualization of a social theory of autopoietic systems, from the 1984 work, *Social Systems*, which is clearer and more illuminating when concerned with the role of the human in the world at large. Rather than examine communication breakdowns and endless paradoxes, it seems more relevant to explore the descriptions of, and fascination with how self-organized systems have produced highly complex societies, and how these systems seem to have developed their own logic, similar to the way in which Pierre Bourdieu describes the logic of the field, in his related theory of society.[21]

Societal systems' perspectives on the human

The historical model of societies that Luhmann presents several times in his works begins with segmented societies, typically tribal societies in which social stratification hardly exists, apart from the dominance of a leader, chief or similar figure, who has power over his subordinates. This is followed by the stratified societal order, often also referred to a feudal order, where inclusion in and exclusion from the different segments of society are dependent on an individual's position in the system (Luhmann 1995, 397ff.). Eventually, the complexity of such societies led to the development of more autonomous subsystems that came into full flower with the functionally differentiated society, which characterizes the modern world, and in which the various functional systems are separate. Ideally, law, finance, education and so on, distribute justice, wealth, merits and such, regardless of whether or not an accused murderer has a degree, is a great artist or pays his bills. However, at the end of his career, Luhmann began to acknowledge that inclusion and exclusion in modern societies are not as detached as they ideally should be in a functionally differentiated society, meaning that both inclusion and exclusion are often tied together in a strings of events, but he still maintains the importance of functional systems (Luhmann 1997, 967). Above all, the historical model is one of many clear renderings of the constitutive power of societies in the lives of individuals.

Luhmann's theory of societal systems which posits that the systems operate according to their own logic and through symbolic, generalized media presents a strong element of the construct, backed by a series of effective examples. Luhmann's fundamental point is that society includes a number of functional systems that 'observe' the world from their own narrow perspectives, centreed around binary codes (Luhmann 1995, 375). The educational system is principally interested in passed and failed exams, the economic system divides the world into payments and debts, science seeks truth and falsehood, while the legal system determines who is right and who is wrong, according to the law. This reduction of the world's complexity allows the systems to operate very efficiently, but it also creates diverse and incompatible views of the world. Luhmann is aware that from the outside, systems do not always appear to operate optimally, even though corrective secondary codes may be implemented by the system; for example, the law may be merciful, and consider the entire life of an individual. There are both positive and negative sides to sharp distinctions between functional systems. The systems are the precondition for the freedom of the individual who is not affected in all spheres of his or her existence by having a fixed position among the societal systems. But it is also well-known that exclusion from one system can lead to exclusion from others (Borch 2011, 109).

Luhmann does not specify a finite number of functional systems in modern societies, but his own work provides a clear idea of which systems he found to predominate: law, finance, art, religion, science and politics are all subjects of monographs, but families and love have also been included as systems that have produced their own binary codes to control inclusion and exclusion (Moeller 2011, 29; Joas and Knöbl 2009, 275ff.). What is of particular importance from the perspective of this book, is that humanity is conceived of differently by different systems, and that a description of what human beings are is an inevitable, but also evolving, part of some of the systems.

Some systems, such as the economic system, only include a vague concept of what humans are, even though the study of human psychology has proven to be a fundamental part of what determines the economy, the idea of an economic system independent of humans could be envisioned, something that is made perfectly clear by the automatic trading on stock markets, and the apparently dehumanized logic of the financial markets.[22]

An important parallel between Pierre Bourdieu and Niklas Luhmann lies in their insistence on the importance of the differences between systems, or in Bourdieu's terminology, fields. Bourdieu counters the criticism of being too focused on economics by emphasizing that his entire project is about showing that the logic of economics cannot provide a satisfactory account of society, but must be supplemented by other logic systems, very much in the way that Luhmann insists on the plurality of functional systems (Bourdieu 1990, 28).

The judicial and religious systems are two of the most clear-cut examples of systems that generate an idea of what a human is. In a legal system, the idea of the human is regulated in a number of ways, for example, by asserting what kinds of punishment a convicted criminal should receive, something that changed dramatically in the late eighteenth century with the abolition of torture. In the twentieth century, law has had to provide answers about the beginning and end of life, for example, by defining a fetus as not being a human being with rights, something that religions have tried to address by either strenuously opposing this, as the Catholic church does, or pragmatically claiming that human existence begins after 120 days, as is customary in Islam (Bowen 1997). At the other end of human existence, the question of criteria for death have also forced legal systems to define when a human is alive, and the adoption of the criterion of brain death by most Western countries reflects Luhmann's definition of a human as the combination of two systems, physical and mental, and the brain death criterion emphasizes the central role of consciousness.

Even more important than legal definitions of 'living' and 'dead' is the development of a legal concept of the human, and of its dignity and rights. Despite the evident fact that the intentions of the *Declaration of Human Rights* are far from being implemented on all points or in all countries, it has been a widespread success in terms of setting a standard that influences issues related to economics, culture, ethnicity and gender, and is backed by transnational courts and a relatively strong implementation in national legal systems (Risse and Ropp 1999, 267ff.).

A decisive challenge to the legal system today and in years to come will be to find a way to maintain the idea of universal rights and unity of the human species, at a time when technological developments challenge the naturalness of humans. Laws restricting the use of human embryonic tissue and limiting the cloning of other species, and a ban on human cloning represent just three of the borderline cases arising from new technological possibilities. The strength of the legal system is such that it may act on a basis that is not scientifically or philosophically sanctioned, but is instead the expression of the will of the political system to let a particular interpretation of humanism that champions dignity and equality dominate. Yet, the question remains, whether this unity can be contained in the long run.

Religions almost always have fundamental definitions of what a human is as their philosophical foundation and cultural influence, but these vary significantly. The three major monotheistic religions, Judaism, Christianity and Islam, place the human at or near the centre of the universe as a privileged being, whereas nature religions, and to a lesser extent, Buddhism, do not view humans as distinct from the rest of the life on Earth, but rather, as part of a larger community defined by the idea of life. In an increasingly secular world, the patterns religions have left remain very active, and little reflected upon, for example, in the complex relations maintained between humans and societies, and nature and other species. In this area, Western culture has a significant capacity to produce 'double thinking', in the Orwellian sense, which justifies its will to power.

Like law and religion, science and art are also concerned with what humans are, but in a different, inquisitive, and open-ended way. Science seeks a further understanding of what humans are, while at the same time engaging with technologies that could alter the very idea of what a human is. Simultaneously, science generates an abundance of theories about the various features of the human being, of its evolution, of its cognitive abilities, and of its social skills. The same open-endedness applies to art, which ideally makes its explorations in an undogmatic way, having the creation of art as its only purpose, which does not abide by truth (or beauty, for that matter), but by the social system of art, and being recognized as art. But as a side-effect to creating art, a long history of expressions regarding what humans are and should be has been created. This tradition also persists in the face of a posthuman horizon, but draws heavily on its long history, in order to be recognized as art, and thereby bridges tradition and vision.[23]

Finally, politics operates through the codes of government/opposition and the medium of power. There are no intrinsic values or stable visions of the human connected to politics, apart from the idea of making collective agreements binding. As always, Luhmann sees systems as functional, because they end discussions that might last forever, if a complete consensus was sought, but the idea of bringing about a form of collective agreement does say something about the view of humans from the perspective of political systems (Borch 2011, 72ff.).

Luhmann's theory is concerned with elements in the world that decentre the role of the subject, and in some respect it makes his theory both posthumanist and capable of adjusting to a posthuman condition. Still, his ability to account for the influence of external circumstances on human existence is important. Cary Wolfe has, with the inspiration of Jean-François Lyotard's paradoxical definition of the postmodern, characterized posthumanism as something that comes both before and after humanism (Wolfe 2010, xv). Wolfe suggests that humans' lengthy involvement with technology and cultural knowledge is something that began long before the idea of humanism came into being, and the prosthetically enhanced human is by no means a new concept. On the other hand, we are facing a new horizon, where the human is in many ways decentreed in its own world, and in need of new concepts for comprehending this (Wolfe 2010, xv-xvi). Following Michel Foucault, Wolfe criticizes the idea of the autonomous human being, as N. Katherine Hayles has also done (Hayles 2002, 319), although the criticism does not mean that all debate and influence are passé:

> What this means is that when we talk about posthumanism, we are not just talking about a thematics of the decentering of the human in relation to either evolutionary, ecological, or technological coordinates (though that is where the conversation usually begins and, all too often, ends); rather, I will insist that we are also talking about how thinking confronts that thematics, what thought has to become in the face of those challenges. Here the spirit of my intervention is akin to Foucault's in 'What Is Enlightenment?'; the point is not to reject humanism tout court—indeed, there are many values and aspirations to admire in humanism—but rather to show how those aspirations are undercut by the philosophical and ethical frameworks used to conceptualize them. (Wolfe 2010, xvi)

Wolfe's position is not uncommon in the debates revolving around the diffuse term 'posthumanism', where many variations of similar positions are being formulated. What is particularly important in this quotation is the desire to acknowledge the epistemological consequences of a world view in which humans have a different role than they have traditionally held, while maintaining that humanity is something extremely precious. This dichotomy of wanting to part with the idea of a non-evolving human while keeping the human intact continuously challenges the conception of the human.

2

An Emerging Cultural History of the Twentieth Century

Luhmann's model of the human, combining two different systems that are dependent on a third kind of system, is also suitable for describing how, historically, the focus has shifted throughout the twentieth century, to reflect what will make for a new, as well as a last human. The development may be described as emergent, as the horizon revealed by biotechnology was very different just as few decades ago, in terms of realistic possibilities for changes to humanity. Thus, former visions of change gain new relevance in the face of a changing perspective on the future.

As with most attempts to periodize history and cultural history, the borders between the different phases are not absolute, but they still identify elements and conditions that existed in one period, and not in another. Even if Mary Shelley could have imagined the creation of a new human, she came nowhere near to describing those techniques and understandings that modern technological developments have brought with them. And, while Friedrich Nietzsche imagined a change in thinking that would create a superhuman, he did not envision the new human as a part of a totalitarian project that might change society, based on a central agency of change.

A central claim of this book is that there are three main phases in the thinking about the new human since the late nineteenth century, corresponding to the three types of autopoietic systems in Luhmann's theory, and which have profoundly influenced the types of changes that could be envisioned. The first phase runs from the 1880s to the 1930s, and has the changed mind at its centre. The second phase begins in the 1920s, and has the vision of controlled changes of entire societies as its underlying condition, and the possibility of creating a new human through politically controlled processes of change. This phase essentially died out by the end of the Cold War. Finally, since the 1970s, biotechnology has made it clear that biological traits are not only an object of study, but also something that may be manipulated at a level hitherto unimaginable.

I believe valuable insights may be gained by linking the different ideas of change, and jointly studying their different visions, whether optimistic or pessimistic, rather than focusing exclusively on the promises of technology, for example. First, it is important to not describe visions of human change today as something that has arisen as a consequence of technology, but rather as something that has also fascinated people in the past. Second, the other phases and dominant ways of thinking about human change are important as reservoirs for understanding how change in one domain of human existence may influence other aspects, both positively and negatively. The three phases in the thinking about the new human do not necessarily best describe the political or cultural history of the twentieth century, but on the other hand, neither are they contingent on, nor detached from this, but are simultaneously rooted in the deeper questions of human identity, which has a scope in the twenty-first century that it did not have before.

The spiritual change in modernism

The rising influence of secularization and the development of the theory of evolution in the mid-nineteenth century helped to create a vision of a new and improved human being who cast away self-imposed limitations. There were clear expressions of secular ideas that confronted religion, as is cogently formulated in the writings of Friedrich Nietzsche, but they also gave rise to more complex and even irrational interpretations of how evolution, religion and mysticism might work together. For example, Eve Metzner and Roman Lesmeister describe how the Russian writer and founder of the Theosophical movement, Helena Petrovna Blavatsky, tried to connect occult thinking inspired by Hinduism and Buddhism, and an application of the Darwinian theory of evolution to the psychological sphere. Without denouncing the evolutionary links between humans and the great apes, she suggested that humans could continue to evolve toward a higher cosmic level, in order to achieve brotherhood, unity, love, and beauty (Metzner & Lesmeister 2002, 140).

Less humane ideas of change also thrived, most notably in the arts, in certain avant-garde movements, particularly in Italian Futurism, led by Filippo Tommaso Marinetti, who rejected the values of the past, and celebrated the pulse of modern life as central to new values. Speed, in particular, for which train, cars and planes had set new standards, was essential to the futurists, as was their insistence on a new condition, which in turn demanded a new mindset or approach to the world. Furthermore, aggression, war and all things mechanical were foregrounded as what was interesting, powerful and new (Marinetti 1998, 251f.). The rhetoric of Futurism is radical and anti-humanist, but does not make excuses for itself in a world that it finds fundamentally absurd, and without absolute truths and values.

Dadaism was also founded on the void of meaninglessness, without claiming to have a vision for the future or standards for what might follow the breakdown of the old values. The related Surrealism was essentially more political, and saw the unconscious and dreams as pathways to a new mental state, and as the foundation of an artistic practice that primarily legitimizes itself by being interesting, rather than true or good.

It is widely known that the sense of a breakdown in values following the First World War was articulated through literature and art in a number of ways, and, through movements that were either focused on expressing the absurdity of existence, or sought to find new ways of creating form and meaning, both made the continuation of art possible, and inevitably also expressed moral values. This art expresses the idea of a change in mindset, following the legacy of Nietzsche and others. At the same time, this is also a change that does not have specific content or a sense of necessity, and therefore, the other aspect of modernism was a renegotiation of which values were worth keeping. What is also central to this perspective is that the idea of a change was primarily situated in the human mind, and to a lesser extent, touches on the changes in a society. The idea of a physical change in humanity was not central in the way that it is today. Rather, as Matthew Biro suggests, the cyborg-like humans that the Dadaists presented were more of a critique of industrialized warfare and the hordes of invalids that it generated, while other representations, by Hannah Höch, amongst others, criticized the influence of commodities on people. But as Biro concludes, Dada did foreshadow both the question of hybrid identity and the cyborg-like comprehension of reality that has been taken up by a number of contemporary artists (Biro 2009, 258).

Marcus Krause and Nicholas Pethes have argued that experiments with humans had a significant role, going back as far as the avant-garde of the 1920s, when leading figures of Dada and Surrealism, such as Salvador Dalí and Luis Buñuel, created representations of experiments on people. This interest has also persisted throughout the history of film, and now also includes cloning and altering genes, inspired by the evolution in biotechnological capabilities (Krause and Pethes 2007, 27).

The idea of humanity as still undergoing evolution, and the mind, which is at the centre of this evolution, has been taken up by the evolutionary psychologist Merlin Donald, amongst others. In *Origins of the Modern Mind*, he argues for a number of changes in human cognitive abilities. These developments cannot be seen as isolated from the cultural contexts in which people exercise these abilities, particularly since language and other forms of symbolism have played a central role in bringing humanity to a new stage, when contrasted with Homo erectus, from which modern humans are descended.

At the conclusion of his book, Donald takes on nineteenth century biology, which classifies humans with the great apes, which he finds 'absurdly, grotesquely wrong in its classification' (Donald 1991, 382), because despite the close genetic relationships, our cognitive capabilities are completely different, which not only make humans unique creatures, they also make it necessary to consider what will happen in the future, especially in light of the enormous changes that new media have provided, in order to give access to a shared bank of knowledge and information:

> We act in cognitive collectivities, in symbiosis with external memory systems. As we develop new external symbolic configurations and modalities, we reconfigure our own mental architecture in non-trivial ways. The third transition has led to one of the greatest reconfigurations of cognitive structure in mammalian history, without major genetic change. In principle, this process could continue, and we may not yet have seen the final modular configuration of the modern human mind. Theories of human evolution must be expanded and modified to accommodate this possibility. (Donald 1991, 382)

When looking back at visions of human evolution and the change in human attitudes from the beginning of the twentieth century, Donald's angle offers an argument for taking visions of a change in cognitive abilities quite seriously, and suggests a great deal of foresight on the part of the artists and writers who described such scenarios. A change in the human mind was not the only kind of change that was foreshadowed, as ideas of physical change also occurred, but a change in the way the world is perceived remained the dominant vision until the early twentieth century. However, that was soon to be expanded further.

Changing humankind through society

While the discourse on 'the posthuman' emerged rather late, there were several uses of 'the new human' during the middle of the twentieth century, when 'the new' could be used as political rhetoric in conjunction with a nation's citizens, or the members of an ethnic group. At other times, the rhetoric was not as explicit, but the idea of changing humans through the pressure of a changed society was central, particularly to a number of communist states. Even though there are many differences among the sizes and scopes of the projects for change, it is clear that there were profound visions of creating different, 'new' humans, and that these were self-described as worthwhile and noble undertakings. Historically, this is in many ways the most important phase that this study addresses. Whereas the consequences of the modernist conception of a new human are difficult to evaluate, apart from their influence on the arts, and the consequences of the biotechnological revolution are still mostly projections of events that may happen in an uncertain future, it is evident that the idea of a new human created through societal change was a part of movements responsible for making millions of people suffer and die.

There is a sliding scale in both the use and the consequences of the rhetoric and politics of the new human. From the ideas of a 'new Chinese man', the fatal experiments in Cambodia, and the long and varied use of the 'new Soviet man', there is quite a long way to the ideas of 'the new negro', who was trying to liberate African-Americans from the lingering cultural bonds imposed by slavery, or the use of 'the new Jew', whose impact on the use of military force to protect Israel is open to interpretation (Cheng 2008; Hellbeck 2006; Locke 1997).

In Part Three, I present some of the most important uses of the rhetoric of the 'new human', in particular those based on events that occurred in the Soviet Union, China, Cuba and Cambodia, but it is also necessary to note examples of a less totalitarian character, which were still profound in their visions, such as the cultural change initiated in Turkey by Kemal Atatürk's project of Westernizing the former Ottoman Empire. That is a case that may be even more remarkable, as it is not a finished project, but presents a cultural divide that makes its influence felt today.

Another decisive process of cultural change took place through colonialism and decolonization, which included economic benefits to the colonizer among its many goals, gave rise to a number of ideas for reform and the development of cultures, and which ultimately also affected humans through profound changes in society. During the colonial period, other interests held by the colonizers make it less relevant to speak of a grand project for societal change, but missionary work, Western administrations and educational systems were established, as were important elements of massive changes in societies.

Decolonization brought about a renegotiation of these changes, and the older, indigenous cultures made efforts to determine how much of the influence of the colonial period should be rolled back, if this was at all possible, and how much should be integrated into a new vision of a future national identity and culture, which would possess elements of both the original culture, and the influences of the colonizing powers. In literature, this has sparked debates on the use of language and the preference for either a foreign, but shared language on the one hand, or a multitude of languages and dialects rooted in the people's own cultures, on the other (Achebe 1975).

On the sidelines of these attempts to steer national processes of change, other organizations in, or rather outside of society, contributed to the understanding of the new human in the twentieth century, namely, the cult groups that detach themselves from society, in order to realize their vision of a changed way of living. Such groups are often characterized by having a strong and charismatic leader, and are held together by the promise that a changed way of living will lead to both personal and collective gains. In a number of cases, such cults have ended tragically, as was the case with the Jim Jones cult, and the suicide and massacre in Guyana in 1978, in which more than 900 members of the cult lost their lives (Hall 2004, 254ff.). In other cases, one might question the real motives of the guiding vision, which may be more about the interests of the cult's leaders than enabling real change. For example, this is the case with the Scientology movement, which has a core narrative of the thetan as a traveling soul that members put in the service of the movement for thousands of years, while at the same time offering to take steps toward a higher level of insight, a process often connected with a series of economic transactions (Ankerberg 1996, 526). However, the very impact and scale of such movements is symptomatic of the desire for a vision of a new human.

Even in societies where there has been no attempt to bring a grand project to life, the idea of a radical change in society was influential. From the Russian revolution until the end of the Cold War, there were numerous models of societal reconstruction to both inspire and to serve as warnings against experimenting with society's influence on individuals. The historical consequences mean something in this respect; this phase is the one that has influenced the most people, and killed many in their attempts to create a new human. Metaphorically, a lot of eggs have been broken without any omelets to show for it; literally, the human cost is beyond imagining. Thus, the literature that will be analyzed, relating to this phase, is a retrospective that chronicles the human response to the pressures of society.[24]

Genetic transcendence as a horizon

While changes of a cognitive and social kind may be very real and easily observable over time, they are not as tangible as the changes that biotechnology can produce, and promises to be able to produce. Advances in biotechnology, to a large extent attempted only on other species of animals, have revealed a horizon with an array of daunting perspectives ranging from the absolutely welcome to some very frightening scenarios. A longer life with fewer diseases would be cherished by most, but the risks of mutations, new diseases, eugenics programmes, and the complete devaluation of the human are just some of the perils that are also foreseen.

The most significant breakthrough in biotechnology has been the discovery of the human genome, and in particular, the mapping of the human genome, which was completed in 2003 (Lander 2011). This has also made it possible for every human to think of him – or herself not just in terms of what exists here and now, but also as the manifestation of an underlying code. In an unexpected way, this brings a certain form of dualism back into the world, not between body and mind, but between code and corpus. Parallel to this, a broad range of techniques for altering genes has been developed, particularly those used on crops, while cloning techniques have been carried out on a number of species, including the famous sheep, Dolly, which was cloned in 1996. Bringing dead pets back to life by creating their clones has already become a commercial undertaking, although not exactly a common enterprise.[25] In most countries, strict regulations have been imposed on the use of these techniques on humans, a consequence of which is that it is not some technological limitation that is holding back experiments, but the willingness to use such techniques in ethically murky waters.

The term 'posthuman' designates a species different from humans, but evolved from them. This should not be confused with posthumanism, which is a broader idea regarding how humans value themselves and their environments (Badmington 2010). Usually, life above the bacterial and fungal level is divided into three groups, consisting of plants, non-human animals (or just 'animals') and humans (Savulescu 2009, 214). But the idea of the posthuman and the road to it has generated the need for a number of other terms. In Julian Savulescu's useful typology, the next step after the human is the *enhanced human*, a category which Savulescu and others emphasize is very complex, because of the difference between culturally accepted and unacceptable means of improvement. A healthy life with ample exercise and nutritious food will improve individual capacity for a number of activities, but so would the use of various pharmaceuticals that could increase muscle strength and stamina, but the latter are only accepted by society as therapy, not enhancement.

The next beings in Savulescu's chain are *transhumans*, which have been changed and enhanced so much that they have significant non-human characteristics. Chimeras that have been created by combining genes from a human and another species would be an example of a possible, but not-yet extant transhuman being. The integration of man and machine, or a cyborg, also falls into that category, which again has a sliding scale. Pacemakers and surgically mounted hearing aids would hardly be regarded as making a decisive difference, nor would the artificial ear that the artist Stelarc has had inserted and grown under the skin of his lower arm make him a transhuman.[26] Again, the technical limitations of the moment and the near future are not the reasons the frequent fantasies of cyborgs have not been realized.

In contrast to transhuman creatures, the *posthuman* would be a being or a species that has its roots in the human species, but which differs so much from Homo sapiens it may no longer be said to belong to the same species.[27] Juan Enriquez and Steve Gullans thus see the coexistence of different members of the hominid family as the normal condition, and the solitary existence of Homo sapiens as an exception in a long history (Enriquez and Gullans 2010, 'Intro').[28]

Savulescu is careful to remind us how difficult it is to define what a human is. Genetically, there is little difference between humans and the great apes, which share up to 98.4 per cent of their DNA (Savulescu 2009, 242), and there are a number of challenges to articulating a simple and scientific definition of a human. At the same time, it is evident that there are significant features that differentiate humans from other species. Here, Savulescu notes the capacity to make generalizations and act normatively as characteristic of human life (Savulescu 2009, 242f.), knowing that this does not resolves the problem of defining humans.

Savulescu's viewpoint on ethics and analytical philosophy may make it unsurprising that cognitive capacities are foregrounded, and these are exactly the capabilities that challenge humans in this new situation. Humans justify their place in the world and the privileges that accompany it, in contrast to those of other life forms, which, in practice, humanity dominates, and assigns statuses as means and ends. But being challenged by the thought experiment of a posthuman species is not the only reason the idea of a posthuman is problematic and uncanny; it also colours other ethical arguments. Whereas a normal child is an implicit wish of any parent, Savulescu questions whether parents who would prefer a healthy, normal child to a child with a disability, might find it even more desirable to have an unusually intelligent or even posthuman child (Savulescu 2009, 242). This creates a grey zone, as there is a considerable difference between wanting one's child to be as intelligent as possible, and having the best of all other kinds of traits, including creativity, social intelligence and so on, but still within the spectrum of what is humanly possible under normal conditions. However, a posthuman child with an abnormally long life span and extremely high intelligence may fit poorly into the family and the society into which it is born. One of the weaknesses of Savulescu's arguments is that they do not pose the kinds of questions that Fukuyama insists on, such as whether one would care to live in a society in which the posthuman is replacing the human. On the other hand, Savulescu exposes a certain hypocrisy in the contingent normality, which has changed over the course of history, often quite drastically, as new standards and new techniques have emerged.

There are many principles of caution connected to the use of new biotechnology, which some groups claim hold back an otherwise positive development. The so-called 'transhumanists' argue that technology should be deployed, in order to improve humans in various ways, including their health, longevity, psychological wellbeing and cognitive abilities. Some, for example Nick Bostrom, stipulate that such enhancements should be implemented universally, so that no 'last human' is left behind. Bostrom also envisions a world of posthumans as just one of four scenarios, ranging from annihilation, regression and a status quo, to the coming of a posthuman condition in which people will typically live for at least 500 years (Bostrom 2009, 204).

The idea of the complete annihilation of humanity is a possibility, which is frightening in a different way than the transformation into a posthuman condition. The end of world is, in fact, one of the compelling narratives of Western civilizations, forming a part of both major religions and secular visions. Mary Shelley's novel, *The Last Man*, is as mentioned one example that does not involve a transformation or succession to humanity, but simply its end. Similarly, the second half of the twentieth century saw a justified concern for a nuclear Armageddon in which the world would end with a bang, rather than the whimper imagined in T. S. Eliot's 'The Hollow Men'. With the end of the world order of the Cold War, this scenario has evaporated, or at least retreated. However, there is now the risk of new, incurable and deadly diseases that could be engineered by terrorists.

Bostrom also recognizes the possibility of a plateau in the evolution of humanity, where nothing radical happens, and he ascribes this view or hope to Francis Fukuyama, but in light of technological developments, he considers this status quo unlikely. Another unlikely scenario would be a regression, owing to a collapse of the planet's civilizations, which would push humans back to a more primitive state. Bostrom notes that such collapses of civilizations have many historical precedents, but he does not believe that it would be a stable, final outcome of the history of humankind. Advanced societies would make a comeback, or humanity would be annihilated (Bostrom 2009, 194ff.).

The unlikeliness of each of the foregoing scenarios is an implicit argument for a posthuman condition that has been dramatically altered in terms of longevity, health and intelligence. Bostrom does not exclude the possibility of a reversion from a posthuman condition to a human condition, but rules it unlikely, in the same way that we can hardly imagine returning to a prehuman condition. In a world beset by poverty and inequality, it is unlikely that new technologies would be implemented broadly,[29] although governments' capacities to direct such processes should not be underestimated (Fukuyama 2012, 163). Nevertheless, it would be difficult to control the use of biotechnology, given the number of countries in the world, the many non-governmental organizations and private companies, and cult-like groups that might acquire the resources for cloning humans, for example.[30]

Since the end of the Cold War, globalization has been a driving force in the world's economic changes, and despite its negative aspects, it has so far caused a significant rise in the wealth of major countries such as China, India, Russia and Brazil, while the development in Africa is more uneven. The proposed successor to the East–West conflict of the Cold War in the form of a North–South conflict has not materialized as a major conflict, owing to the positive economic development in many parts of the world. Instead, at the beginning of the twenty-first century, climate change is viewed as the dominant global problem in need of a political solution. This has led to a different vision of the future, marked more by pessimistic outlooks than by optimistic prognoses of the use of modern technology. At the same time, this ecological awareness has drawn attention from biotechnological developments. One likely reason for this lack of awareness is the disturbing aspect of human change, whereas ecological disasters at least do not change the idea of human identity. Societal control of the use of biotechnology has already created, and is likely to increase a discrepancy between the cautious – and as most people believe, sensible – deployment of new technology on humans, and technological potential, so the possibilities will increasingly exceed the willingness to use them. There is no doubt, either, that various techniques, including gene sequencing or therapeutic measures, will be attractive, and that the cost of using them, the ethical challenges they pose, and the right to have access to medication and other therapies, will not only pose an enormous ethical challenge, but an economic one, too.

Aldous Huxley's *Brave New World* remains one of the most visionary works of literature of the twentieth century, not so much because of the novel's accurate predictions of the future – given its setting in the year 2540, the validity of the predictions remains open to speculation, although it is probable that the techniques used more than 500 years from now will be much more advanced than those the novel presents – but because it reflects on changes to all domains: mind, body, and society. There is, as in George Orwell's kindred novel, *Nineteen Eighty-Four*, a strong and uncanny description of a stratified society controlled by a cocktail of meaningless entertainment and ideological control, and in Huxley's work, there is also the decisive additional step of the description of how psychopharmacology and new means of reproduction control intelligence and other capabilities.

Huxley wrote *Brave New World* at a time when the genetic code was just on the verge of being discovered, but the idea of manipulating it, as is possible today, was still far off, yet he describes the willed use of imaginative means of controlling bodies and minds to make them fit into a social order, which is even more prophetic, given the abilities that have been, and are being developed today.[31] Furthermore, Huxley also observes the consciousness and spiritual life created by this control, and a class of 'wild' people is used to criticize the controlled life of the world state, just as the references to Shakespeare's classics play a decisive role in creating a basis for a critique based on notions of humanity as needing more than a frictionless society to thrive, and instead requiring the kinds of subversive foundations that literature so richly provides (Huxley 2005, 207; Thomsen 2011, 213).

Bioethicist Leon Kass noted, after having commented on Huxley's work, that his own idea of a dystopia would be created not by going against the idea of the humane, but by carrying our humane ambitions of eliminating disease, hunger, conflict and pain to an extreme, but at a high price, in the form of 'homogenization, mediocrity, trivial pursuits, shallow attachments, debased tastes, spurious contentment and souls without love or longings'. (Kass 2002, 5). If these features represent an accurate negative definition of the human, would the positive formulation of this involve heterogeneity, excellence, creativity, strong relations, refined tastes, genuine satisfaction and a desire- and love-filled spiritual life? Maybe Kass does not get it all right, but who would honestly say that he got it all wrong? Above all, this perspective on Huxley's fiction suggests that a number of emotions are connected to the vision of a new or changed human, which cannot easily be formalized or evaluated by focusing on simple enhancements, but that address the right to assert that the human is also connected to certain values and abilities, which are ultimately embedded in the societies in which we live, and their historical evolution.

3

History, Technique, Imagination

Ideas regarding human change have taken many forms throughout history, the full range of which is beyond the scope of this book. In this chapter I introduce a number of ideas regarding changes in the human species, and the different ways these have been used. After that follows a discussion of a typology of the means of altering humans, which, in various ways, have been, are being and are imagined to be used, spanning improvements by the individual and the development of cultures, advanced, man-machine interaction, and the changes to genetic expression. In the concluding section, the roles of literature and art are discussed, with regard to both their capacity for criticism and their inability to support human change.

The new human in history

There are two very different ways of looking at the history of visions of human change. One focuses on the numerous inventive, imaginative ideas that humans have spun for centuries, and which provides a rich background for twentieth century visions. But it would also be justifiable to emphasize the long periods during which this theme did not play a great role, particularly because rituals and religion provided satisfactory and socially stabilizing explanations of the world. So, although human change is not a topic that has dominated any cultural discourse at any time in history, it has emerged as a fascinating and often uncanny theme that has, in various ways, influenced the repertoire of the collective imagination of Western cultures.

Nearly all cultures and societies include, or have included ideas of something mystical and inexplicable as part of their world view, just as the idea of some sort of transformation has been central to explaining why death is not a definite end, but also a new beginning (Eliade 2005). While the world's dominant religions have claimed to have addressed the problem of the individual's death by promising an enchanted transformation to another state of being (or less enchanted, if one has sinned or created bad karma), the idea of postponing aging and making it possible to live indefinitely on Earth has had a minor but significant appeal. The hope for a 'fountain of youth' is a staple in the collective memory, which goes against the teachings of the dominant religions, and is more relevant as a subtext to some of the hopes for what biotechnology might be able to achieve for humanity. Variations on a source of eternal youth have been found in Greek and Roman cultures, such as the legend of Zeus's wife, Hera, who bathed each spring to maintain her youth (Blazer 2009, 4). These visions have flourished both in cultures dominated by the idea of an eternal life as described by monotheistic religions, and in monistic cultures with no ideas of an individual afterlife. Expeditions have even sought to find an actual source of the fountain of youth in Ethiopia, and in Florida, where a theme park is named after a Spanish explorer: 'Ponce de Léon's World Famous Fountain of Youth'. In modern times, the idea of a fountain of youth has become a popular myth that is referenced and used in various media, without their having a historical model for it. In literature, Jorge Luis Borges used the idea of a fountain of youth in the short story, 'The Immortal', in which eternal life is bestowed on a Roman soldier, who then lives through many ages, but comes to see immortality as curse (Borges 1998, 185). Oscar Wilde's *The Picture of Dorian Gray* is another significant fantasy about not aging, just as Peter Pan has been influential across literature, film and cartoons. Today, expeditions to a geographical location of the fountain of youth would be a joke, but the connection between a biotechno-logical search for halting aging and death, and the myth of eternal youth is quite evident.[32]

The idea of a new human created through cultural effort is one of the major subtexts of the Renaissance, and its adoption of secular role models for the advancement of culture. The idea of being able to recreate or shape humanity was taken a step further when John Locke's description of the human as a blank slate became a paradigmatic example of an understanding of the plasticity of human nature, later influencing some Enlightenment thinkers (Cheng 2009, 8). The relative significance of heredity and environment has been on the agenda ever since, and even though the importance of genes has received more recog-nition in the last few decades, the individual's dependence on upbringing and the cultural environment of which it is a part remains pivotal. Nevertheless, the idea of the blank slate provided a foundation for visions of being able to alter central human traits through education and societal changes, something that has recurred throughout the twentieth century, and which yielded disastrous results during the French revolution. The weaker concept of human nature was also central to Karl Marx's description of the human as a product of the class division of society, which, in the industrial era, caused alienation that, according to Marx, could only be resolved by changing the organization of society (Pinker 2002, 159ff.).

One of the principal disagreements concerning human nature is whether the vision of a new human aims to free humans' inner nature, or to create a society with a particular order that does not necessarily legitimize itself by claiming to have any insight into human nature. Evidently, the idea of human nature is also controversial, and there are few, if any, who believe that the corrupting effect of civilization should lead us to a return to nature. On the other hand, the idea of a blank slate has too many arguments against it, which do not lead to an idea of an absolute human nature, but a dynamic stability with a set of properties. Thus, hopes for a natural order of society are utopian, and seem doomed.

In the realm of fiction and literature, Mary Shelley's *Frankenstein, or the Modern Prometheus* is a work that has become iconic because of its ability to expand on what humanity may become capable of doing. The reference to Prometheus is a gesture to the god-like powers required to create a new human made from of clay, as in the case of Prometheus, but Shelley's novel suggests that science might be able to match what was once the domain of gods.[33]

Frankenstein's monster has had an enormous ability to fascinate, and thanks to movies, it has also become a popular cultural reference (Graham 2002, 62ff.). What is often ignored by the popular iterations of *Frankenstein* is the complex depiction of the monster, which, in the films as well as the book, is presented as sensitive and empathic, but turned cruel. The basic narrative is simple, the portrait of a being that is rejected because of its abnormality, but Shelley nuances the issues at stake by introducing reflections on the natural, the sublime and the human, which is often most forceful when coming from the mouth of the monster. At one point, he demands that Frankenstein provide him with a female partner, which is asking no more of his creator than what Christian mythology relates that the first man was given. Frankenstein declines, even though his creation promises to take his female to South America, and live apart from humans:

> If you consent, neither you nor any other human being shall ever see us again: I will go to the vast wilds of South America. My food is not that of man; I do not

destroy the lamb and the kid to glut my appetite; acorns and berries afford me sufficient nourishment. My companion will be of the same nature as myself, and will be content with the same fare. We shall make our bed of dried leaves; the sun will shine on us as on man, and will ripen our food. The picture I present to you is peaceful and human, and you must feel that you could deny it only in the wantonness of power and cruelty. Pitiless as you have been towards me, I now see compassion in your eyes; let me seize the favourable moment, and persuade you to promise what I so ardently desire. (Shelley 2000, 129f.)

The rhetoric is well-polished, and Frankenstein is presented with a romantic vision of life that is simultaneously a criticism of humanity. The 'monster' is the one who wants to live as a vegan in harmony with nature, without exploiting it for its own purpose as humans do, and there is a subtle point in identifying this trait as being particularly human.[34] Then, the creation mentions the inhumane qualities that Frankenstein would be displaying, should he refuse to accede to its wishes, that is his exercise of power and cruelty, again, traits that historically describe any number of human deeds, but are rarely used to describe what is specifically 'human'.

Ultimately, in Shelley's novel Frankenstein's creation is a monster that cannot be integrated into society. In terms of literature, this problem leading up to a dramatic ending functions well. If Shelley had written a novel about a normal being, and perhaps just somewhat more beautiful, intelligent and empathic than humans are at their best, this would have been a completely different story; in some respects, perhaps an even more frightening story, since monstrosity can be singled out and dealt with, in contrast to something that comes close to being human. Such a creation would present itself as more uncanny, as it would undermine the idea of defined borders between human and non-human. It is also significant that the creature becomes monstrous because of Frankenstein's technical inability to create a normally proportioned human from the stitched-together body parts (Shelley 2000, 58). Had Shelley let him do that, she would have created an even greater ethical dilemma for the reader, who would see its other in the creation, instead of a very different being.

The Last Man complements *Frankenstein*, by presenting the end of humanity as the end, and not as a new beginning. Shelley's 'method' of making humanity extinct is an epidemic that kills all people, and which lets her develop the theme of the human need to live in a society. But it is also significant that there is no thought of something beyond the last man that transcends the human, but only the endpoint of the final generation. Shying away from imagining further evolution is in line with the teachings of the Western religions, which would consider the idea of the posthuman as blasphemy.

With the publication of Charles Darwin's *The Origin of Species* in 1859, speculation on the future of humanity and human development was put on the agenda, although not by Darwin himself. One branch was Social Darwinism and the concept of eugenics, a term coined by Darwin's relative, Francis Galton, in 1883. In the realm of literature, there were numerous speculations regarding what humans might become, most prolifically by Samuel Butler. In *Erehwon* ('nowhere', backwards) of 1872, he imagined how machines might acquire consciousness, thereby addressing the Romantic construct of the automaton (Benesch 2002, 189), as well as being a forerunner to later ideas of cyborgs and humanoid robots.

At the beginning of the twentieth century, the Danish Nobel laureate Johannes V. Jensen, who was deeply inspired by evolutionary thought, wrote a historical novel about Denmark's King Christian the Second, *The Fall of the King*, set in the fifteenth and sixteenth centuries, in which Jensen introduces a minor character who experiments with human evolution. The more or less mad scientist and physician, Zacharias, reveals to the protagonist Mikkel Thøgersen a creation that he claims is a son of the king, but also a human that has been evolved through a special technique:

'His head has proved to be singularly expansible. I remove the skull, you see, and let the membrane over the brain develop into skin, and then I provide rich nutrition and a high temperature around the head. That's why the bell is necessary. In fact, Carolus still enjoys crawling into his bell, where he has sat for so many years, although it is now getting too small for him. He has the best head in Europe'. (Jensen 1992, 253)

Carolus's body is diminutive, and thinking gives him pain, something that astonishes Mikkel, who connects problem solving with joy. Mikkel later talks too much at a bar and indirectly causes the burning of Zacharias and Carolus, a scene that Jensen narrates in detail over a page and a half, of humans vainly clinging to life, mirroring another central scene in the book, where the aristocracy cruelly retaliates on a peasant uprising.

Earlier, Zacharias is presented as an eccentric who tells strange stories and confesses his desire to understand and control nature. As in Shelley's novels, Jensen is concerned with aberrant individuals who cannot be accepted, and where normality lacks a firm base, yet is hypocritically used to set norms, even if it is supported by neither religion nor law. Nature's otherness is seen as something with its own dynamics that humans must fight, but by which they are always defeated, thanks to death. Yet the defiance of nature is a strong and defining force in the mind of Mikkel Thøgersen:

.... Yes, the earth knows all, even though it remains silent. We have our way for a time, and the more lighthearted we are the more we dance about on it. But all flesh is created in defiance of nature, in opposition to the law of gravity. Humans have even lifted their forequarters up from the earth, cheating gravity out of a couple of limbs. God fattens up living things so that they will fall even harder to the ground, for God and Satan are one and the same person. But the earth ... (Jensen 1992, 35)

Then Mikkel is hurled back into reality, and sees a child lying on the ground. One of the fundamental paradoxes Jensen explores in his novel is the dual perception of the human as a unique creation that can pursue lofty goals, but simultaneously finds itself in so many humbling situations. The inclusion of a fantasy of a 'new human' is very telling in this novel, in terms of a change in the outlook.

Olaf Stapledon's two highly ambitious novels from the 1930s, *Last and First Men* and *Star Maker*, present a more radical vision of human change, which to a large extent is engineered by humans themselves. In a narrative beginning with the apocalyptic downfall of our present culture, Stapledon chronicles how humanity evolves into a series of distinct, different successors to the human as we know it. Perhaps not always aiming for the most realistic vision, Stapledon imagines quite extraordinary developments, including flying humans and a extremely prolonged childhood spanning up to several centuries, but eventually tackles questions of how human interaction and the malfunctions of society might be overcome. One of the many interesting elements Stapledon brings into play in *Last and First Men* is the deliberate creation of a new species, owing to dissatisfaction with the current state of humanity:

In working out the general proportions of the new man, his makers took into account the possibility of devising more efficient bone and muscle. After some centuries of patient experiment they did actually invent a means of inducing in germ cells a tendency toward far stronger bone-tissues and far more powerful muscle (Stapledon 1930, 193)

Apart from the foresight of imagining the programming of cells and working with the properties of the body, the slowness that Stapledon imagines and the importance of patience stands out. This contrasts with the rapidity of the actual development of new techniques, and also of their use in experiments, short of being deployed on human beings. The contrast is sharpest when compared with Ray Kurzweil's almost joyful calculations of how accelerated returns will make projected, future developments take place much quicker than expected (Kurzweil 2004, 28). Nevertheless, reality has to some extent caught up with Stapledon's visions. Experiments with the human body are taking place, including very specific efforts to increase muscle strength (Enriquez and Gullans 2010, Chapter 5).

The colonization of the universe is also a part of Stapledon's vision that has been adopted by numerous writers after him, most notably Arthur C. Clarke. Even more relevant to one of the key themes of this book is the idea of access to a collective consciousness, which evolves late in Stapledon's fantasy:

> In addition to the brain organization necessary to this perfection of individual human nature, each member of a sexual group has in his own brain a special organ which, useless by itself, can co-operate 'telepathically' with the special organs of other members of the group to produce a single electro-magnetic system, the physical basis of the group-mind. In each sub-sex this organ has a peculiar form and function; and only by the simultaneous operation of the whole ninety-six does the group attain unified mental life. These organs do not merely enable each member to share the experience of all; for this is already provided in the sensitivity to radiation which is characteristic of all brain-tissue in our species. By means of the harmonious activity of the special organs a true group-mind emerges, with experience far beyond the range of the individuals in isolation. (Stapledon 1930, 320f.)

The balance between inventiveness, imagination and the presentation of something extraordinary, and the description of a possible, realistic and perhaps also more subdued vision of the future seems to affect the influence of such novels. Stapledon does not strike the balance so well in terms of developing exciting but incalculable scenarios of what might happen, but like Shelley, Jensen and numerous others, his work is being revitalized thanks to current developments in human biotechnology.[35]

While Shelley, Jensen and Stapledon imagined the new human in terms of a physical transcendence, Friedrich Nietzsche, along with Fyodor Dostoyevsky and other intellectuals from the second half of the nineteenth century elucidated how a changed attitude toward the world may cause a change in character so thorough that it makes sense to call the outcome a new human, whereby these writers and philosophers laid foundations for ideas that remain both influential and controversial.

Nietzsche stands as a pivotal figure in evoking a spiritual modernization of humanity that will yield a new human. An ardent critic of religion, Nietzsche, in works such as *Also sprach Zarathustra*, lends his voice to the idea that the human is something that must be overcome. This passage is unmistakable in its message of an evolution not yet finished:

> Behold, I teach you the overman! The overman is the meaning of the earth. Let your will say: the overman shall be the meaning of the earth! I beseech you, my brothers, remain faithful to the earth and do not believe those who speak to you of extraterrestrial hopes! They are mixers of poisons whether they know it or not. They are despisers of life, dying off and self-poisoned, of whom the earth is weary: so let them fade away! Once the sacrilege against God was the greatest sacrilege, but God died, and then all these desecrators died. Now to desecrate the earth is the most terrible thing, and to esteem the bowels of the unfathomable higher than the meaning of the earth! Once the soul gazed contemptuously at the body, and then such contempt was the highest thing: it wanted the body gaunt, ghastly, starved. Thus it intended to escape the body and the earth. Oh this soul was gaunt, ghastly and starved, and cruelty was the lust of this soul! But you, too, my brothers, tell me: what does your body proclaim about your soul? Is your soul not poverty and filth and a pitiful contentment? Truly, mankind is a polluted stream. One has to be a sea to take in a polluted stream without becoming unclean. Behold, I teach you the overman: he is this sea, in him your great contempt can go under. (Nietzsche 2006, 6)

The loyalty to the Earth and the swearing off other worldly hopes are Nietzsche's credos, but ultimately they are empty and have no content apart from the denial of any values except the belief that the freedom from religious dogma and illusions will set humans free. In a certain way, the monist Nietzsche is tied to the dualist Plato, in connecting epistemology with a philosophy of life: a life lived with the right insights is valuable in itself, whether it means breaking free of an illusion, or believing that one can see through the veils of phenomena. Nietzsche's failure to recognize the evolution of language, culture and communication through social processes, and his praise the lost past of antiquity, stands out as a blind spot in his criticism of culture (Nietzsche 1968, 438ff.).

While The Fountain of Youth and Frankenstein's monster suggest changes of a physical character, in the forms of the absence of aging and a being designed by humans, the idea of a new human has played a significant role in the political rhetoric of the twentieth century. As will be discussed in greater detail in the beginning of Part III, different visions of change in society have flourished, with the underlying assumption that the change would also bring about a new kind of human, with different character traits than the old human. It is also important that these changes were thought of at a time when today's biotechnological horizon of change was nowhere in sight. This kind of change is important for both historical and contemporary reasons: historically, because more than any other vision, this kind of political rhetoric has influenced how societies have been changed, legitimized by a vision of a future conditions, the kind of legitimization that Jean-François Lyotard criticized in his attempt to discern the postmodern from the modern (Lyotard 1984, 34). Influences on twentieth century literature have also played a prominent part in the accounts of atrocities committed throughout the century, and their place in literary history has become more and more pronounced. Thus, Horace Engdahl has argued, with reference to Elie Wiesel, that the witness literature of the twentieth century is the latest major innovation in the history of literature, and the recognition of a number of such works, particularly over the past two decades, has been hard to ignore (Engdahl 2002, 5f.).[36]

The contemporary relevance of the political rhetoric of the new human lies in the significant warning that individual and society are closely connected, and a strong focus on biotechnological innovation and 'improvements' could potentially neglect contemplation of their societal consequences. As biotechnology has advanced, numerous scholars, scientists and artists have speculated on its uses and its consequences, and how it could dramatically change the future of humanity. In *Our Posthuman Future*, Francis Fukuyama self-critically describes how the developments of biotechnology were unforeseen, and would have changed the argument in the criticized but influential *The End of History and the Last Man*. Fukuyama acknowledges that the first book was predominantly about societal change, and did not take into account how a dramatic change in the living conditions of individuals could have a profound effect on other domains (Fukuyama 2003, xii).

Other scholars have described the development of technology as having already made the human posthuman, in the sense that depends on technology. That is the case made by N. Katherine Hayles in *How We Became Posthuman*, while futurists such as Ray Hammond and Ray Kurzweil anticipate a radical change in the human condition as a result of the advances in artificial intelligence, which, according to Kurzweil, will exceed human intelligence within four to five decades.[37] The posthuman constitutes an interdisciplinary subject that includes different approaches to clarifying the consequences of various technologies and developments, and to discern between those that are welcome and those that are not. The last point is divisive, and brings in discussions of value. Fukuyama is among the skeptics who wish to defend the idea that an otherwise criticized concept of human nature still makes sense, and is inseparable from human dignity. At the other end of the spectrum there are philosophers such as Nick Bostrom, who sees the possibility of a new human as positive, although he is aware of the pitfalls. Bostrom has taken part in organizing a transhuman society which advocates and debates the use of advanced technologies, and that does not see fundamental or significant problems in the creation of conditions in which the idea of the human as a creation of nature, and nature only, ceases to make sense.

Transhumanism has no prominent place in the public debate; and often, stories of humans who wish to be frozen after their deaths, using cryonics, and hope to be revived in a later age, attract most of the attention of the mainstream media. Such stories also paint a picture of transhumanism as a project for the few and the privileged. The organization Humanity+ tries to present a different version of a foundation for a transhumanist movement. Their overarching purpose is an improvement in the conditions of human existence. They support the ambition to live longer, and argue that the extension of the mean lifespan by two decades, which was achieved over the last century, should encourage striving for more, otherwise, why value former achievement?[38] Furthermore, they support cultural exchange that indirectly recognizes the stress being put on the idea of the unity of humanity, which arises from the idea of improved humans and posthuman beings. Finally, the organization wishes to secure the rights of individuals to be able do as they wish with their bodies, and to provide access to new technologies. Again, this is a crucial point, where one without the other could create a society very different from one with rights and access to technologies. But the question is whether Humanity+ is naïve in hoping for universal access to often costly technologies, or whether they merely use their good intentions as a non-binding argument for removing barriers for experiments. At least there is a potential conflict of interest in the 'Transhumanist Declaration', which the organization supports. The declaration is filled with good intentions, but reveals little concern for the interaction between the groups it mentions:

> 7. We advocate the well-being of all sentience, including humans, non-human animals, and any future artificial intellects, modified life forms, or other intelligences to which technological and scientific advance may give rise.

> 8. We favour allowing individuals wide personal choice over how they enable their lives. This includes use of techniques that may be developed to assist memory, concentration, and mental energy; life extension therapies; reproductive choice technologies; cryonics procedures; and many other possible human modification and enhancement technologies. (http://humanityplus.org/philosophy/transhumanist-declaration/)

The transhuman movement is far from being a powerful organization at this point in time, but it is worth noting that leading universities such as Oxford and Harvard take the question of the human future in this perspective very seriously.

N. Katherine Hayles argues that a positive trait of the posthuman is that in a situation where humans and technology are both evolving, it will no longer be possible to dream of controlling future development, and instead of teleology, emergence will be the dominant way of thinking about the future (Hayles 1999, 288). Hayles' argument is compelling, because it avoids the idea of perfection (see discussion of this in the next section), but one must question whether Hayles puts too little emphasis on the roles of stability and continuity in the life conditions of the individual and its ability to establish a strong sense of self. Here again, the dilemma of strong and weak individuals arises. Nietzsche took the part of the strong, and their ability to handle change and chaotic situations, while for many reasons, Hayles devotes less attention to the fundamental consequences of this aspect. Above all, Hayles' ambition is to describe a posthuman condition that is not necessarily either anti-humanist or apocalyptic (Hayles 1999, 288), but it is also obvious that this condition is a highly unpredictable, and the consequences are more radical and manifold than in other scenarios for human development that do not consider the ubiquitous use of technology. Hayles acknowledges that she has a particular focus on cybernetics, rather than genetic and biological approaches to the question of the posthuman (Hayles 2010, 322). Regarding her reasons for evading the latter perspective, Hayles argues that one cannot do everything, which is certainly correct, but the biological dimension is such a significant part of the discussion that it is difficult to ignore.

Western culture has been much more influenced by imagining the end of the world than by the possibility of a dramatic new direction in the history of humankind. There is an uncanny feeling to imagining a more advanced culture, or a being more advanced than the human, which would put existing humanity into a broader perspective as just one element in a long evolution. The major monotheistic religions do not have a place for this kind of thinking, either, but support the idea of the human being in its present cultural and biological state as the endpoint of evolution. Despite its influence, evolutionary theory has only had a limited influence on broader visions of a different future for the human species.

Historically-oriented culture displays a fascination with bygone advanced civilizations – such as the Etruscans, the Mayas, and the Incas – without this being connected to the idea that today's dominant cultures might someday share their fate. However, apart from their much more advanced supporting technology, contemporary cultures feature one significant difference, namely, their participation in a lengthy process of globalization, which, despite cultural differences, has left no culture uninfluenced by others. The transcending of contemporary cultures would not be prompted suddenly from without, but as part of an internal process of the social systems in question, where, from a historical perspective, it would then be reasonable to speak of a change so profound that the idea of a new human would make sense. This might be the case with the way technology makes information available in new ways, the beginnings of which may be seen in the form of smartphones and internet connections. Another commentator on the idea of the posthuman, Tim Lenoir, seconds N. Katherine Hayles' view of the hybrid of human and posthuman that does not favour either domain:

> .... the emergence of the 'posthuman' is not a matter of technological deter-
> minism, of the needs and necessities of computer processor improvements
> anastomosing the unwitting aid of human agency with biotechnology to
> produce a new life form. As Kate Hayles has reminded us, the posthuman, like
> the human, is a hybrid entity constructed through networks that are materially
> real, socially regulated, and discursively constructed. (Lenoir 2002, 210)

A more specific prophecy based on technological developments has been formulated by Ray Kurzweil who, in *The Singularity is Near*, foresees, partly based on the predictions of Moore's law, a situation in which machines will become more intelligent than humans, hence the idea of a singularity of the world that would make the dichotomy between life and technology obsolete. The many consequences this might include, along with other technological innovations, the possibility of making backups of entire brains, which would make a system of consciousness immortal. But it would also be a world where humans, if the term still applies, would have to deal with being surrounded by superior intelligence in many forms.

Kurzweil does not understate his arguments, and his time schedule based on technological developments may not hold, but the influence of computers on human living conditions is difficult to downplay. Furthermore, he sees it as a positive thing, that the human being will be forced to acknowledge that it is not a privileged species with special rights; ironically, humankind's ability to produce complex machines is what has put it in the position of a being that will be surpassed in intellectual capability. Therefore, Kurzweil's vision of the world is one that will have human 'fingerprints' all over it, although not controlled by humans.

Regardless of whether Kurzweil proves to be correct in his predictions, the underlying values on which his vision of the future is founded are thought-provoking. Kurzweil is by no means an anti-humanist or a nihilist, and he argues for a number of values that, according to him, should guide future development. Death is regarded primarily as a tragedy that cannot be relativized, even though one of the primary functions of religion is to give meaning to death (Kurzweil 2005, 372). He even counters the argument that death makes life bearable and even meaningful by arguing that life will become really meaningful and bearable in the Singularity.

A consequence of the Singularity is that one's body will not be a stable part of one's identity, and it will be possible to change bodies. As Kurzweil notes, using an argument that also corresponds to Luhmann's systemic view of the human, the body is perpetually replacing its parts, and it must be thought of as an informational structure that goes beyond its DNA, and encompasses memory and the particular constitution of intelligence and knowledge an individual has produced, which is what separates information from knowledge (Kurzweil 2005, 372).

When Kurzweil discusses the source of meaning of live and of evolution, his ideas of the meaning of existence are both abstract and specific. He sees the creation of order, or higher intelligence and knowledge, as the joint purpose of both humans and the universe. Over time, this will foster a vision of the cosmos based on resistance to the Second Law of Thermodynamics, which states that in a closed system there will be more and more entropy: that is, disorder and chaos. Expressed metaphorically, life itself is a resistance to this law of nature. Kurzweil presents mesmerizing and clear-cut arguments, but they are also focused on values that say little about life as it is actually lived. For Kurzweil, 'knowledge' is the unifying term, and under this, music, art, science and technology may be summarized as categories where the creation of patterns has a privileged position, and from which superfluous information is eliminated.

Kurzweil's presentation, in the form of a future dialogue on the dangers and opportunities connected with the achievement of Singularity, is both entertaining and humorously liberating, and includes Charles Darwin giving his candid views on the subject (Kurzweil 2005, 367). The Singularity will not end all problems, there will still be risks, including software viruses, and risks of terrorism and crime; yet for Kurzweil, the underlying premise seems to be that the overwhelming power of computing and technology will be so unimaginably vast that things will work out in the end. Kurzweil sees the effort to overcome the limits of biology as a defining human trait (Vance 2010). While this is highly debatable, there is also the question of how to understand this view of humans as striving for connecting elements that, until now, have mixed rather poorly. There is a clear connection to earlier periods in the history of ideas, when the material world was viewed as a prison, from Plato, through a number of religions and Romanticism. It is not difficult to see the hope for a Singularity as an extension of this frustrated desire. Ashlee Vance remarked that:

> On a more millennialist and provocative note, the Singularity also offers a modern-day, quasi-religious answer to the Fountain of Youth by affirming the notion that, yes indeed, humans — or at least something derived from them — can have it all. (Vance 2010)

Until now, visions of transcending biology have been based on the idea of a human essence, idea, soul or similar. In the idea of a Singularity, the coupling of visions of evolution and of eternity promises the best of both sides.[39] These sorts of promises are rarely kept.

With his 1977 article, 'Prometheus as Performer', Ihab Hassan was among the first to to address posthumanism and visions of radical human evolution, and to use the term 'posthuman' (Hassan 1977, 214), having already written, in his 1971 article, 'POSTmodernISM', on the prospects of a radical change of the human (Hassan 1971, 25ff.). The article concerned topics that both relate to both posthumanism and the idea of the posthuman, and typically of Hassan, the article is unconventional in its style: in this case, written as a play for different textual forms. But the content of the article is informed both by developments in artificial intelligence and by the reflections of a number of scholars, including Martin Heidegger, Claude Lévi-Strauss and Michel Foucault, regarding the relationship between humans and technology. Echoing Lévi-Strauss, Hassan's article states that the history of the Earth began and will end without the human, while Foucault is quoted for his perhaps now much-too-quoted statement that the human or the subject is a relatively new invention that may be approaching an end. More importantly, Hassan defends himself against some of the criticism of his use of the term:

> At present, posthumanism may appear variously as a dubious neologism, the latest slogan, or simply another image of man's recurrent self-hate. Yet posthumanism may also hint at a potential in our culture, hint at a tendency struggling to become more than a trend. (Hassan 1977, 212)

In many senses, Hassan is an optimist, especially when he argues against Foucault and Lévi-Strauss that the end of humanism is not the end, but a step toward an improved understanding of humans as part of a larger context, which will lead to a higher level of reflection, and where art, technology, and 'the existential search for a unified sensibility' will play significant roles (Hassan 1977, 208ff.). Even then, dilemmas remain, when it comes to determining what would count as improvement.

Means of change

In a discussion of change, the goal of the changes and how such goals may be described in a way that makes them ethically convincing are of central importance. Such descriptions may be explicit, as parts of debates in the sciences, politics and art, but they may be just as telling as parts of an underlying justification for a practice that strives to achieve certain goals.

The classic division in the field of bioethics is that of *therapy* versus *enhancement*, which is often also associated with acceptable therapy and unnatural enhancement, although the usefulness of the distinction has been criticized (Resnik 2000, 374). I argue that change needs to be considered in three main divisions: *normalization, improvement* and *perfection*. This provides a more dynamic and realistic way of thinking about different visions of change. 'Normalization' is a stronger term than 'therapy' because it reflects group norms, rather than the normal condition of the individual in question. At the same time, normalization is a concept that is easily connected with some of the most significant policies of the twentieth century, ranging from the eugenics of some Western societies, to the imposition of new norms in totalitarian societies.

The concepts of normalization, improvement and perfection are useful for analyzing current ethical debates. Technologies that screen fetuses for genetic abnormalities are widely accepted, and many expectant parents respond to test results indicating that their child would have Down's syndrome or other, increasingly detectable genetic anomalies by having the fetus aborted. In this instance, the ideal of 'the normal' is reinforced across society to a very high degree, and this is a cause for concern, should future genetic diagnostics disclose traits that may be interpreted as abnormalities, or even when present-day gender diagnostics are responsible for the disproportionally high rate of male births in China, for example.[40]

Normality and therapy are also central concepts when using technologies to repair humans, currently with the use of pacemakers, artificial body parts, laser surgery and so on, in order to restore the individual to normality, but not too much further. This becomes clear when considering the cosmetically improved human who balances between normality as established by groups, ideals of both the individual and the group, and the possible individual improvements. The lines between therapy and enhancement are difficult to draw, and the norms are not carved in stone.

The use of psychopharmacology is another accepted way of helping people to re-establish a normal balance in their lives, whereas the use of drugs to attain a state of euphoria is not accepted, partly because of the conviction that there are inevitable negative side-effects to using chemical substances. But if there were no side-effects, why should one not actively promote their use?

Perfection is a complicated term to work with, but nevertheless, it is important. In 'The Soul of Man under Socialism', Oscar Wilde noted that perfection was what humans should strive for, and ideas of perfection permeate a number of ways of thinking about changes in body, mind and society (Wilde 2001, 128). Mary Shelley lets Victor Frankenstein consider how a tranquil mind is a sign of a human in a state of perfection (Shelley 2000, 59). Critics of the use biotechnological means of change, such as Michael Sandel and Maxwell Mehlman, explicitly use the idea of perfection as a prominent part of their argument against the hope for improvement (Mehlman 2009, Sandel 2007), whereas the idea of enhancement is a more modest category, brought into play by advocates of the use of technology for more than therapeutic goals (Bostrom and Savulescu 2009). However, the utmost perfection related to the question of the posthuman would be immortality, which is also clearly distinct from merely prolonged life. While a number of challenges have already familiarized humans with dilemmas surrounding normality, improvement and perfection, there is the horizon of the genetically improved human, which is a challenges the thinking behind each of these categories, and which could be guided by the desires expressed by our current practices: healthy, resilient, constantly repaired, physically attractive individuals who may also have a high degree of intelligence and empathy. That would be the positive vision, seen from the level of the individual, but it would be naïve to think that guiding human genetics toward certain goals would not have significant consequences across a number of societal domains. Conversely, it is important to emphasize that technology-based change is only part of a nexus of different means of effecting human change.

The great mental plasticity of humans, owing to their long infancy and great capacity for learning, rather than a reliance on instinct, makes them unique among species on Earth, and the consciousness of being able to do something active to improve humans has a long history that should be part of the perspective on the horizon revealed by technology and biotechnology. The possibilities for human change take six main forms: 1) development of the individual's body and psyche through cultivation and learning, 2) changes to cultural organization and communication that affect individuals, 3) changes in the genome over time, either through natural or deliberate selection, 4) influencing the body and psyche with chemical substances, 5) changing the genome through biotechnology, 6) integrating machines and humans. Each of these six ways of changing humans may be significant and laden with traits that may be regarded as both positive and negative.

Individual cultivation

The extraordinary ability of humans to cultivate themselves through diet, activities and learning has had a central role in cultural history, from the attributes lauded in antiquity, to the political values around which modern societies are organized. It is also evident that the forms this cultivation has taken, the ends that it has served have changed over time, and it has been decisive in determining the balance between the benefits to the individual and society, which remains relevant.

In Greek antiquity, the difference was most pronounced between Athens and Sparta, where upbringing and education in both states were highly developed, but of a very different nature. Both states knew how to turn boys into soldiers, but the difference between the promotion of art, philosophy and democracy in Athens, and the much narrower focus on warfare in Sparta is also clear. From a modern viewpoint, taking small boys from their families to be trained as soldiers seems to be particularly cruel and unnatural, but also raises questions about the norms and goals established by society. Discussions of normality can never be carried out in a vacuum, and one's argument will always bear the stamp of one's own culture, providing what Carl Schmitt called 'the normative power of the given' (Schmitt 2003, 73).

In 'What is Enlightenment?', Immanuel Kant formulates an ethics calling for the individual to be treated as an end, and not as a means (Kant 1991, 60). At the same time, this thought has had a significant influence on education and upbringing, as well as on societal utopias and the hope of bringing society to a utopian state where economy does not restrict individuals. Yet, the relationship between self-improvement and societal needs played a significant role in the twentieth century, with regard to people's bodies, from the awareness of the importance of being physically active, a series of injunctions against overindulging in alcohol and food, smoking, and injecting various substances, and the societal pressure to keep bodies healthy and free of fat and smoke, in order to not burden public health care (where such systems exists). This was a significant development toward putting pressure on the individual to cultivate itself, in order to be considered 'a good life', worth sustaining.

Cultural improvements

Just as few questions are raised, concerning self-improvement, as long as it remains within certain limits, the idea of cultural advancement is a forceful narrative of civilizations, although it is just as often counterbalanced by narratives of decay. Oswald Spengler's *The Decline of the West* is one example of this, just as the series of developments bundled together as 'globalization' may be described in terms of both positive and negative cultural change, depending on how one values the changes in national and local identities that it brings.

Questions of cultural improvement are extremely complex, in particular because the pros and cons may be argued on a level of detail where the different elements may be impossible to compare. The value of some progressions is only briefly debated. Women's suffrage, equal rights for all, regardless of race, and protection from violence are just a few issues that looked different in many societies, one or two centuries ago, but for which it is difficult identify drawbacks. Other changes are more difficult to assess; for example, whether the cultivation of competiveness is good or bad, or a bit of both. The decline of violence, described by Steven Pinker in *The Better Angels of Our Nature*, is another account of a change that makes it difficult to establish grounds for essential human traits, but situates them in a historical narrative of change (Pinker 2011).[41]

From a long, evolutionary perspective, cultural development is inseparable from the evolution of the human into what it has become. Among others, Merlin Donald has suggested that culture and the use of language must have had a significant role in the development of a larger and more advanced human brain. Even more importantly, it is not possible to develop one's potential without being a part of a culture in which the transfer of knowledge and access to specialized resources are crucial (Donald 1993, 269ff.). Twenty-five thousand years ago, people must have been quite different from today's humans, because their cultural software had a different and much more primitive constitution, lacking, for example, ideas of mathematics and complex organizations. Donald views cultural advances in the form of science, technology, language and many other aspects in a positive light, despite there also being negative consequences attached to these developments, such as a very high degree of specialization, and dependence on technology (Donald 1993, 207f.). But ultimately, this view of humans emphasizes their ability to transcend their fundamental biological conditions, and emerge as cultural beings whose cognitive abilities are largely formed by culture, just as culture has been a driving force in the evolution of cognitive abilities.

With respect to contemporary societies, Donald indicates that right now a huge leap is taking place in human cognitive environments, where the 'old' brain of the human is placed in a new media ecology that gives access to an unprecedented wealth of information. Donald's thesis is that the brain will adapt to this condition, and his description of what might happen in the digital age is comparable to former leaps forward (Donald 1993, 4). Whether this constitutes a new human is not certain, but Donald's descriptions of structural changes in working memory, a deeper relationship with, and dependence on collective memory, and a change in brain structure through the different uses of its parts, make it possible to suggest the idea of a new kind of human arising as a result of the digital revolution.[42]

Another decisive point Donald makes is that biological evolution has always been slow, and that most evolutionary features are kept and supplied by new features. Thus, a number of central operations that are vital to the human organism are still carried out by the hippocampi, whereas the frontal lobes, particularly large in humans, are where a large part of contemporary change is taking place. Therefore, cultural development and changes in social systems will have a greater effect on humans over the short term, while it is not possible to separate the idea of the individual from the cultural process of which it is a part.

Cultural change is by no means neutral, but profoundly affects people's cognitive abilities, and influences the wider evolution of the species. At the moment, the increased information that individuals process makes for a significant change, where the idea of given body of knowledge may give way to the ability to recognize patterns. Almost 50 years ago, Marshall McLuhan made a prediction about the cognitive needs of a culture with an overload of information:

> What is indicated for the new learning procedures is not the absorption of classified and fragmented data, but pattern recognition with all that that implies of grasping relationships. (McLuhan 2011)

Pattern recognition is also the title of the first novel in a trilogy by William Gibson, which addresses this view of the world. In the *Neuromancer* trilogy, the wild fantasies of a matrix in which body, mind and machine are inseparable have given way to a much more down-to-earth setting, but it is one in which the eerie sense of not being at home in the world and its wealth of information is the dominant feeling, thereby highlighting a central, inevitable trade-off between being progressive, and maintaining a recognizable comfort zone. Nevertheless, recognizing changes in culture, and their effects on people's lives and their mental 'software' can hardly be underestimated.

Selection

While individual and cultural changes may be relatively uncontroversial when presented as harmless, positive, and future-oriented, it is also easy to provide examples of their murkier sides, rendering the question of human change through the cultivation of the human gene pool more controversial and more complicated. First, it is crucial that there be a number of mechanisms at work that make the element of selection a part of reality, and for there to be both 'natural' and unintentional, as well as 'cultural' and intentional selections taking place, and the difference between these may sometimes seem very minor. In animal herds, as well as in the human selection of partners with the purpose of securing the continuation of the species, individual strength and socials norms are central regulating factors.

Taking a humorous approach to the topic of natural selection, the creators of the 'Darwin Awards' have collected tales of accidental deaths caused by the deceased themselves, whom they thank – with a glint in the eye and a good deal of dark, sarcastic humor – for removing themselves from the human gene pool, having proven by the circumstances of their deaths that they will not be missed.[43]

The distance from the humorous to the eerie is not far. In his *Guns, Germs, and Steel*, Jared Diamond, in a well-meaning way describes primitive societies as having selection mechanisms that, owing to the harsh living conditions and dangers, favour intelligent individuals in ways that members of developed societies do not encounter. This poses questions regarding the consequences of this way of looking at humans, in terms of those who are not subjected to Darwinian pressures in advanced societies (Diamond 2005, 21).

Humans have a long history of involvement in selecting to obtain a desirable population. In animal husbandry, this has been applied for centuries, both to ensure a fit population and as a part of experiments to create new breeds. For humans themselves, the culturally universal ban on incest is also part of an effort to select, in order to secure fitness and ensure the previously-described normalization, and the heartbreaking practices found in most cultures, of killing newborns that are unfit to live normal lives is part of the human heritage.

Fitness and normalization may not account for all the selections of evolution. Judith Rich Harris suggests that selection in the animal kingdom takes place for three reasons. Two of the mechanisms are well-described, namely fitness and sexual appeal (Harris 2006, 64). Harris's argument is that parental selection of their offspring is a third significant evolutionary force that may yield relatively rapid changes, since, according to Harris, this selection seems to be driven by aesthetic criteria. Harris uses examples involving skin colour and body hair to underpin her argument, and she connects the last development – again, recognizing it as a hypothesis – with the once slowly-growing awareness that humans are different from other animal species. Harris suggests that hairlessness could signal that one was not prey, and that the rapid extinction of the Neanderthals might be related to their body hair identifying them as prey for humans (Harris 2006, 66). Harris's points about parental selection are particularly relevant in situations where technology facilitates new methods for the selection of fetuses. In parts of China, the birth ratio of boys to girls is off by up to 60 per cent from the natural gender distribution, and the large number of abortions owing to diagnoses of Down's syndrome demonstrates that people make choices that are not far from those Harris depicts, and underscores Jürgen Habermas's concerns regarding 'liberal eugenics' and a return to the eugenics of the early twentieth century.[44]

One central element in the long history of selection is that its development has progressed at a pace such that no radical break has been experienced from generation to generation, but, given the insights that new technologies may deliver, in the form of gene sequencing and the selection of eggs and sperm from particularly gifted donors, the situation has the potential to change very rapidly, and the social norms regarding what is accepted as normal could alter.

The world is also changing in ways that render a future vision of increased normalization inaccurate. Evolutionary biologist Spencer Wells mentions that in the modern world there has been a mixing of genetic lines to an extent never before seen. He calls this 'the third big bang in the human history', which goes back to the time of the African slave trade, and it is the reason Irish genes may be found in Africa, and it is a development that has continued with even greater rapidity today, where travel between countries and cultures has cleared the way significantly for an increased mixing of genes from ethnic groups that had no contact with each other before. Wells points out that a global icon such as professional golfer Tiger Woods is a human being who, owing to his complex genetic heritage, could only have been born in the twentieth century (Wells 2002, 193).[45]

While Wells sees many positive traits in the new patterns of combining genes, he notes that there is a certain irony (for a scientist concerned with the genetic heritage of humans) in the overlap between the increased technological capacity to trace an individual's genetic heritage and the fact that the existing situation means that it will be increasingly complicated to connect the individuals of today and tomorrow with their pasts. The new human with a detached relationship to the past might be a reality, but Wells warns us to not forget the journey that brought us to where we now are. Wells' call is another example of the importance of collective memory concerning identity and ethics.

All in all, natural and controlled selection are parts of human heritage, but new means now at our disposal may be so powerful that they can make changes on a completely new scale, and raise questions of how they should be used and who should decide how this is accomplished. And, if diversity has value, how does that fit with normalization, improvement, and perfection?

Infusions

It is quite evident that the human body is a system that requires ongoing maintenance, or the system will come to a halt, and with that is the end of consciousness. But apart from oxygen and the most basic nutrition – about which accepted wisdom regarding what is healthy and harmful has periodically changed – advanced pharmaceuticals may extensively affect both body and consciousness. Ideas of normality have guided societal regulation of what is and is not considered acceptable, but also sometimes regulated to an extent that this control may be questioned, as the prohibition on alcohol in 1920s in the United States showed. Thus, the use of pharmaceuticals is legal if they are used to eliminate pain, but is unacceptable for pleasure or performance enhancement in sports. Side-effects, particularly addiction, often provide a strong argument against certain uses of substances. In the same vein, psychopharmaceuticals are regarded as good if they can heal, but bad if used to produce an exalted state. Again, there are many pragmatically valid reasons for being cautious, from spending resources that might be better used, to complicated and manifold side-effects. One literary documentation of this is William S. Burroughs' *Junkie* with its account of the damage done by, as well as a fascination with drugs.

Philosophically, it would be more difficult to argue against allowing the use of substances that make one more comfortable, happy, aware, resilient and quick thinking, if there were no substantial negative consequences to them. With the development of more advanced pharmaceuticals, it is likely that such scenarios will become more prevalent, making the arguments for denying enhancing drugs difficult to respect, from the viewpoint of the individual.

Societal restraints on enhancing drugs are widespread, but it is also probable that some societies or organizations will be tempted to increase their competitive strengths. In the same way that nutritious food, nutritional supplements and exercise are some of the recommendations that help to create a more fit population, and hence greater productivity, it is not unlikely that substances that will enable people to think faster, concentrate longer and generally be more productive could become part of a race for fitness among nations. The outcomes might resemble the situation described by Aldous Huxley in *Brave New World*, which illustrates how simple gains may be followed by complicated losses, or even more ominously by Robert Louis Stevenson, in his *Strange Case of Dr Jekyll and Mr Hyde*.

Designing and cloning

The development of biotechnological techniques for analyzing and manipulating genetic material is of one of the two most radical, and in many ways potentially frightening means by which humans might change themselves, the other being integration with machines, which will be addressed in the next section. The situation is without historical precedent, and to most of the writers discussed in this book, the level of sophistication of these techniques was inconceivable. It is possible to describe the implementation of these techniques as both slower than expected and as a rapid development. Until a few years ago, there were no known attempts to design the genes of a human, but babies with three parents have moved significantly closer to existing, which constitutes a milestone in the use of designing human genes, and the co-development of ethical boundaries and technical possibilities is being negotiated in most countries, to ensure a legal foundation for the use of this biotechnology.[46]

In principle, cloning does not lead to a change in a genome, although minor mutations always occur. This is a technique that has been used on various species for commercial purposes, both to ensure a fit population (e.g. of cattle), and as a way of recreating deceased pets. Cloning techniques are difficult to develop from species to species, and are laden with risks, but it is likely that the risks will decrease over time. At the same time, it is well-known that nature itself can clone, in the form of identical twins, triplets, and even larger numbers, although human cloning is forbidden. One or two clones do not seem uncanny but 50 to 100 identical humans would probably disturb most.

Given the advancements in cloning techniques and the relatively low costs of using them, it is not unlikely that in the not-too-distant future a clone of a human individual will be produced. If this barrier is transgressed, the consequences would be manifold: people would be able to clone themselves, as French writer Michel Houellebecq has expressed his wish to do (Houellebecq 2003); clones could be made for the purpose of growing spare organs, a topic about which Kazuo Ishiguro has written in the novel, *Never Let Me Go*; it would be possible to clone people with special features ranging from athleticism and beauty, to intelligence and creativity, the order of reproduction could be altered, as suggested in Huxley's fiction; and it would be possible to recreate deceased persons. The 1978 movie, *The Boys from Brazil*, was an early fictional work addressing this topic, exploring what would happen if a series of clones of Adolf Hitler had been produced and distributed around the globe in family conditions resembling those of the German dictator.

Concerning the alteration of the genome, things become more complicated. What is currently most important is the rapid growth of knowledge about the human genome, which may be used analytically on many levels. It is an important tool in criminal investigations, while the interest in interpreting genes is rising, and will affect people's knowledge about inherited diseases, for example, just as the gene sequencing of fetuses is likely to become normal, as the cost of the analyses drops. Parents tend act on the knowledge they gain,[47] which could be one of the qualification for demarcating an era of a new human, in the sense that individuals would be preapproved, based on a thorough genetic analysis.

While more knowledge of genes is being generated, it is also increasingly evident that previous ideas of finding very specialized genes that could explain specific character traits are incorrect, and that a complex interplay of genes accounts for certain dispositions, making it very difficult and potentially dangerous to attempt a specific outcome of gene manipulation. Ultimately, development would be driven by areas where the stakes are high, with longevity as a frontrunner. Gene therapy is in vogue, holding forth promises of being able to radically slow the processes of aging.[48] Should such therapies become available, and successfully extend the human life span considerably, it would be difficult to dismiss this as not being a gain for humanity in some respects, but it would also become a changing factor in society and the ways people live their lives.[49] An uneven distribution of such therapies, and new anxieties about dying in accidents might be side-effects.

Machinery

A final and equally controversial way of changing humanity is through the integration of mechanical technology, particularly cybernetic technology, which would also affect consciousness. Many elements of the integration of such technology are a part of our world. Artificial joints, for example hips, seem uncontroversial, as they replace simple mechanical parts. Pacemakers have long assisted heart activity, and are already a slightly more invasive addition to the body that can even react to altered physical and emotional states. And, one of the latest practices involves implanting hearing aids in children who would otherwise be deaf.

A key feature of these technologies is that they are integrated, and cannot be simply removed, but become part of the individual's identity. Here too, questions of therapy and enhancement arise, as the creation of 'normal' states of heart activity and hearing do not affect the everyday much, whereas enhancements, particularly those designed to integrate information technologies into the human body, would involve a decisive break with normality. However, regulation of hormone production and metabolism are also areas where technology could signal a further integration.

Donna Haraway's definition of the cyborg as a hybrid of machine and living organism, and as 'a creature of social reality as well as a creature of fiction' that has the ability to change its perspective on the world, captures different aspects of visions of change (Haraway 2004, 7). Both aspects are active in their potential, and in their more limited material expressions. The perspective on the present includes changing the status of a number of dualisms that are central to our culture:

> … certain dualisms have been persistent in Western traditions; they have all been systemic to the logics and practices of domination of women, people of colour, nature, workers, animals – in short, domination of all constituted as others, whose task is to mirror the self. Chief among these troubling dualisms are self/other, mind/body, culture/nature, male/female, civilized/primitive, reality/appearance, whole/part, agent/resource, maker/made, active/passive, right/wrong, truth/illusion, total/partial, God/man. The self is the One who is not dominated, who knows that by the service of the other, the other is the one

who holds the future, who knows that by the experience of domination, which gives the lie to the autonomy of the self. To be One is to be autonomous, to be powerful, to be God; but to be One is to be an illusion, and so to be involved in a dialectic of apocalypse with the other. Yet to be other is to be multiple, without clear boundary, frayed, insubstantial. One is too few, but two are too many. (Haraway 2004, 35)

Haraway views the breakdown of the dichotomy between machine and living organism as a central consequence of advanced technology, leading to a view of the world as consisting of communication systems that, in principal, have no ontological difference. Yet, one must still consider the difference between body and consciousness. As long as it is the body that enters into a symbiotic relationship with machines, and not the consciousness, there remains one last border to transcend, even if this transcendence might be impossible to discern, because the integration might be seamless, and the sense of self would not be lost, even if the conditions of its being were changed dramatically. However, we have yet to experience that, and most people can handle the dichotomies that are actively acknowledged, even if they are losing their undisputed validity.[50] The curious dilemma is that even though there is little enthusiasm for becoming cyborgs, it is difficult to deny that many have become so, at least to some extent (Hables Gray 2012, 27f.).

The many kinds of thinking about human change have developed historically, and added more varieties to the list of possible means of broadly influencing the body, consciousness, and society. As the newer and more technologically advanced methods for change present themselves as the most forceful, it is easy to forget in how many ways humans have both dreamt of change and actually pursued change and improvement through those means they had at hand, based on the values that they believed in. Older methods still influence us, and newer kinds that we cannot yet imagine will appear, adding more complexity to the desires and the moral grounds on which change is pursued or avoided.

Literature's critique

In a number of ways, literature thrives on criticizing the idea of human change and the new human. The idyllic does not contain the tensions that have histori-cally produced the most remarkable literature, and literature cannot portray beauty in the same way that the visual arts may create objects that merely fascinate with their own appearance. Literature's seemingly inherent logic or need for being critical, and its limited capacity to produce positive visions of the future, may render literature excessively pessimistic, in a way that might be regarded inherently problematic. If certain developments in the world could be described in hindsight as positive, why should the potential of the future not be part of similar descriptions? Literature may be progressive in its exploration of form, but conservative in its ability to generate ideas of better worlds. This dilemma will be particularly addressed in the works of Michel Houellebecq; but in general, this this is one of literature's blind spots. That being said, literature's often nuanced critique and well-founded skepticism are central functions of the art.

Concerning visions of the new human, literature delivers various specific kinds of critique: ideas of utopias ultimately shaped as hopes for a new human, and which are carried out on a societal level; circumstances that present humans as isolated beings whose social relations and cultural history are not considered; the aesthetic criticism of a tensionless life, where boredom becomes an argument against the promises of a new human.

A common idea of a utopia is a place where history no longer matters, a place where history has come to an end. Visions with roots in both the Bible and Karl Marx's ideas present states of being where nothing fundamentally new is supposed to happen. Such a condition does not form the basis for exciting literature or for narrative structure. But there is also the question of whether such a utopia of paradisiacal conditions is desirable. H. G. Wells presents an argument urging people to reconsider the idea of a utopia:

> The Utopia of a modern dreamer must differ in one fundamental aspect from the Nowheres and Utopias men planned before Darwin quickened the thought of the world. Those were all perfect and static States, a balance of happiness won for ever against the forces of unrest and disorder that inhere in things. One beheld a healthy and simple generation enjoying the fruits of the earth in an atmosphere of virtue and happiness, to be followed by other virtuous, happy, and entirely similar generations, until the Gods grew weary. Change and development were dammed back by invincible dams for ever. But the Modern Utopia must be not static but kinetic, must shape not as a permanent state but as a hopeful stage, leading to a long ascent of stages. Nowadays we do not resist and overcome the great stream of things, but rather float upon it. We build now not citadels, but ships of state. (Wells 2011, 1)

Wells' idea of a utopia is a facetted criticism of the static utopia, and of a condition where nothing important will occur again. At the same time, there is a paradox built into this conception of a developing utopia, as it will always leave behind something of lesser value, and one's contemporaneity must be regarded as less valuable than the future, unless the very ideas of evolution and progress are so highly valued that they are themselves parts of the utopia. However, this is not an idea that seems to permeate public discourse at the present. Progress is being made in many technical disciplines, but they do not translate into a grander narrative of progression, perhaps because what makes life worth living is bound up with much more complex elements that cannot be substituted by progression in one field or another.

In 'Terminal Men', Nicholas Pethes writes about science fiction's fascination with genetic change and cyborgs, with an emphasis on the subgenre of 'medical thrillers'. One of his conclusions is that the world represented is rarely a complete dystopia or a scientific utopia, but a world in which the human in its present form cannot live:

> As such, human beings according to today's notion are not suitable inhabitants of this future scenario anymore. Medical thrillers are, as István Csicsery-Ronay has put it, 'mutopias': they tell of a community of mutant and mutable humans that does not provide a stable ground for the traditional narrative on humanity. Popular novels on genetic experimentation with human beings are neither utopias of a coming paradise nor the apocalypse of humanity transformed. Instead, they serve as a mutopian stage for the collisions of these extremes—a collision that is in fact going to change the image of man on the level of the narratives he is telling about himself. (Pethes 2006, 180)

At the same time, Pethes finds the literary genres exploring human evolution important, especially medical thrillers, in that they create scenarios where the ability of humankind to guide its own evolution is addressed from a number of perspectives. Pethes underscores the complexity of the field, and demonstrates how difficult it is to define a particular human trait.

Literature's critique of utopias and idyllic scenarios is part of its value, and this plays an important role in describing futures to be avoided, key examples of which appear in the novels by Huxley and Orwell. Also central to a literary universe are the conflicts and distinctions that give it a substantial vibrancy. On the other hand, one might also ask whether it is a problem that literature has difficulty in taking part in visions of the future that demonstrate improvement, gains that are without significant losses, and that do not involve the dichotomy of utopia and dystopia, but merely show incremental improvements in the conditions of human life. There is no doubt that the world is full of problems and injustice, just as existential problems concerning meaning and death, both now and in the future, provide literature with ample material. Literature does not have to be univocal, and it can present a double perspective that criticizes both the present and an imagined future alike, thereby revealing the positives sides of both.

It is significant that literature thrives much better on apocalyptic and dystopian scenarios than on visions of improvement. Particularly with regard to the physical changes that biotechnology assists, it is difficult to find works of fiction that convincingly address prolonged lives, improved treatment of disease, and improvements to physical, emotional and intellectual capacities. For many good reasons, some of which are that these changes and the means of achieving them are laden with risk and eerie consequences, one might still argue that literature has a problem if it cannot deal with such phenomena when they constitute improvements. Literature is thus often put in a position where it is in opposition to the general perception of improvement in a public discourse. But literature has the capacity to present nuanced positions, because it does not have to convince and draw conclusions, but can operate through multiple perspectives and in different registers within the same work, ranging from seriousness to dark irony. Creating future visions in order to criticize the present is a common approach at which Kurt Vonnegut (for example) excelled. His novel, *Galápagos*, chronicles a future when the human brain has shrunk, enabling people to be happier than we are in our present state of evolution, with our 'oversized human brain' (Vonnegut 1985, 16). Robert T. Tally notes that *Galápagos* is a narrative of both apocalypse and change, which widens the sense-making peace with the universe found at the individual level in *Slaughterhouse-Five* (Tally 2011, 146). Ultimately, there is no philosophical foundation for this kind of optimism on behalf of the human species, but there exists a sense, as Tally sees it, that mankind will endure, despite all its flaws. Tally also points out that the role of the writer in this situation is something Vonnegut himself commented on, in a 1973 interview, when he described the writer as 'specialized cells in the social organism. They are evolutionary cells. Mankind is trying to become something else; it's experimenting with new ideas all the time'. (Vonnegut in Tally 2011, 147).

Literature has also taken a more positive stance is in the exploration of communicative systems. Following Marshall McLuhan's credo of seeing media as an extension of humans (McLuhan 1994, 21), the literature concerned with cyborgs and human-machine interaction has found a way to describe a future that offers new perspectives that are vastly different from the ordinary world of today, by positing a way to transcend the barrier to the individuality of consciousness. But even such fantasies may be exhausted, and it is striking that William Gibson has turned away from fantasies of a radical integration of consciousness with other communicative systems, in favour of a more traditional and contemporary involvement with the influence of technology on humans.

A variation of the problem of the idyllic is the problem of boredom in the perfect world. Things would be nice, but ultimately dull, and from the way we make sense of the world, it is difficult to describe a perfect world as not being void of significant meaning. Alan P. Lightman's novel, *Einstein's Dreams*, takes the life of Albert Einstein at around the time of his publication of his first theory of relativity in 1905 as the loose and poetic framework for a series of fantasies of how the world might be, if the conditions of time and death, in particular, were different. Lightman thereby creates a series of meta-utopias. One chapter begins like this:

> Suppose that people live forever. / Strangely, the population of each city splits in two: the Laters and the Nows. / The Laters reason that there is no hurry to begin their classes at the university, to learn a second language, to read Voltaire or Newton, to seek promotion in their jobs, to fall in love, to raise a family. For all these things, there is an infinite span of time. In endless time, all things can be accomplished. Thus all things can wait. Indeed, hasty actions breed mistakes. And who can argue with their logic? (Lightman 1993, 117f.)

Lightman describes many utopias where the fundamental conditions that one might hope would be changed have in fact been altered; but at the same time, there is always a criticism lurking in text. The chapter quoted above ends by describing how the repetitiveness and the impossibility of doing anything new leads people to commit suicide.

An important aspect of Lightman's book is that it revolves around a revolution in the conception of the universe, but renders worlds that are by and large difficult to regard positively, and the utopian ideas end by accepting the world as it is. In the same manner as Lightman, and also very humorously, Julian Barnes describes, in *A History of the World in 10½ Chapters*, how repetition takes its toll, even in a perfect world. In the case of Barnes's alter ego, it is a universe where Leicester City repeatedly wins the Cup by 5–4, and where Barnes can make a round of golf in 18 strikes (Barnes 1990, 309). But this world soon becomes uninteresting, and even as he drops golf and takes up tennis, he soon becomes so good that he also beats everyone at that sport. Perfection is wonderful, but only for a time. Barnes's fascination with the problems that secularization should have done away with also recurs very explicitly in his non-fiction work, *Nothing to be Frightened of*.

The Danish author, Jens Peter Jacobsen, who was the first to translate Darwin into Danish, expressed similar thoughts in lyrical form, regarding the boring character of perfection in the poem that begins: 'Eternal and unchangeable/ is only the empty' (Jacobsen 1993, 100), which identifies the dynamic and changeable as the only things that are of value, but which one is also bound to lose. Jacobsen's atheist perspective on life is stoically presented in a poem from his final, tubercular years. The poem is materialistic and unsentimental, yet ends with a gesture of faith in ideas growing from the deeds of individuals, and thereby to the ongoing life of cultures and societies (Jacobsen 1993, 102). Here, the divide between individual and collective that Niklas Luhmann also emphasizes becomes a consolation for the inevitability of death, in accordance with the conviction that endlessness cannot make sense.

To avoid being locked into repetition, there is a need for alternative conceptions of time. On the one hand, literature is locked into grammatical and narrative conceptions of the world that make alternative ideas of time unrealistic, although the exploration of such alternatives is a recurrent theme, expressing impossible desires for a new ontology. Jorge Luis Borges presents a number of visions of different worlds where time functions differently than in our world, while in *Slaughterhouse-Five*, Kurt Vonnegut very radically and elegantly gives the alien creatures from Tralfamadore the ability to both live in linear time that comes to an end, and to move around in this otherwise mechanical time, as though they had been given the remote control to the movies of their own lives. This setup creates the possibility for new paradoxes and explanations, for which a writer of fiction cannot be held accountable, even if one were to see this conception of time as a way of describing a utopia that takes the best of two irreconcilable concepts of the world. However, this interpretation is implicitly commented on by Vonnegut, as he presents the Tralfamadorians as a particularly bored species that abducts human beings from the Earth to display them in a zoo (Vonnegut 1969, 25). Time poses a number of problems that eventually add up to questioning whether eternity or death is the more frightening idea.

While literature struggles to express positive visions of the future, it is also quite evident that Western culture has not stopped functioning as the result of the undermining of beliefs that were once its foundations, and even thrives on skepticism. It is telling that Renaissance authors such as Shakespeare, Cervantes and Montaigne all expressed a deeply-rooted skepticism about ideas of an inherent and benign human nature, and that they participated in revealing false ideas regarding a solid foundation for a philosophy or an interpretation of the world. As their own canonical status is very high, they may be said to part of a paradoxical, subversive foundation for Western thought (Thomsen 2011, 213).[51] The skeptical tradition carried on into Romanticism, with its complicated relations to fragments and transcendence, whereas both Karl Marx and Sigmund Freud founded two central discourses that both underline the conflicting conditions of human existence, and emphasize various paths to improvement. It is also worth noting that Marx's analyses of the roots of this conflict, rather than his utopian thinking, remain his most valuable contribution, again demonstrating how conflicting and subversive foundations may be regarded as part of that on which Western culture builds. It is in these aspects that literature has a particular role in expressing complex, sometimes paradoxical ideas of how to make sense of the world, and the way it is moving forward without ever aspiring to perfection.

4

The New Human and the Medium of Literature

Throughout history, literature has demonstrated that it is one of the strongest, if not the strongest, medium by which a collected presentation of the human condition may be offered in a mode that considers the past, interprets the present and, as the passage of time has often shown, forecasts future events or warns against what may happen. However, correspondences between the literary world and the world in which we live may not be the most important consequence of literature. Literature's capacity to present a particular vision of conditions that are highly relevant to thinking about the new human, through its inherent formal potential, is perhaps its most important contribution to the field. In this chapter, I make the case for four aspects of literature, that enable it to accomplish something different and often more valuable than other kinds of discourses. These concern the use of memory, both individual and collective, re-enchantment of the world, the engagement with an aesthetic ideal that does not strive for perfection, and a particular way of presenting the complex relationship between individual and collective. Each of these is in turn related to the formation of identities and modes of coupling aesthetic expressions and ethical norms.

Memory and re-enchantment

Literature is one of the primary means for enabling humans to make memories public and to adopt other people's memories. It is also a medium with a particular way of presenting the world and memories of it, which, in its ability to depict lived life, may in some ways be inferior to other media, such as a representational painting, a photograph or a film, but in other ways, literature can use its lack of mimetic expression to overcome the distance to the past; a distance that is almost always inherent with the use of images and sound.

Since the early 1990s there has been a boom in the academic interest in memory.[52] One explanation for this is a revaluation of memory against history, and the adoption of a constructivist paradigm in many humanist disciplines. Memories are being regarded as something produced, regardless of whether they are parts of a personal recollection or a community effort to transfer memories of a given phenomenon. In contrast to history, memories exist in the present, and even if false memories occur, they still occur as events in the present. This is also the dominant view of the research in the psychology of autobiographical memory, whereas earlier models that saw memory as an archive from which a recollection was retrieved have been replaced by more complex models, where the recollection is an event influenced very much by the circumstances of the present, even though there is still a dependence on archived material.[53] Other reasons for the interest in memory lies in the possibilities created by new media, in particular the internet, which makes it possible access material that was unavailable only a few years ago, just as globalization has given rise to a new cosmopolitan awareness and challenged the nation state as the frame of reference for collective memories (Olick 2011, 31).

Even more important reasons than the intense interest in memory studies may be found in the gradual change in the way of thinking about identity, which is essentially is a shift from a romantic idea of a self with a unique identity, which also underlies popular discourses such as those regarding 'self-realization', and political ideas of group identity. Within a constructivist paradigm, identity becomes much more a question of individual experience and education, and of the complex history of personal and collective memories that comprise the matter that has shaped the individual. In this respect, sociology and psychology have also been able to demonstrate how personal memories are connected to collective imagination as new influences, as suggested by Maurice Halbwachs' theory of dependence on collective memory (Halbwachs 1992, 40), and as the idea of 'life scripts' as a cultural model used by individuals when they think about their own lives, comparing them to a shared idea of the 'normal' and 'good' life of a given culture (Bohn and Berntsen 2008). On the other hand, traumatic events also have the power to shape personal memories, particularly because such shared memories, for example, the 9/11 attack, or the moon landing of 1969, are possible to communicate, and therefore to repeat time and again.

In *Contingency, Irony, and Solidarity*, Richard Rorty describes some of the consequences of the shift in the concept of personal identity that goes back to

Freud and Nietzsche, although Rorty does not believe that their thinking has yet had its full cultural impact (Rorty 1989, 40). Borrowing a metaphor from a poem by Philip Larkin, Rorty explores the idea of identity as a ship's bill of lading, with some things being taken aboard, and others being offloaded over time. Furthermore, such a composite and often contingent list will create a singular expression and print of an individual's life. But Rorty differs from Larkin in the sentiment expressed over this condition. Whereas Larkin's poem regrets that such a list is only valid for one mortal person, and does not express something more general or essential, Rorty does not share this concern for his not being an imprint of something else, or being unable to see one's life mirrored in something larger, but simply lives with what it is. Instead, he turns to Nietzsche and Freud, who, in different ways, concerned themselves with whether or not a life was interesting. Nietzsche's stance is that most people's lives are trivial to the extent that they leave no trace behind, unlike the strong geniuses who have the ability to create new conditions for what it is possible to think and do, as Foucault also suggested (Foucault 1984, 107f.). On the other hand, Freud may be regarded as having 'democratized' genius, by pointing out that all people have an unconscious that cannot be dull, but operates as an uncontrollable and irrational source for all kinds of human thoughts and fantasies (Rorty 1989, 36).

While individuality, although not necessarily a deeply original one, may be a given, the relationship between identity coalesced from a composite, and the complex arrangement of memory functions is at the centre of the concept of identity beyond a romantic conception of selfhood. This is important with regard to thinking about a new human or a posthuman, as the challenge of determining what kinds of selves one should strive after becomes even more pressing when facing the means of changes described in the previous chapter.

Memory and history may be distinguished from one another in many ways, but one of the most significant distinctions is that history actively searches for the truth in the past, whereas memories are emotional events that have no obligation to their own verity. In *Postwar*, Tony Judt points out that these two ways of approaching the past, while never completely separate, have different cultural consequences: 'Unlike memory, which confirms and reinforces itself, history contributes to the disenchantment of the world'. (Judt 2006, 830) The distinction is important, because the rationality of history and the seeking after truth have a much better chance of legitimizing themselves, in contrast to the irrational and emotional enchantment. But the potentially negative side of the ideals of the Enlightenment and its belief in rationality pave the way for questioning how experiences of the world as enchanted, marvelous or mystical can legitimize themselves, however loosely defined these metaphors may be, although in many ways no more loosely than the idea of rationality.

If such approaches to the past intensify and expand the experience of the world, should that not suffice? But even if there is, or could be some kind of agreement that a balance between rationality and irrationality, history and memory, purpose and purposelessness was desirable, the concrete forms of these balances and their many consequences are not possible to formulate or comprehend in their entirety. For example, the mythologizing of wars is one sort of significant memorial phenomenon with both positive and negative effects, as myths build communities and connect people to historical events, but also exaggerate conflicts and vilify other groups. On the other hand, the irrationality of memory, in the form of nostalgic retro-cultures, is an expression of a relation to the past that does not so much represent the past or a truth about it, but uses it as an element to make the present more complex and fascinating.

Joshua Landy and Michael Saler's anthology, *The Re-Enchantment of the World: Secular Magic in a Rational Age*, considers a number of ways of achieving what the title suggests. Their central argument is that there remains a need for enchantment in the modern world, but that it must be provided in various ways, as no almighty power is credible and sufficient for 'filling a God-shaped void', as Landy and Saler put it (Landy and Saler 2010, 2). According to the authors, one of the central ways of finding re-enchantment is through language and its ability to create fictional worlds and as such literature functions as a medium of wonder (Landy and Saler 2010, 8).[54]

Another reason for an interest in memory may be found in its capacity to explain certain experiences of the world. Hans Ulrich Gumbrecht has challenged the traditional hierarchy of the humanities by asking why interpretation and meaning are valued more than the experience of being present, but he does so in a way that connects memory and intensity to the description of how certain experiences may be framed and explained. His main argument, presented in *The Production of Presence*, is that the focus on presence-effects has not been given due attention, because of the imperative to make sense of all things. Gumbrecht declares his debt to Martin Heidegger's philosophy, but what is particularly remarkable is the way his examples that present 'moments of intensity' often depend on a context that frames the experience, and alludes to something that is not present, thereby invoking a more complex conception of time. This means that these moments are not thoughtless surrender to the present, but parts of a more complex way of achieving such effects. This is the case when plays in sports are framed by the memory of other intense moments and comparable plays, when the materiality of a book bears witness to processes that have left their mark but that do not unfold in the present, or when watching a No-play, where the knowledge of repetition and tradition provides a fruitful contrast to moments void of meaning, and in a number of instances that create a particular feeling, which Gumbrecht quotes the swimmer Pablo Morales on, as 'being lost in focused intensity' (Gumbrecht 2004, 104). There is no promise of making sense, just a condition with some special qualities.

Merlin Donald has described the importance of collective memory as a decisive trait of the human and its evolution. Our ability to develop cognitive skills is inseparable from our ability to benefit from a reservoir of shared knowledge. If one accepts Donald's and other researchers descriptions of the connection between evolution and collective memory, it gives collective memory and culture decisive roles in constituting what a human is, and in defining whether there is something 'human'. This is particularly important when imagining a new human that might arise through a change in the uses of collective memory, and through a change in its content (Donald 1991, 311ff.). For Donald, the borders between individual memory and collective memory are floating, and may be compared to a network, where parts of the entire system may be changed.

In light of the digital revolution that has taken place within the last decades, it is only fair to question how humanity's relationship to the collective memory has changed, and how it will change in the future. These new conditions have both the potential to produce nostalgia for a time when not everything was online, and for seeing the access to the world of information as the beginning of a new form of enchantment of human existence. Literature has created scenarios and fictive consciousnesses that address this new media landscape, in order to investigate the kinds of relationships between individual and collective memory that are desirable, and how the endless streams of information from the world should be processed and lived with.

The proactive conception of improving human recollection is a final aspect of which memory plays an important role for the visions of the posthuman. Two of the central categories of human enhancement that might occur without significant side-effects (although that remains to be seen) are intelligence and memory. Transhumanists argue that there would be many benefits to increasing the general intelligence of a population, and that in many ways, we are already striving for that (Sandberg and Bostrom 2009). The goal itself is not problematic, but rather, the means for attaining it are, in particular if selection of embryos or the use of biochemical substances are some of the tools.[55]

Akin to increased intelligence is the possibility of raising the human capacity for recollection, which is also a condition for making good use of one's intelligence. But at the same time, the structure and function of human memory is very much connected with the way identity, emotions and life stories may be experiences and expressed, and many other questions related to life-philosophy seem linked to the memory.

In literature, one of the canonical and eye-opening stories about the relation between memory and forgetting is Jorge Luis Borges' 'Funes, His Memory', which portrays a man who has a complete recollection of everything he has ever experienced. Every memory is so detailed and filled with endless elements to which he must give his attention, it is impossible for him to think abstractly and reach conclusions. 'To think is to ignore (or to forget differences)', Borges writes, half ironically, half sincerely, trying to show that too much memory would be a catastrophe for the individual (Borges 1998, 137).

The study of autobiographical memory shows that positive memories tend to significantly outweigh negative memories; although the latter play an important role, they are fewer (Bohn and Berntsen 2007). A central question might then be, 'how should the memory function of humans be changed, if it becomes possible to do so?' An improved memory for performing difficult intellectual tasks is very different from a memory system that may be optimized for producing wellbeing over time. But what if these could be improved, if traumatic memories could be removed from individual memory, or if the balance between good and bad memories is not currently optimal for human happiness, but could be changed?

Speculating further, one could imagine improved control of useful knowledge, and a better ability to block unwanted memories. But such fantasies go profoundly against commonly held conceptions of balances in life, and what is meaningful and important. The counterargument might be, 'As long as there is loss in the world, should it not be mourned?'

The impact of collective memory on individual memory should not be forgotten. To a large extent, autobiographical memory is created in relation to ideas of what the 'normal' and 'good' life is in a given culture (Bohn and Berntsen 2008). These ideas form a life script of major events that normally occur. Deviations from this may be interpreted either as loss or failure to achieve certain goals, or as meaningful and courageous departures from the normal paths. Concerning human change on a number of levels, it is central that the culturally determined life scripts could be influenced and altered to accommodate new standards for a longer life, to deal with debilitating conditions such as Alzheimer's, and a stratification of society – and hence life stories – could arise, according to how advanced treatments are available.

Literature has a long tradition of describing and reflecting on life courses, and there are no signs that the novelistic genre's links to the biography will change, and this will evolve accordingly, and give meaning or the lack of meaning an expression. The importance of memory and re-enchantment should also be understood as integrated with the two other themes that guide this book, namely, the specific capacity of literature to explore the relationship between individual and collective, and art's capacity to incorporate the imperfect into an aesthetic ideal.

The aesthetics of imperfection

In Martin Seel's *Theorien*, there is a passage discussing the reason a society based on an aesthetic ideal would be problematic. Because beauty cannot be defined, it cannot be generalized, and Seel argues that it would be problematic to establish a society under the laws of beauty, since there are no laws of beauty (Seel 2009, 236). At the same time, beauty is of central importance to Seel, and the idea of a good society is one that enables the creation and experience of beauty. Here, aesthetics and ethics intersect in a way that is profoundly important in an era where human engineering is not a farfetched idea. Aesthetics is problematic as a foundation of society, but it is also an important component of life.[56]

Normalization, improvement, and perfection are three key terms that are attached to thinking about the evolution of humans and of their cultures. In particular, the idea of perfection is both an impossible, utopian idea, and one deeply rooted in religion, philosophy and even the aspirations governing how to live one's life. The idea of perfection in relation to many kinds of engineering and selection has, and could have, profound consequences. However, there is also a prominent drawback to all the positive features that are drawn from the ideas of perfection. These shortcomings of perfection have been particularly evident as parts of the aesthetic regime of modernism, and to a large extent, still retain a central position in their ability to connect the seemingly incompatible notions of imperfection and beauty. This connection and its particular importance in literature will be developed in this section, by describing the aesthetics of modernism in the light of the imperfect, building on Franco Moretti's notion of 'the flawed masterpiece', leading to the vision of the dominant literary form, the novel, as a fundamentally imperfect form. There are many modernisms, underpinning works ranging from the cool aesthetic of white buildings with straight lines to complex novels filled with references to the past. One sentiment associated with modernist architecture is boredom with the perfect, straight lines and whiteness, which paved the way for postmodernism, as well as a feeling of awe of the determination to create works that had no reference and no nostalgia attached to them, as is evident in the importance of Donald Judd's boxes. But this kind of empty perfection could not endure as an aesthetic ideal, if it ever was one.

In *Signs Taken for Wonders*, Franco Moretti interprets T. S. Eliot's *The Waste Land* as a work in conflict with itself. On the one hand, the form of the work relies on references to mythical narratives, particularly the myth of the grail inspired by James Frazier's *The Golden Bough*, and through this 'mythical method', the work aspires to exclude a comprehensive description of the world. But in its relatively short span of 433 lines, the poem cannot but give a sense of the all-encompassing, the elements lack a sense of necessity, and seem to be parts of a strategy of assembling contingent material, which Claude Lévi-Strauss has described as characteristic of the making and use of myths (Moretti 1988, 220). Even as he emphasizes these features, Moretti expresses no doubt that Eliot's poem is a modern masterpiece, precisely because it both attempts to represent meaningfulness or a modern mythology, and fails to do so, just as James Joyce's *Ulysses* does. In this respect, it is significant that Moretti delivers an argument for an aesthetic ideal that connects categories such as 'the flawed' and 'the imperfect' with the idea of a masterpiece. That does not mean that anything may qualify as a masterpiece, but 'the flawed masterpiece' is a term that accommodates descriptions of works that are characterized by dissonance, contingency, and fragmentation, without dismissing their potential as canonical works that hold a central position, in terms of what literature is able to accomplish. Works by Marcel Proust, Ezra Pound and a number of their successors may only be regarded as masterpieces if this concept also accepts the imperfect. The same holds true for twentieth century art, with Pablo Picasso and Jackson Pollock as two principal exponents of this.

Beauty remains something that is being strived for, as contemporary popular culture displays in so many instances, but the complexity of beauty is easy to use against the idea of perfecting human life, either through dreams of immortality or through the appearance and other qualities of individuals. That does not mean that it is impossible to imagine a world where other concepts of beauty prevail, but with that change, a great deal of what humans describe as valuable would also change. An expression of this may also be seen in the dominance of the novel as the main literary form.

The nineteenth century is considered to be the great age of the novel. The genre found stable forms, following its breakthrough and many subsequent experiments in the eighteenth century, and it has remained the dominant genre to the extent that poetry and drama have been marginalized by the wider literary audience. However, the nineteenth century was also a period when repletion rather than renewal and experiment dominated, when compared to the range of novelistic forms seen in the eighteenth and twentieth centuries (Moretti 2006, 106).

Georg Lukács wrote his *Theory of the Novel* influenced by the impressions of the First World War, and with the sense of looking back at an epoch that had come to an end:

> In Tolstoy, intimations of a breakthrough into a new epoch are visible; but they remain polemical, nostalgic and abstract. / It is in the words of Dostoevsky that this new world, remote from any struggle against what actually exists, is drawn for the first time simply as a seen reality. That is why he, and the form he created, lie outside the scope of this book. Dostoevsky did not write novels, and the creative vision revealed in his works has nothing to do, either as affirmation or as rejection, with European nineteenth-century Romanticism or with the many likewise Romantic, reactions against it. He belongs to the new world. Only formal analysis of his works can show whether he is already the Homer or the Dante of that world or whether he merely supplies the songs which, together with the songs of other forerunners, later artists will one day weave into a great unity. (Lukács 1971, 152f.)

Lukács did not provide the analysis he mentions, but concludes his book with this monumental gesture toward an epochal shift of a kind that he does not characterize further. The heroism and individualism of the novel, even if it is presented in a non-affirmative version, with the novel of disillusion, was unsatisfying, whereas the depictions of nature and death counterbalance the convention-centreed content on which the genre had thrived (Lukács 1971, 146).

For Lukács, the modern world is one in which there is no truth, but he acknowledges that it is not possible to write literature or create literary forms based solely on negativity (Lukács 1971, 106). Pure nihilism and misanthropy do not generate form, but the attempt to overcome paradoxes – such as finding the meaning of a world that ultimately makes no sense – does so. The history of the novel is therefore also a history of writing about past forms in a way that distances one from the past while confirming its influence, by making it present in the works. This is clearly the case with Cervantes' *Don Quixote*, and with the heroism of the picaresque novels, Gustave Flaubert's dependence on the *Bildungsroman*, or James Joyce's combined use of the Homeric epics, the Medieval and Renaissance worlds portrayed by Dante, and the genres of English literature, in *Ulysses*.

The use of material from the past is one of the divisive points in the art and literature of modernism as the avant-garde renounced the past, while modernists had a more inclusive attitude toward the use of form and material that may represent an unviable world view, thereby only emphasizing the impossibility of finding a 'correct' view of the world. One could cautiously claim that, similarly, such attitudes toward the future of the work of art may be found in overarching visions of what the human can be and should become, where the idea of a new beginning will always determine in what way the ties to the past should be understood: does the dominant idea tend toward a clear-cut break, or a complex integration?

The idea of abandoning the novel as an expression of a certain world view had many proponents in the first half of the twentieth century. In addition to those already mentioned, it is remarkable how a very young Claude Lévi-Strauss was influenced by Louis-Ferdinand Céline's *Journey to the End of the Night*. In a review he began by calling it 'without doubt the most important work published for a decade', most likely referring to Marcel Proust's *In Search of Lost Time* as the previous great event in French literature. Lévi-Strauss quickly goes on to point out that the book is difficult to classify, and he asks, rhetorically, what Céline's work should be called: 'Novel? Autobiography? Story? Feuilleton?' (Lévi-Strauss 1993, 121). The ability of the work to transgress the expectations of the genre, and to provoke a profound uncertainty about what one is dealing with is, for Lévi-Strauss, as it was for Lukács, a positive trait. Thus, his review concludes that one should be proud to witness the birth of such a work, and Lévi-Strauss rightly claims that although the book is, at least for its time, shockingly coarse, there are passages of reflection that counterbalance this (Lévi-Strauss 1993, 121).

The farewell to the novel as a form was shown to be slightly exaggerated, as it has increasingly come to dominate contemporary literature, with its roots still planted in the traditions of the nineteenth century and exist side by side with modernist and postmodernist narrative modes. Realist fiction also has a far more wide-ranging influence on literary culture than do formal experiments. Later in the twentieth century, ambitious attempts to set a new agenda, such as the 'new novel' of the 1960s, spearheaded by Alain Robbe-Grillet, who sought to present a more objective and dehumanized view of the world, have been unable to diminish the dominance of the more traditional novel, either in literary history or in the book market.

Like Virginia Woolf, Lukács found that the novel is biographical in its form, and even if modernity is characterized by a skepticism of metaphysics, divinity, nationality and other social constructs, little has changed regarding the fact that humans live their lives from birth to death as part of the fauna of the Earth, and that the mortality of the body is a basic condition that will not likely change. But that means that the perspective arising from biotechnology is even more central to literature that will have to accommodate itself to a situation where there is a potential for future changes, not only in society and communication, but deep within the human body, in a way that challenges what individuals and lives are.

Bridging individual and collective

Literature is better able than any other art to present the relation between the individual and the collective, and to show dependences and distances alike. Its ability to shift its point of view, and to move from specific descriptions to generalized observations is unique, as Dorrit Cohn's *Transparent Minds* has shown. Literature can move smoothly from a specific situation to a general reflection, and this gives literature, as medium and an art form, a particular ability to render the conflict between individual and collective.

One exemplary instance of this is the ending to James Joyce's short story, 'The Dead',[57] when the protagonist, Gabriel, is looking at the snow falling on Dublin, while speculating as to whether he has lived a lie. From this scene, the story follows Gabriel's innermost thoughts, which become a monologue about the idea of Ireland as a totality, and where specific images of graves and land are bound together by the imagery of the snow that indiscriminately covers everything in the same whiteness, both 'the living and the dead' (Joyce 1996, 224). In John Hughes' adaptation of the story, this is illustrated with imagery taken from Joyce's words, as well as some that have been added. Hughes also adds a significant textual element to the narration, which serves as an interpretation of what Joyce is trying to conjure up, but that images can never fully grasp or present: 'Think of all those who ever were, back to the start of time'.

Literature's ability to navigate among different points of view and levels of generalization is even more important, when considering how new conditions of humanity will affect communication between individuals, and their reactions to their social environment. While it is relatively easy to formulate ideas of improved properties relating to health, intelligence and longevity, ultimately it makes no sense to write about the new human without considering its relations to other people in concrete social situations, rather than merely picturing an isolated being on a mountain top, as Nietzsche envisioned Zarathustra. At the same time, it is difficult to imagine the end of individuality as anything other than a dystopian situation. That may reflect a limitation of the human imagination, but overcoming the idea of the difference between the individual and the outer world is extremely difficult to envision in a positive way.

As will become evident in the readings that follow, literature has responded in many ways, to express the complex relationships between people, and between individual and collective, particularly during times of cultural transformation, and in ways that have a significant impact on the form of the literary work. The attitudes also range from depicting new conditions as crippling relationships between people, demonstrating the alienation that can be experienced as a result of inadequate communication. However, there are also expressions of desires for a more nuanced and complex relation to the world which serves as a critique of the present state of communication and relations. In 'Imaginary Homelands', Salman Rushdie's famous call for opening up the world more that he emphatically pictures how a barking dog might feel, and that this situation is akin to how literature fails to be ambitious enough to show the world fuller and richer than before, is also an underlying agenda of the discourses surrounding the new human (Rushdie 1991, 21).

In the following chapters, the literary forms presenting visions of change will be examined along the lines presented here, regarding how memory, re-enchantment, imperfection and social life are parts of an equation that is not easily solved when dreaming of a new human.

Part Two

Self-modernization

One strength of narrative literature is that it always presents individuals living in time and space, and every contingency that must be thought out abstractly must find concrete manifestations in the narrative. In contrast to philosophical discourse, which may speak of transcendence and change with reference to the norms and conceptions of the world, and the human detached from other humans, literature is historically conditioned to combine abstract thinking with specific situations. At the turn of the twentieth century, much revolved around a change in human consciousness in the face of a general crisis of values. This also had profound effects on fiction. Andreas Huyssen sees this expressed in Rainer Maria Rilke's *The Notebooks of Malte Laurids Bugge*, and the emptiness experienced by modern humans:

> Malte describes himself as a nothing that begins to think, a blank piece of paper waiting to be written on. The voiding of the self appears as a precondition for the new mode of writing the text itself aspires to. (Huyssen 2004, 671)

Other seminal novels from the period displayed a fascination with the idea of the new human that might emerge, as no values could claim superiority, but Huyssen remarks that they also present a longing to build a new future (Huyssen 2003, 44).[58] In Nobel laureate Henrik Pontoppidan's 1904 novel, *Lucky Per*, its ambitious protagonist, Per Sidenius, depicts the masses walking by his window, dreaming of a new, industrialized, secular society:

> And down there, the unsuspecting crowd – that raw stuff of Denmark's future, the dead clay that he, like God, dreamed of creating in his own image, breathing into it the life of his emancipated soul. (Pontoppidan 2010, 289)

Sidenius fails to realize his vision, is unable to make his plans for society come true, but ends as a recluse, determined to be true to his own world view.

Pontoppidan's work was influential in its German translation, and among others, Robert Musil, in *The Man Without Qualities*, continues to describe the evaporation of true meaning and values that could occur in a new era. In Musil's work there is a pervasive sense of living in a transitional period, where the emergence of a new spirit would change everything, while the characters are still stuck in the modes of the old world (Musil 1994, 231).

There are several seminal works that might have been included in this study, but I will concentrate on examining how works by Virginia Woolf, William Carlos Williams, and Louis-Ferdinand Céline contribute to the thinking surrounding new modes of being in the world, which are closely related to visions of a new human. None of these present unproblematic versions of the future, and it is precisely through their internal conflicts between a dialogue with a troubled past and an uncertain future that they create literature that underlines the conflict. Their works are not dedicated to the subject of the new human, but are therefore even more fascinating in their complex desire for change.

5

Virginia Woolf

Virginia Woolf was certainly no post- or transhumanist, but an ardent defender of the human, as demonstrated in one of her last essays, 'The Humane Art', on Horace Walpole. However, the essay also focuses on loss and on dehumanizing developments, at least from the Woolf's perspective, for example, the loss of the art of writing letters, which new technologies had placed under pressure (Woolf 1966a, 105). The sense of changing times is pervasive in her works, and finds a number of expressions in both thematic considerations and formal experiments that strive to convey a different perspective on life. Woolf believed in progress, but in a way formulated in 'How It Strikes a Contemporary', which both acknowledges that things are improving in a way that one would not trade for being alive 100 years ago, while claiming the right to be nostalgic, and mourn the way people exist and are unable to connect with the world around them (Woolf 1966b, 157).

Woolf famously stated that 'human character' changed around December 1910, whereby she mockingly put an exact date to what was obviously a much longer and more complex process (Woolf 1966a, 320). What she referred to was more a change of character in literature, rather than the real world; but ultimately, literature is also a means for exploring new ways of being human that have an impact on life itself.

The desire to renew art and life was a staple of modernist poetics. Ezra Pound said it louder than anyone else; but in her own way, Woolf was also guided by hopes for a departure in form from the traditional: 'I have an idea that I will invent a new name for my books to supplant 'novel'. A new – by Virginia Woolf. But what? Elegy?' (Woolf 1980, 34)[59] In Great Britain during the preceding century, the novel was the essential vehicle for presenting lives and building identities, therefore this was not merely a hope for a break with a specific form of entertainment, but a profound hope for changing the mental software that permeates people's minds.

Woolf's arguably most unrealistic figure, Orlando, may easily be seen as an expression of the desire to transcend the confines of normal existence, and it will be analyzed as such in this chapter, along with the more subdued yet clear visions of the new, on the part of protagonist Jacob Flanders, in Woolf's *Jacob's Room*. This is followed by a reading of 'A Sketch of the Past', which formulates hopes of experiencing the world differently. Finally, Woolf's search for new forms of narration should be seen in light of the complex relations between individual and world, and the desire for a wholeness in which it is no longer possible to believe.

Orlando and Jacob as new humans

Most of Woolf's work does not defy the limits of what is realistic and possible. So, even if the ties to ideas of a new human are mostly linked to a change in consciousness, it is remarkable how *Orlando* revolves around a figure that utilizes the freedoms of fiction to imagine an individual who can travel through time, and who defies the sharp distinctions between male and female. As Jean O. Love remarks, *Orlando* is not a typical novel by Woolf, but even though its references to Woolf's own life seem more distant than in her other work, paradoxically, it should be understood in connection with Woolf's relationship to Vita Sackville-West, whereas a novel such as *To the Lighthouse* transforms recognizable episodes from Woolf's life into a work on the human condition in general (Love 1980, 192 *et passim*).

The uniqueness of the protagonist is by no means subtly presented in *Orlando*:

> The sound of the trumpets died away and Orlando stood stark naked. No human being, since the world began, has ever looked more ravishing. His form combined in one the strength of a man and a woman's grace. As he stood there, the silver trumpets prolonged their note, as if reluctant to leave the lovely sight which their blast had called forth; and Chastity, Purity, and Modesty, inspired, no doubt, by Curiosity, peeped in at the door and threw a garment like a towel at the naked form which, unfortunately, fell short by several inches. Orlando looked himself up and down in a long looking-glass, without showing any signs of discomposure, and went, presumably, to his bath. (Woolf 1973, 87)

It would be an overstatement to describe *Orlando* as a book in which Woolf finally imagines a universe with other possibilities, that like Orlando, can live for centuries. Nevertheless, the desires this character expresses should not be underestimated in Woolf's constant conflict with loss, death and the limits of the human capacity to understand and communicate.

The ambiguity relating to gender, presented very explicitly throughout the novel (Woolf 1990, 193), is a subject that has been given even more prominence today, to an extent that the acceptance of transgender individuals has made its way into laws, enabling individuals to obtain passports that indicate this complex identity, instead of 'male' or 'female'. Woolf could not have foreseen this, yet it brings new life to *Orlando* as being more than a fantasy, but as a work that directs our attention to a very real topic that questions one of the most fundamental binarisms to have permeated views on culture and nature.

While Orlando's supernatural qualities confer the benefit of immortality, this does not bring unconditional happiness, as the Woolf underlines the relationship between the character of the individual and the age in which it lives:

> But the spirit of the nineteenth century was antipathetic to her in the extreme, and thus it took her and broke her, and she was aware of her defeat at its hands as she had never been before. For it is probable that the human spirit has its place in time assigned to it; some are born of this age, some of that; and now that Orlando was grown a woman, a year or two past thirty indeed, the lines of her character were fixed, and to bend them the wrong way was intolerable. (Woolf 1990, 158)

At another point, Orlando chooses a life of extreme solitude, taking up reading instead of human company, but eventually breaking free from her confinement to seek a love that is not abstract (Woolf 1990, 168).

A central conflict in Woolf's writings is that the universe presents itself as disenchanted, and without transcendence and meaning, to satisfy the desire for coherence and meaningfulness. This is also evident in *Jacob's Room*, where Jacob Flanders is gently exposed in the youthful hubris of his belief in himself as a human with a new and privileged understanding of the world:

> They were boastful, triumphant; it seemed to both that they had read every book in the world; known every sin, passion and joy. Civilizations stood round them like flowers ready for picking. Ages lapped at their feet like waves fit for sailing. And surveying all this, looming through the fog, the lamplight, the shades of London, the young men decided in favour of Greece. / 'Probably,' said Jacob, 'we are the only people in the world who know what the Greeks meant'. (Woolf 1992, 101f.).

The irony in the description is not hidden, but at the same time, it describes the young men's genuine feelings of possessing an overwhelming insight, as though they were a new breed of humanity marked by a privileged access to the lost ideals of true being that they attributed to the ancient Greeks. Woolf goes on to remark that Jacob did not even read Greek, but throughout the novel, the desire to feel other eras, to be different, is a significant element.

Tragic irony is even more pronounced when the novel portrays the anonymous deaths of thousands of young soldiers, where all the hope of the passage above is lost. Woolf goes to great lengths at end of the novel to express the experience of the intangible collective. The dehumanized deaths at sea and on the battle field are evoked by giving agency to battleships and canons, while soldiers are like tin soldiers (Woolf 1992, 216). Similar effects are used when describing the detached world of a government that commands people at a safe distance from the killing fields (Woolf 1992, 240).

The final passages of the novel, where the emptiness of Jacob's room is filled with Bonamy's cries, are also set against the backdrop of the long history of the rooms of the building, and what has taken place there. This is followed by a reference to the Greek world, presented as though it was a present reality, then the sounds of the busy streets, followed by an unnatural, united action of the trees: 'And then suddenly all the leaves seemed to raise themselves'. (Woolf 1992, 247) Thus, the novel plays with multiple viewpoints, each evading an identification with Jacob, and establishing both dehumanized perspectives and collective observations, while simultaneously making Jacob's absence even more acutely felt.

The desire for a new life lurks in many parts of Woolf's novel. It may take a subtle form, as in the musings regarding how 'human life would be a different affair altogether', if artificial flowers could make real flowers dispensable, as Woolf notes that real flowers fade, which has many effects on those who buy them, who must buy them again and again, subtle reminding humans of their own mortality (Woolf 1992, 112).

The theme of the individual and collective is brought forth particularly strongly in Chapter Nine, where Woolf describes the effects of Jacob reading Plato and Shakespeare, with the noises of the street as a background:

> The dialogue draws to its close. Plato's argument is done. Plato's argument is stowed away in Jacob's mind, and for five minutes Jacob's mind continues alone, onwards, into the darkness. Then, getting up, he parted the curtains, and saw, with astonishing clearness, how the Springetts opposite had gone to bed; how it

rained; how the Jews and the foreign woman, at the end of the street, stood by the pillar-box, arguing. (Woolf 1992, 150)

The intermingling of voices from the past that ultimately are distant and non-dialogical, even if Plato writes in dialogue, presents a double estrangement from the social world, underscored by the lack of understanding among people represented in the novel. There are voices from the present and from the past, but ultimately, they do not move Jacob's mind as much as might be desired. Christine Froula notices how the essayist-narrator of *Jacob's Room* 'frames a kaleidoscopic array of private and public scenes,' and that Jacob Flanders has an elusive character (Froula 2005, 63). Froula goes on the conclude that Woolf, like T. S. Eliot, makes an epic gesture in her novel by alluding to classical texts while conjuring up an image of a civilization that has experienced a severe rupture, as 'the ending of *Jacob's Room* symbolically delivers us to the first moment of all future historical time' (Froula 2005, 81). Therefore, the literary form is more than just an experiment, but connected to a search for a new orientation of the soul (Froula 2005, 84).

Time, history, and collectivity are interwoven objects of desire to be experienced differently and more fully than real life can offer. In *Jacob's Room*, these romantic desires are ultimately put into the perspective of the First World War, which effectively put an end to not only to Jacob's youthful delusion of being able to transcend former generations, but to his life; moreover, in a meaningless way. At the same time, the form of the novel flirts with its capacity to actually present a different perspective on the world, letting the reader experience a different kind of reality while coolly distancing itself through the narrator's recurring, sober voice. Nevertheless, to the end of her life Woolf sustained hopes for experiences of the world that would defy the blandness of the everyday.

Unreal patterns and real moments

In Woolf's posthumously published autobiographical essay, 'A Sketch of the Past', there is a key passage that describes a conflict that is as old as the history of human thought. As Plato struggled to explain the reason that the world seemed simultaneously messy and ordered, Woolf's problem is that she experiences a high level of coherence in the phenomena of the world that are of a character and beauty that might lead one to imagine that a higher power, a collective will, or at least some kind of artistic intention underlies them. She also clearly states that she cannot believe that she is any such agency in the world, least of all a god:

Hamlet or a Beethoven quartet is the truth about this vast mass that we call the world. But there is no Shakespeare, there is no Beethoven; certainly and emphatically there is no God; we are the words; we are the music; we are the thing itself. (Woolf 2002, 85)

Woolf goes on to write that she experiences a shock when this apparent paradox becomes clear to her. Without suggesting that she resolves this paradox, it is possible to regard her narrative constructs as partly related to the mystery of how patterns and coherence enter the world in an exploration of forms that enable an understanding of the complex interactions between people and their states of consciousness and actions in the social realm.

However, coherence is not everything, and, as it could be a mirage, Woolf turns to another phenomenon. As Pericles Lewis emphasizes in *Religious Experience and the Modernist Novel*, Woolf's theory of certain intense moments, 'moments of being', becomes her primary attempt to formulate an antidote to the disenchantment that she otherwise experiences (Lewis 2010, 156). As Lewis further claims, there is distinct resemblance between the terms Woolf uses to describe her experiences, and the vocabulary of religious experiences, just as conceptions of the sublime seem closely related, even if Woolf ironizes her own use of such terms (Lewis 2010, 157ff.). Thus, in many ways, Woolf is influenced by the legacy of Romanticism and its perspective on the infinite and the sublime, yet finds herself in a situation where such concepts are of little use when it comes to bringing about a correspondence with reality. Seen this way, the story of the new human is that of tragic being, the inhabitant of a disenchanted world, where the search for intensity and moments that raise one above others are perhaps the closest one gets to re-enchantment.

Could the interest in collective narratives, multiple voices and so on, be seen as parts of re-enchantment? Self-organization is one of the key terms that influence the study of complexity in the sciences, often involving an attempt to find underlying principles that may be transferred from one system to another, from avalanches to stock crashes. In *How Nature Works*, Per Bak argues that certain kinds of self-organization may occur, and that regardless of the kind of system, the distribution of events within the system may be described along similar patterns, which could be a general principle of organization, as he tries to demonstrate with a number of different kinds of systems (Bak 1997, 31). In light of the situation Woolf describes, the idea of self-organization is remarkable as it does not posit any central agency that controls the organization, but seeks to explain why order may arise in a way that actually creates those patterns about which Woolf speaks so highly (Woolf 2002, 85).

In addition to Bak and other contemporary scientists, Charles Darwin, too, at the conclusion of *The Origin of Species*, explicitly emphasizes the beauty inherent in the evolutionary view of nature, thereby relating a theory of the organization of life and nature to the re-enchantment of the world, by observing self-organizing principles at work (Darwin 1985, 459f.). Virginia Woolf took evolution is taken seriously, very emphatically so, in *A Sketch of the Past*, as she connects her personal identity to the long line of her ancestors:

> His hand explored my private parts too. I remember resenting, disliking it – what is the word for so dumb and mixed a feeling? It must have been strong, since I still recall it. This seems to show that a feeling about certain parts of the body; how they must not be touched; how it is wrong to allow them to be touched; must be instinctive. It proves that Virginia Stephen was not born on the 25th January 1882, but was born many thousands of years ago, and had from the very first to encounter instincts already acquired by thousands of ances-tresses in the past. (Woolf 2002, 82)

Woolf did not believe in reincarnation, but a passage like this, with its traumatic origins, demonstrates a will to re-enchant the view of the world by seeing oneself as not just a part of the universe, but as a specific, evolved being that relates to unnumbered generations in an unbroken nexus of life.[60] This is also a key point in 'It Strikes a Contemporary', where she laments how each generation is cut off from the past. This attitude should also be seen in relation to Woolf's loss of her mother, which she describes in 'A Sketch of the Past' as a loss that was with her every day until she published her first novel, at the age of 40 (Woolf 2002, 91). The individual death remains individual, but death may be considered a part of a larger process that has some kind of consoling or enchanting element to it, even if this does not entail a definitive meaning of life and death.

The connection between evolution and beauty is taken up by Richard Dawkins in *The Greatest Show on Earth*, which goes to great lengths in its reading of the final paragraph of *The Origin of Species*, and its thoughts on grandeur and beauty (Dawkins 2009a, 399ff.). In many ways, it is an alluring contribution to the idea of what constitutes beauty. It shifts the focus from objects to processes, from individual events that may be perceived, to traces that may be seen as parts of an evolution and of time that extends far beyond history. And, evolution challenges the idea of a platonic, eternal basis for beauty to which even Baudelaire subscribed, in his vision of modernity. However, this also reinforces the breach between individual and collective, and the mixed desire to both experience oneself as a unique individual and as part of a larger whole. Learning to do that, or finding ways to express a path between these, is at the heart of Woolf's formal experiments with form of the novel.

Poetics of the polyphone

Woolf has a deservedly secure place in literary history as one of the modernist renewers of the novel. While in many ways she is often overshadowed by the more obvious extremes of James Joyce's novels, and the extreme complexity of both *Ulysses* and *Finnegans Wake*, her more subtle ambition to present a multitude of voices may be seen as an equally radical formal innovation. This ambition recurs in her work as an expression of the conflict between individual and collective, which led her to pursue a number of formal experiments that could accommodate this, not in an attempt to give up the idea of individuality, but to see it represented in a larger frame of reference that could better represent the complexity of human identity. These explorations led her to different approaches to tackling the same basic problem.

At its heart, the novel, *Jacob's Room*, is a biography of the life of Jacob Flanders, told from various perspectives: There is the authoritative, narrative voice that explains how the world works, and there are representations of Jacob's often youthfully enthusiastic views of the world, as discussed above. Between these is a medley of voices that helps to create a portrait of the time, and to include all the everyday communications and considerations of mundane phenomena that are often overlooked in Jacob's lofty ambitions for his life.

Mrs Dalloway has Clarissa Dalloway as its centre of gravity, confirming the biographical roots of the novel, but with a chorus of other voices that are again bound together by a narrator, as is the case with *Jacob's Room*. The principal story takes place over the course of one day, but there are numerous references to other times, thereby evoking the sentiments of transcending not only the individual and collective, but also past, present and future. The sentiments that these divides evoke are beautifully captured in numerous passages, where the relations among humans in a modern city are lauded, but are also used to meditate on the nature of the collective:

> One of the triumphs of civilisation, Peter Walsh thought. It is one of the triumphs of civilisation, as the light high bell of the ambulance sounded. Swiftly, cleanly the ambulance sped to the hospital, having picked up instantly, humanely, some poor devil; some one hit on the head, struck down by disease,

knocked over perhaps a minute or so ago at one of these crossings, as might happen to oneself. That was civilisation. It struck him coming back from the East–the efficiency, the organization, the communal spirit of London. Every cart or carriage of its own accord drew aside to let the ambulance pass. Perhaps it was morbid; or was it not touching rather, the respect which they showed this ambulance with its victim inside–busy men hurrying home yet instantly bethinking them as it passed of some wife; or presumably how easily it might have been them there, stretched on a shelf with a doctor and a nurse... . Ah, but thinking became morbid, sentimental, directly one began conjuring up doctors, dead bodies; a little glow of pleasure, a sort of lust too over the visual impression warned one not to go on with that sort of thing any more–fatal to art, fatal to friendship. True. And yet, thought Peter Walsh, as the ambulance turned the corner though the light high bell could be heard down the next street and still farther as it crossed the Tottenham Court Road, chiming constantly, it is the privilege of loneliness; in privacy one may do as one chooses. (Woolf 1964, 167)

Woolf takes her interest in the collective further, in the form of her next novel. *To the Lighthouse* does not have an individual at its centre, tellingly indicated by the difference between the title of this and her two earlier novels, and it further develops the use of multiple voices to the extent that the transition from one voice to another is not clearly marked. Here, the connections between individual minds and voices in her earlier novels, where they are distinct from one another, is taken to the new level of a lyrical portrait of coexisting impressions of reality, a fantasy of a shared space,[61] which nevertheless remains a fantasy that cannot change the fact that reality is not like this.

With its use of fantastic elements, in the form of Orlando's journey through time, *Orlando* is a significant exception in Woolf's authorship, whereas the formal experiment of *The Waves* finds a mode where the central individual is present without dominating. For example, while Jacob Flanders has his own voice, the real protagonist in *The Waves* is represented indirectly through six other voices, supplemented by nine intermezzos describing costal landscapes. The biographical, the importance of the social, the turn toward the raw, material world, and the decentreed impression of the individuality of the individual are here expressed within the form of the novel.

Woolf's approach makes it possible to envision a sort of re-enchantment of the world by presenting human communication and the lack of access to the other as mysteries of our world that are more than just everyday experiences. Pericles Lewis suggests that the aesthetics of her novels present ways to discover and present the sublime 'in the encounter, not just with natural or supernatural forces, but among people'. (Lewis 2010, 160) As Lewis concludes, the modernist sublime for Woolf is not a man on a mountain top, but a woman at a party.

Elsewhere, I have explored the concept of the 'social sublime' as an experience that may be found in a number of seminal works throughout the history of literature, but that has a significant representation in modernism (Thomsen 2008, 114). Lewis's interpretation of Woolf's connection with the modernist sublime is consistent with that concept, since it relies on recognition through the specific experience of the vastness of the social world in a way that gives way to a shock or sense of elevation of the world, which, for Lewis, may be described as having the potential for a re-enchantment of the world (Lewis 2010, 160).

Another path to re-enchantment is through personal memory that overcomes the disenchanting gaze of the historical approach. The Memoir Club, and Woolf's own interest in biography and autobiography are other, more conventional and intimate means of pursuing a view of the world and individual life, in contrast to depersonalized attempts to imagine wholes and evolutionary processes. Still, both the innovative forms, including multiple perspectives, and the individual story seem to primarily offer the comfort of form, rather than a breakthrough in terms of a different way of being in the world. In that light, the mysterious deviation in the path of Woolf's authorship that *Orlando* represents seems to be primarily connected to an expression of a desire for a new human.

Michael Whitworth has argued that Woolf was knowledgeable about contemporary scientific findings, for example Einstein's theory of relativity, which was popularized in 1918 (Whitworth 2005, 184). Whitworth also posits that while Woolf did not employ scientific terms, she was influenced by parallels that could be drawn from the sciences. The insight that atoms are not dead matter, but have their own lively behavior, corresponds to Woolf's descriptions of the social world where nothing is stable, either (Whitworth 2005, 180). *The Waves* may also be understood in connection with the modern scientific views that regard waves as complementary to the behavior of individual particles, again giving meaning to viewing humans as separate yet connected, as Whitworth claims is demonstrated by Woolf's significant use of the wave metaphor:

> Bernard recognizes that the universe can be understood as a collection of finite particles, be they particular places and times, or particular words, but he recognizes that to describe it thus leaves out something wider and broader, the waves that flow through the particles. Not only the interaction of language with the world, but the interaction of one person with another is described in these terms. (Whitworth 2005, 182)

One of the effects that may be inspired by physics is the re-enchantment of a world that can no longer be regarded as mere matter that obeys mechanical laws, but that is far more dynamic, all the way down to the tiniest parts of a universe, where even time is much more complex than one might have imagined only a few decades ago. The problem is that these insights do not apply to a world that in the eye of the ordinary beholder behaves in terms of Newtonian physics. The attempt to push the reader to consider new ways of thinking about coherence is part of an ambitious attempt to see the world differently and more accurately, which entails hopes for a new human character to take possession of the world. Thus, Woolf's hopes for a new human rest on a continued presence of the past, and on a deep passion for the complex minds of others.

6

William Carlos Williams

William Carlos Williams' *Spring and All*, of 1923, is one of the most overlooked and alluring masterpieces of modern literature. 'Overlooked' should be qualified, as some of Williams' most frequently read poems, including 'The Red Wheelbarrow' and 'At the Ballgame', appear in the book, but they are rarely read in their original context, where the wild, coarse prose fragments stand in sharp contrast to the meditative and economical verses of the 27 poems in the book. Where the pastoral tone of 'The Red Wheelbarrow' captures what is undoubtedly a sincere appreciation of the everyday and the ordinary, and demonstrates how they cause elation in the individual, the prose pieces speak of desire for the new, of new beginnings, of continued evolution, and of new eras in art and literature, elements that are lost when reading the poems alone.

This chapter examines the fascination with new scientific insights, and the daunting perspectives they inspired in *Spring and All*. Williams' critique of perfection, combined with his ability to celebrate the ordinary, are central factors in the canonization of his work. In the following analyses, these aspects are contrasted with the desire for all things new. Finally, the conflicts between the avant-garde art on which Williams comments in *Spring and All*, and his appreciation of the everyday are seen as similar in structure to those Virginia Woolf displayed, with regard to individual and collective, and the search for a greater whole.

Evolution, Einstein, and the ecstasy of the new

Spring and All is a complex book that oscillates between philosophical and choleric prose fragments, and the numbered poems, which usually have no

clearly stated subject, and present themselves with more harmonious diction.
The first ten pages of the book are entirely devoted to prose, divided into unsys-
tematically ordered chapters, after which, prose and lyrics interchange. The first
page sets the tone by introducing ambitious themes to which the book returns
repeatedly. The opening paragraph mocks the idea that anything remarkable
could arise from the present, and then the following paragraph speaks of the
distance between author and reader, and the reader's distance from the world.
This abstract thought is made concrete by listing a number of uneven elements,
in a manner that evokes Walt Whitman, in *Leaves of Grass*:

> Or rather, the whole world is between: Yesterday, tomorrow, Europe, Asia,
> Africa,–all things removed and impossible, the tower of the church at Seville,
> the Parthenon. (Williams 1986, 177)

The unstable vision of the world is presented along the lines of time, space
and cultural orientation, as both Christian and ancient sites of devotion are
mentioned in a casual, yet grandiose manner. In the subsequent lengthy
paragraph, Williams turns to poetry, and typical critiques of Williams' own
poems are delivered in a mock-ironic voice, describing them as anti-poetry,
offensive, incomprehensible and rhythmical. In terms of the theme of this study,
sentences such as these are particularly fascinating: 'They are heartless, cruel,
they make fun of humanity. What in God's name do you mean?' (Williams 1986,
177). Such lines underscore the importance of the idea of the human, and also
how to envision what humanity is, with or without a religious underpinning.
After the mock rant against Williams' own poetry, the first of a series of hints of
the beginning of a new era follows:

> But today it is different / The reader knows himself as he was twenty years ago
> and he has also in mind a vision of what he would be, some day. Oh, some day!
> (Williams 1986, 177f.)

After considering solipsism, and the reason the poet loves his fellow humans
anyway, the imagination is foregrounded, as the place where it is possible to be
'locked in a fraternal embrace, the classic caress of author and reader. We are
one'. (Williams 1986, 178).

The next pages are devoted to considerations of what a new world might
mean, and a bizarre fantasy of killing everything of the past in an echo of
Futurist rage is put forth, before paradoxically praising all races and cultures of
humanity. Later, the arrival of spring is declared, but perhaps as something that
takes place in the imagination, even though Williams declares, in capital letters:

'EVOLUTION HAS REPEATED ITSELF FROM THE BEGINNING. / Good God!' (Williams 1986, 181) But what is new is that the imagination becomes open to something new, and not just the reiteration which evolution has led:

> In fact now, for the first time, everything IS new. Now at last the perfect effect is being witlessly discovered. ... / Yes, the imagination, drunk with prohibitions, has destroyed and recreated everything afresh in the likeness of that which it was. Now indeed men look about in amazement at each other with a full realization of the meaning of 'art'. (Williams 1986, 181)

It is always possible to discuss the extent to which such pronouncements regarding the new should be taken seriously as profound visions, or as a mockery of such hopes for a radical alteration of the world. This uncertainty is part of a productive tension that the book builds up, yet it is difficult to overlook the centrality of the theme of the new as reflecting a radical change in the ability to perceive and think.

In his poetry, Williams captures the schism between feeling that, on the one hand, everything has changed, and there are new rules governing every aspect of the new century, from natural laws to the laws of morality, and on the other hand, recognizing that in many ways, life continues as always, and that poetry and science do not change the need for wheelbarrows on a farm, where chickens do what they have always done.

Apart from the obvious references to the theory of evolution, which had already matured by that point, for Williams and many others of his day and age, an important background to thinking of the world as new was connected to the public impact of Albert Einstein's theory of relativity. In 1921, Williams wrote a poem celebrating Albert Einstein, entitled 'St. Francis Einstein of the Daffodils', which he went on to revise several times. In a note, Williams remarked:

> It is always spring time for the mind when great discoveries are made. Is not Einstein, at the same time, saintly in the purity of his scientific imagining? And if a saint it seems to me that the thorough logic which St. Francis saw as sparrows or donkeys, equally to be loved with whatever other living aspect of the world, would apply equally to Einstein's arrival in the United States a number years ago to celebrate the event in the season's shapes and colors of that moment. (Williams 1986, 543)

Williams' ode to Albert Einstein is not among the best or most interesting in his authorship, but it displays how Williams, more than many others writing during the same period, was influenced by the breakthroughs in science. The line 'It is April and Einstein!' reads like a commentary to T. S. Eliot's famous opening of *The Waste Land*, 'April is the cruelest month', which was written in the same years, and of which Williams had learned through their common friend, Ezra Pound, prior to its publication in 1922.

The well-known combination of abstract references and descriptions of surroundings in Williams' poetry is presented very directly, although not particularly elegantly, in this instance:

> It is Einstein/ out of complicated mathematics/ among the daffodils–/spring winds blowing/four ways, hot and cold/among the flowers! (Williams 1986, 133)

There is nothing original in seeing Einstein as an icon of the imagination of science and the ability to think differently. On the contrary, Einstein has become an icon to the extent that his extremely counterintuitive insights into time, space, and matter are now taken for granted, without giving him due credit for his revolutionary break with Newton's mechanical world view, and the positivism that dominated the late nineteenth century. The way Williams writes of 'complicated mathematics' in the poem's pastoral setting might be seen as a mockery of the abstract in favour of the concrete and natural, but that would hardly make sense, given the positive views of Einstein that Williams otherwise expressed. Instead, this is a manifestation of the allure of a world that may be perceived as both straightforwardly beautiful and accessible, and as containing depths and traits that are difficult to explain.

Williams' fascination with Einstein's theory of relativity is probably explained by the way in which it renounces the mechanics that were essential to the Newtonian universe, leading to a re-enchantment of the universe that does not sacrifice science in the process. However, even if it was possible to take in the wonders of the largest forces of gravity and the seemingly incomprehensible behavior of the smallest particles of the universe, there remains the problem that the individual does not have sensory access such alternative views of the world. The bending of time and the unpredictable workings of atoms are unseen. As in Woolf's work, the generally believable visions of the world suffer from not being subject to direct experience, but only through the imagination. However, that does not reduce the sensory world to something inferior.

Beauty imperfect

In *The Revolution in the Visual Arts and the Poetry of William Carlos Williams*, Peter Halter quotes an early poem by Williams, entitled 'PERFECTION', which begins: 'O lovely apple! / Beautifully and completely / rotten' (Halter 1994, 20). Williams' insistence on drawing out the beauty of the ordinary, which is a hallmark of hypercanonized poems such as 'The Red Wheelbarrow' and 'This is just to say', is here extended to an appraisal of a rotten apple, where even the rot must be taken as a part of its perfection, perhaps in its ability to reconnect with the rest of the world by degrading. It is possible to read the poem ironically and understand the rot as the only thing that is perfect, but altogether, it is plausible to establish a connection between imperfection and beauty. Halter notes a similarity between the collages of contemporary avant-garde art and Williams' poetry, but also notes that the despair and nihilism of Dada, for example, are not dominant in Williams' poetry, which tends to be affirmative (Halter 1994, 23f.).

Another variation on the interplay between beauty and perfection may be found in the poem, 'To a solitary disciple', where a church is described as though to an apprentice learning to see things properly.[62] The central feature of the poem is the variety of ways in which the construction and the ornaments of the building itself, in all their perfection, are less important than all the phenomena that may be observed in the interplay between the church and its surroundings, such as the light that takes on a particular colour at an exact time of day, or the spire that seems to touch the moon, and so on. The dynamics of the colours, the particular mood at dawn create a beauty worth speaking or writing of. This contrast with the monument itself, which exalts a metaphysics to which Williams does not subscribe.

Deploying a Whitmanesque tone in *Spring and All*, Williams plays with the idea of perfection in a way that is contradicted by the confused and contradicting proclamation:

'Why should I go further than I am able? Is it not enough for you that I am perfect?' (Williams 1986, 219)

But the important perspective of Williams' reflection on perfection is that it acknowledges the flawed order of the universe, between the imagination and the material world, and in the field of art and literature, where poetry and prose are presented as complementary ways of creating. Yet, to fully experience this dynamic, a new era seems to be needed:

> The greatest characteristic of the present age is that it is stale – stale as literature
> – / To enter a new world, and have their freedom of movement and newness.
> (Williams 1986, 219)

Williams searches for situations where opposite desires may be expressed, if
not united, rebalanced, or seen as parts of a larger whole, for example, at the
beginning of poem X, in *Spring and All*: 'The universality of things / draws me
toward the candy / with melon flowers that open // about the edge of refuse'
(Williams 1986, 204). On the one hand, the metaphysical idea of something
elevated or sublime has a place in Williams' poetry. But even if literature is a
medium through which such experiences may be expressed, there is also his
persistent refusal to regard the poet as an individual with a privileged access
to the things of the world. The everyday has a significant place in Williams'
poetry, even if, in his descriptions of actions and moods, he does not deliver
those epiphanies that are also parts of Williams' poetic universe. This is where
the repeated events and experiences of collectivity become important to appreciating the phenomena of the everyday, because they are not just random events,
but may be seen as parts of a larger pattern. This emotion is expressed negatively
in a verse in *Spring and All*, which also puts the author in his place:

> Somebody dies in New York City / every four minutes / to hell with you / and
> your poetry (Williams 1986, 231)

Here, the lure of being able to comprehend or have a different relationship
with the vastness of the social world is displayed in his self-condemnation. The
erasure of individualism is also very much a part of his poems, which are often,
but not always, devoid of a central subject, but instead describe states or scenes,
without identifying any observer, while simultaneously avoiding Whitman's
hyperbolic identification of all America, or all the world.

The question of enchantment in a modern, secular world is taken up from
various angles, in Joshua Landy and Michael Saler's *The Re-Enchantment of the
World*, which presents strategies for achieving or perceiving enchantment that
are not based on an idea of an overarching metaphysics. The attempts to achieve
such re-enchantment are manifold and resonate in Williams' poetry: the human
capacity for creativity is examined through architecture's capacity to be both
positive and surprising, while on the other hand, literature is capable of creating
alternative worlds, although they do have the shortcomings of being imaginary
and fictitious. Finally, there is the perspective of attuning oneself to the world
in which the emergence of form and the sensitivity to intensity become more

important than the experience of meaningfulness (Landy and Saler 2009, 10f.). The poem, 'At the Ballgame', depicts the crowd of spectators at a baseball match at a stadium during the summer. The stadium, as a secular cathedral of sports, provides the frame of reference for descriptions that connect the actions described in the scenery with imaginative interpretations that only make sense as fiction, but are grounded in concrete events. It is also noteworthy that the poem portrays the spectators as 'disinterested', in the Kantian sense of seeking out the beauty of the situation and the spectacle, where together, the crowd of spectators and the athletes create an atmosphere of being that Hans Ulrich Gumbrecht has described as 'lost in focused intensity' (Gumbrecht 2006, 51).

In 'At the Ballgame', the crowd 'is moved uniformly', whereby the essential difference between individual and collective is compromised. The driving force is a 'spirit of uselessness / which delights them'. After this, the vocabulary of sports is introduced as 'the chase, and the escape, the error', which is supplemented with the more general, but highly important 'flash of genius'. The uselessness is underscored again, by stating that the whole thing is 'to no end save beauty', but it is a beauty that, in contrast to the time-bound existence of the game, is 'eternal'. The vision of the crowd's composite nature as individuals joined together, and its capacity to establish a dynamic of its own, is taken to a meta-historical level, by comparing it to 'the Inquisition, the / Revolution', before the idea of beauty is made general and metaphysical as 'beauty itself'. The poem concludes by emphasizing the feeling of summer and the crowd, by using repetition in the third and second to last stanzas: 'It is summer, it is the solstice' conjures up the warmth and light of the situation, while 'the crowd is// cheering, the crowd is laughing' signals that people are being entertained. But this ode to light and its qualities is surrounded by an emphasis on how beauty is connected to 'the power of their faces', and later, the rhetoric becomes paradoxical in a productive way, when the cheering of the crowd is described as 'permanently, seriously / without thought', which very much the resembles the idea of being lost in focused intensity, and a modern form of enchantment (Williams 1986, 233f.).

'Imagination' is a, if not the, central theme in *Spring and All*. It is not precisely defined, but is used throughout the book, particularly in its concluding section. At the same time, it inevitably refers back to Romanticism, which praised the imagination as something that was not nature, but could deliver sublime moments and unexpected experiences in ways other than those the senses could produce. In Williams' own time, there were many who were interested in the importance of the subconscious and the imaginary with regard to the general constitution of the human, and the possibilities of art. Williams was inspired by the French art scene, and a contemporary of the Surrealists who, in André Breton's *The Surrealist Manifesto* of 1924, praised the liberating powers of the imagination (Breton 1972, 4ff.). But Williams also has his own elaborate development of the concept. At the beginning of the book, in the very short 'Chapter 2' (which is preceded by chapter VI and followed by chapter XIX), it says:

> It is spring: life again begins to assume its normal appearance as of 'today'. Only the imagination is undeceived. The volcanos are extinct. Coal is beginning to be dug again where the fern forests stood last night. (If an error is noted here, pay no attention to it.) (Williams 1986, 182)[63]

Geological time is invoked and mingled with the change of seasons, and the idea of the rhythm of life is contrasted with the idea of the perpetually new 'today'. At the same time, the imagination has a privileged position that persists throughout the book. After 'At the Ballgame', at the end of the book, the use of the imagination is taken up again, with another series of significant statements about it. The imagination uses the vocabulary of science in a critical and 'radioactive' way that can also be liberating. It is a force, it is immaterial, and as the most important characteristic that is repeated in several different ways, the persona in *Spring and All* emphasizes that the imagination should not be understood as an avoidance or a distancing from reality, but that poetry:

> [A]ffirms reality most powerfully and therefore, since reality needs no personal support but exists free from human action, as proven by science in the indestructibility of matter and of force, it creates a new object, a play, a dance which is not a mirror up to nature but– (Williams 1986, 234f.)

This 'but–' is followed by a comparison of birds' wingstrokes against the air, and the liberated words' affirmation of reality. These are opposites that confirm one antoher, rather than exclude, which is recurrent figure Williams uses in these fragments. Also decisive is the way that Williams' materialistic world view introduces several emergent levels. Human action is different from the material reality, implicitly because it is connected to self-consciousness, and human action can produce new objects that are different from what nature can produce. Thus, it is crucial to Williams to determine ways in which the world can be enchanted, not by reference to metaphysics, but to emergent phenomena that leave empirical traces.

The final poem and words of *Spring and All*, poem XXVII, are a seemingly vague but colourful description of 'Black eyed susan' which is a flower, but in the poem is also to be read as a representation of a woman. In four short stanzas, a number of colours are mentioned: black, orange, purple, and white, twice. A recurrent motif is invoked here, as well, namely the fascination with masses, which in this instance are contrasted to the black woman: 'Crowds are white / as farmers / who live poorly', while Susan is 'rich/ in savagery', and with her culturally complex, and therefore temporally lengthy heritage: 'Arab / Indian / dark woman' (Williams 1986, 236). Spencer Wells' point that genetic diversity has accelerated in recent centuries, to an extent that it could qualify as a third Big Bang in human evolution, fits well with Williams' final ode to the complex Susan, who cannot be placed in a single culture or genetic line, but is completely her own (Wells 2004, 193); not detached from the past, but with more complex references to it. The romantic invocation of the flower that turns out to be a woman also underscores a shift from an ideal of a clear identity to a more diffused way of thinking about the heritage and the future of humanity.

The exhaustion of the avant-garde and the everyday

The French avant-garde around the First World War was one of Williams' primary sources of inspiration, and in his works there is a clearly-expressed desire to give literature and other art forms larger roles in society. The many attempts in his work to change the form of poetry, for example, with a new kind of indented verses, or with the very explicit thematic coupling of renewal in science, nature and art, add up to an intense interest in the idea of the new. At the same time, it is noteworthy that the unpretentious, marginal and everyday play key roles in his poetry. Wheelbarrows, chickens, plums, baseballs, broken glass, and so forth, are central to his most canonical poems, and the connection to Williams' profession as a doctor, which is evident in many texts, also contributes to balancing the aspirations of uncompromising avant-garde art and everyday impulses. In this respect, Williams' work is paradigmatic of two perspectives of the historical avant-garde. One view focuses on its exhaustion, and how the formal experiments and disdain for content were unable to significantly change literature and other arts in the long run, or to create a viable break between before and after that could serve as a foundation for a liberating project that would extend beyond art. A symptom of this is that large parts of the radical avant-garde of Williams' contemporaries – Dada, Merz and Surrealism – are read today as examples of avant-garde, rather than developed art in themselves, while the novel and its realism remain at the heart of literary culture.

A different perspective on Williams' stance on the avant-garde and the everyday would see the significance of the everyday in Williams' poetry as a triumph of the avant-garde in privileging the ordinary, and insisting on the everyday as something that may be as exalted and worthy of praise as anything else. This has to do with that which is not normally connected to what literature thrives on – power, love, hate and so forth – but rather, to the quiet intensity stemming from the individual's ability to connect with its past, and to collective, imagined communities. If for Woolf the sublime is a woman at a party, then for Williams it is being at a packed stadium, and contemplating what depends on a red wheelbarrow.

In his long, 1948 poem, 'The Clouds', Williams engages with the same motifs that permeated *Spring and All*. The attempts to capture the long history of both human culture and the universe itself are put forward as objects of desire, but also contrasted with an appreciation of the present, and perceptions of how the contemporary world presents itself. The clouds evoke a transhistorical phenomenon experienced by the Greeks, Erasmus, Shakespeare and Toulouse-Lautrec, to name few of the figures who observed the volatility of the sky. Unlike rocks or other solid material, clouds form systems that seem to have lives of their own, even if that is only a projection of the human mind.

The idea of an escape from humanity is also presented as a straightforward desire, along with the lure of spiritualism: 'The poor brain unwilling to own the obtrusive body', is followed by a fantasy of what might happen, if a brain could exist without a body, not unlike present-day fantasies of copying the system of the brain and its consciousness into non-biological material (Williams 1991, 173). But is this not a vision within Williams' reach, who instead brings the poem to an end by acknowledging his own mortality, and the persistence of the clouds?

In his analysis of *Spring and All*, Joshua Schuster remarks that 'life' recurs over and over again, whereas 'culture' is absent. With reference to the first numbered poem of the book, he also argues that it:

> asks us to consider a new anthropology — what Williams, just prior to this poem, calls 'the destruction of the species *Homo sapiens*'. (Schuster 2007, 126)

Williams' work is not at peace with itself, which Schuster also demonstrates through the complex relationships between past, present and future, between imagination and reality, and between human and non-human (Schuster 2007, 128). If taken out of context, some of Williams' most influential poems create a predominant impression of a serene and contemplative attitude toward the world, but that would be greatly misleading. When reading *Spring and All* as it was published, it becomes much clearer that it contains challenging visions of how humans can consider their place in the universe as complex and largely determined by more powerful forces, yet leaves the everyday and singular moments open to a particular kind of enchantment. Evolution, rather than divine forces, shapes the natural and the social worlds. Williams does not embrace the idea of making everything new, but instead finds ways of presenting the complexity of life between past, present and future in a way that tries to celebrate the ordinary, while – and this is where a notion of the new human may be valid – appreciating the universe in a way that resembles the elevated moments of Romanticism, but without succumbing to metaphysics or religion.

7

Louis-Ferdinand Céline

The perception of the work of Louis-Ferdinand Céline will always be influenced by the radical views and the tumultuous life of the author around the Second World War, and the heyday of European fascism. It is easily forgotten that this is the same person who worked for the League of Nations during the 1920s, and was concerned with improving living conditions for the poorest citizens (Hewitt 1998, 126). His debut, *Journey to the End of the Night*, of 1932, represents the zenith of his career, at least when it comes to the general appreciation of his work. Recognition of his work came early. A young Claude Lévi-Strauss praised the work for being not just a novel, but a text for and about a new era (Lévi-Strauss 1993, 119). Lévi-Strauss's commentary underlines the notion of a decisive change in the world. Céline and Lévi-Strauss also share a fascinating balance between seeing beyond cultural differences and striving for universalism, while their observations of the world eventually emphasize differences, which in Céline's case alone developed into a dubious political standpoint.

With its harsh, realist language, and a distinctive oscillation between presentations of strong ideas of the nature of the world and disillusioned sighs, *Journey to the End of the Night* contrasts with another canonical work, Marcel Proust's *In Search of Time Lost*, which was completed just a decade before Céline's novel. Where Proust writes elegantly and in a subdued tone of the bygone world of the French bourgeoisie and its occasional travels to Venice, Céline's novel is an expedition from the battle fields of the First World War, to Africa and America, before the life of the less fortunate in France provides the setting for the last part of the book.

While Céline does not have a positive vision of a new human, but instead depicted the consequences of war and industrialism, in his work there are a number of themes concerned with the longing for the new, and for a new way of being in the world. His criticism of nationalism and national identity, his appraisal of, and disillusionment with America, and his sensitivity toward people's inhuman behavior, provide a number of distinct approaches to the idea of a transformation of the mind. Georges Bataille has argued that Celine's ability to foreground the darker sides of society, all that society has rejected, gives his work a particular human significance. At the same time, the relation between individual and collective is portrayed as mixture of the lack of belief in a societal brotherhood, the incompleteness of the individual, and the constant awareness of the misery of the masses (Bataille 1993, 117). In this chapter, the conditions of the migrant, the lure of the American, and Céline's disillusion and intertextual references order the many explorations of the ability and inability to profoundly change life, both for the individual, and for humanity at large.

The few happy hours of the migrant and the burdens of culture

At the very beginning of *Journey to the End of the Night*, the idea of a specific French national identity is thematized and rejected:

> What you call a race is nothing but a collection of riffraff like me, bleary-eyed, flea-bitten, chilled to the bone. / They came from the four corners of the earth, driven by hunger, plague, tumors, and the cold, and stopped here. They couldn't go any further because of the ocean. That's France, that's the French people. (Céline 2006, 3)

The uncompromising anger of the quote, and the reversal of all ideas of French greatness and superiority are combined with view of race that is in many ways modern. Here, the concept of race that was traditionally presented during the golden age of the nation state is rejected as a construct dominated by coincidences. Set against this background, the war against the Germans seems even more idiotic to Céline's alter ego, Bardamu. However, later on, in the journey to Africa, Bardamu reconsiders the importance of race, which continues upon his arrival in America, particularly with regard to American women.

The expatriate occupies a central position in the novel, not only as the generator of the plot in the first part of the story, but also as a backdrop for a reflection on what a human is, and what it could be. While Céline had traveled, at this point in his life he did not have the experience of exile that he assigns to his protagonist, but the places he describes overlap those of his own travels. That Céline himself was exiled and imprisoned in Denmark in the aftermath of the

Second World War brings a sort of belated irony to his descriptions of exile in his debut work.

In a central passage, the manifold effects of exile are described in a tirade of highly laden views of the world as such:

> There was also the change in habits; once again I was having to get used to new faces in new surroundings and to learn new ways of talking and lying. Laziness is almost as compelling as life. The new farce you're having to play crushes you with its banality, and all in all it takes more cowardice than courage to start all over again. That's what exile, a foreign country is, inexorable perception of existence as it really is, during those long lucid hours, exceptional in the flux of human time, when the ways of the old country abandon you, but the new ways haven't sufficiently stupefied you as yet. / At such moments everything adds to your loathsome distress, forcing you in your weakened state to see things, people, and the future as they are, that is, as skeletons, as nothings, which you will nevertheless have to love, cherish, and defend as if they existed. / A different country, different people carrying on rather strangely, the loss of a few little vanities, of a certain pride that has lost its justification, the lie it's based on, its familiar echo – no more is needed, your head swims, doubt takes hold of you, the infinite opens up just for you, a ridiculously small infinite, and you fall into it … (Céline 2006, 185)

The quote is primarily a significant statement about the few privileged hours when the mental software a nation or a culture imposes on an individual has disappeared, and the new one has not yet taken over. In many ways, this is an unrealistic description, as there are no grounds for claiming that exile is experienced as a process of emptying, and only then refilling the individual with new impressions, but instead, it is a more complex transformation of habits and expectations. But within the framework of this fiction, it is apparently important to Céline to insist on this condition, which is also connected with the ability to clearly see things as they are. That too seems like an illusion or an untenable claim, but remains in the novel as an ideal.

Céline also confuses the reader, by claiming emptiness and nothingness as that which may be seen, while at the same time claiming the necessity of having positive and affirmative relations with other people. Elsewhere, this dual view is expressed poignantly, as when the act of going into the street is described as 'a partial suicide', because of the impossibility of being oneself among the masses (Céline 2006, 173). In this instance, it is significant that Céline emphasizes the desire to liberate and experience oneself as a human whose being has not been filtered by culture, even though Bardamu admits that there is no meaningful content beneath this filter, but rather, a certain state that is more physical than conscious.

Bardamu's restlessness in the first half of the book may be seen as an attempt to achieve the state of being liberated from culture, a motif that also recurs in the works of Michel Houellebecq; but in the second half of the book, the journey ends in a scrappy suburb of Paris. The end of the novel leaves no hope for change, as boats are tooting on the Seine, while Bardamu is stuck in a lowly bar. His travels provide a quick fix of liberation, but it is short-lived and in many ways a hard-earned fix, considering what the process of migration entails.

Another significant concept in the previous quotation is the infinite, which recurs throughout the book. Here, existential nausea and the lack of control lead to a sense of endlessness, which, paradoxically, is immediately set aside as being an insignificantly small infinity, although it is large enough to swallow Bardamu. The problem with the infinite is that it builds on an illusion from Romantic thought, in which Céline ultimately does not believe. At the beginning of the book, when Bardamu serves at the front during the First World War, endlessness is already presented as a hoax:

> 'Arthur,' I tell him, 'love is the infinite placed within the reach of poodles. I have my dignity!' (Céline 2006, 4)

The interweaving of love and endlessness, and their subsequent rejection is an example of a revolt against the structures of thought and imagery that permeate a post-romantic society. Abstract and absolute categories are used, but they do not make sense to the skeptical individual. Thus, throughout the book, the feeling of being 'in between' is a significant emotion that Bardamu shares with a number of other characters. It is underpinned by the structure of the novel, where hopes for the new are tried out in a dazzling number of changes of scenery during the first half of the book, culminating with a stay in America, followed by a long period of disillusionment in the second half, and his return to France.

The American city and the new human

Bardamu's time in America has a privileged position in the novel. The war, the study of medicine, and particularly his experiences in Africa, all revealed different perspectives and modes of existence, and none of them were met with great enthusiasm. The arrival in America, which Céline himself had visited while he was employed by the League of Nations, gives rise to a number of almost epiphanic moments, and a general joy in response to the great energy of life in a city 'that was standing absolutely erect' (Céline 2006, 159). Yet, Bardamu soon learns of the downsides of America, which reach their low point when takes a job at a factory.

The newness of America presents itself in various ways. The vertical city is fascinating, and provides a futuristic setting for the newly arrived Bardamu. The fascination with American women had already begun in France, in particular with the nurse, Lola, whom Bardamu also encounters in New York City. However, her interest in him is gone, now that he is no longer a wounded soldier. Even more to the point in this context are his attempts to describe and interpret American women. In one passage, he links them to a new Antiquity, and to a breakthrough in the new ideal for humanity (Céline 2006, 167). In the vivid description, he finds that the American women seem to belong to a new race of humanity, where not only the bodies have changed, but also the way that they move in a gracious and powerful way that he has never experienced before. Like Virginia Woolf, Céline makes reference to antiquity, in his discourse of imagining these new humans:

> And yet, what supple grace! What incredible delicacy of form and feature! What inspired harmonies! What perilous nuances! Triumphant where the danger is greatest! Every conceivable promise of face and figure fulfilled! Those blondes! Those brunettes! Those Titian redheads! And more and more kept coming! Maybe, I thought, this is Greece starting all over again. Looks like I got here just in time. (Céline 2006, 167)

In the next paragraph, Bardamu notes that the women seem even more divine when they hardly notice his presence. He is ill and hungry, and he 'needed the erotic proximity of those splendid welcoming creatures' (Céline 2006, 195). This condition, where he is ready to abandon his selfhood and go with the women into the 'world of dreams', lasts for a few hours, but not much longer (Céline 2006, 168). As with the happy moments of the migrant, a couple of hours are, apparently, his standard limit for such a condition, where life may be lived in relative happiness, even if these conditions in the psychological portrait of Bardamu might also be seen as his own projections and misconceptions of the reality he otherwise praises.

The feeling of having been altered is realized to its full extent when Bardamu is led to a room he has rented. A lengthy passage depicts how he is taken through a labyrinth-like building of a size he has not previously encountered, after which he describes the condition to which it has reduced him:

> Struggling to walk faster in those corridors, I lost what little self-assurance I
> had left when I escaped from quarantine. I was falling apart, just as I had seen
> my shack fall apart in the African wind and the floods of warm water. Here I
> was attacked by a torrent of unfamiliar sensations. There's a moment between
> two brands of humanity when you find yourself thrashing around in a vacuum.
> (Céline 2006, 173)

Here, Céline repeats the structure of his description of the happy hours of
the migrant, but it is negatively valued. The comparison with his experiences
in Africa also suggests how that was of a similarly shocking character, while
the rhetoric almost imperceptibly shifts from a psychological description of
inner turmoil to a calm, philosophical explanation of what occurred, thereby
reproducing the familiar oscillation between doubt and confidence in Céline's
writing. It is also evident that here, Céline circles around the idea of a spiritual
transformation, where the self can be suspended for a time in a sort of transitory
phase preceding a new condition, which is further emphasized by the use of
'brands of humanity'.

After moving into his new room, Bardamu observes the people living in the
building across from his in intimate moments, and he is depressed by the lack
of joy in life that they exude, and which he himself also has trouble finding. The
days pass, and he is puzzled by where the strength to do anything comes from,
since it cannot be based on some sort of meaningfulness. In the end, it may be
related to some sort of madness instead:

> And maybe it's treacherous old age coming on, threatening the worst. Not much
> music left inside us for life to dance to. Our youth has gone to the ends of the
> earth to die in the silence of the truth. And where, I ask you, can a man escape
> to, when he hasn't enough madness left inside him? The truth is an endless
> death agony. The truth is death. You have to choose: death or lies. I've never
> been able to kill myself. (Céline 2006, 173)

The many changes of location, the self-forgetfulness, and the daydreaming
about women, are all strategies to create little lies about necessity, which make
life work, but which ultimately always reveal themselves as empty. That is the
reason the transition from one mode of being human to another is never the
quantitative move that Bardamu hopes for, merely a confusion of the senses
and the routines of life, before his system has comprehended the normality, the
repetitions and the lack of meaning and energy in these.

What is perhaps more important than meaning is energy, because it may be
felt and experienced, and cannot be written off in the same way that attempts to

generate meaning can. Intensity presents itself as a value, but is also a something that cannot be taken for granted. Bardamu's experience of America is also intricately linked to its architecture, which expresses a modernity never before seen, and gives rise to two kinds of emotions. It is both inhuman and generates solipsism, while also enabling a hitherto unseen concentration of human life to emerge, which carries with it all the effects of the social sublime that Woolf and Williams also explore.

The inertia of biology and society

In *Journey to the End of the Night,* the value set on human life is presented as not necessarily high in America, and as Bardamu laconically remarks, dogs are taken good care of in Alaska, '[w]hereas nobody gives a damn about immigrants, of whom there are always too many' (Céline 2006, 164). Being reduced to a body and not a person is one of Bardamu's key experiences that situates him in the paradoxical situation that he knows what he is, but still needs to strive against that insight.

The need for the 'fix' of adventure and change is closely related to his body's capacity and need for change, as the description of the migrants' few happy hours suggests. Likewise, it takes a healthy body to crave change:

> Days and days passed, my health picked up, but, as my fever and delirium abated in those comfortable surroundings, my craving for adventure and daring exploits revived and became imperious. At ninety-eight point six everything is boring. (Céline 2006, 164)

The weakness of the mind and the lack will when confronting the challenges the body must face is a recurrent theme in Céline's work. The dehumanizing effects of American industry are portrayed with the hyperbole of becoming a machine, as is the more profound sense of how exterior factors influence social relations among people who otherwise share the same conditions:

> Everything trembled in the enormous building, and we ourselves, from our ears to the soles of our feet, were gathered into this trembling, which came from the windows, the floor, and all the clanking metal, tremors that shook the whole building from top to bottom. We ourselves became machines, our flesh trembled in the furious din, it gripped us around our heads and in our bowels and rose up to the eyes in quick continuous jolts. The further we went, the more of our companions we lost. In leaving them we gave them bright little smiles,

as if all this were just lovely. It was no longer possible to speak to them or hear them. Each time three or four of them stopped at a machine. (Céline 2006, 194)

Further along in this passage, Céline further blends the sensation of the bitter realization of being no more than a physical body, with a vision of being captured along with the other workers by the industrial machine that creates a new organism, which in turn may be seen as only a fragment of the whole Earth as an organism:

> Still, you resist; it's hard to despise your own substance, you'd like to stop all this, give yourself time to think about it and listen without difficulty to your heartbeat, but it's too late for that. This thing can never stop. This enormous steel box is on a collision course; we, inside it, are whirling madly with the machines and the earth. All together. Along with the thousands of little wheels and the hammers that never strike at the same time, that make noises which shatter one another, some so violent that they release a kind of silence around them, which makes you feel a little better. (Céline 2006, 194)

The experience of silence in a space that is not silent is presented as a tragic experience of adapting to an inhuman environment, while the silence comes to signify desires for not really taking part in life, but instead conveys the absence of purpose in life, and the lack of joy. The bodily inertia is a basic condition of life, but that too becomes futile and counterproductive, as the mind cannot make sense of that; suffice it to realize that, in the end, 'your own substance' is all there is. The will and the intellect are supposed to be able to overcome, the body but encounters insurmountable forces.

The end of *Journey to the End of the Night* forms a distinct contrast to the ending of another classic of French literature, Honoré de Balzac's *Old Goriot*, which epitomizes the spirit of carving out a career for oneself in the hierarchical society of the nineteenth century. At the end of his novel, Balzac has his protagonist, Rastignac, standing at the Père Lachaise cemetery overlooking Paris and the quarters of which he so much wants to be a part. The setting is a point of vantage above the city, described by the cityscape, lighting up in the evening (Balzac 2009, 263). Most importantly, it ends with the sentiment of future action being promised by the hero of the novel, who will take up the battle with society. Céline's novel presents contrasts to these points. As in Balzac's novel, the protagonist is also recuperating from the death of someone close, in this case, not old Goriot, but the murdered Robinson – both deaths underscoring the fragility and brevity of life, as well as its injustice. But the scene takes place inside a shabby bar along the banks of the Seine. There is nothing to see, no way to convey the impression of a privileged point of view, but instead, the ending focuses on a tugboat that toots as it passes one bridges after another. Bardamu then imagines that its tooting is an appeal to the whole city, or even the whole world, to end all talk, which at this point is the most Bardamu can hope for (Céline 2006, 435). The lust for adventure is extinct, and his hopes of generating energy through the realm of the social are also lost. This loss is also the loss of faith in the human, as communication with other humans is what most strongly and most consistently defines humans in Céline's novel, but carrying with it all the ambivalence of seeing the encounter with the crowd in the street as a little daily suicide, and as a necessary break from isolation. A middle way would be to find a partner, a privileged relation among humans, where love and friendship bring the individual out of its solitude, while shielding against the chaotic and indifferent world. In a way similar to Michel Houellebecq's exploration of relationships', Céline also demonstrates moments of romantic happiness, or at least the sincere adoption of the illusion of its possibility, but eventually, his fiction has no place for presenting a stable outcome to such encounters. In his next novel, *Death on the Installment Plan*, Céline writes of the possibilities and impossibilities of creating a new type of human in a cult-like setting, however the outcome is not a new human, but a failed experiment (Céline 1971, 434ff.).

Céline portrays cultural and personal memory as neither a means of reconciling with the world, nor a means of making it truly fascinating. But there is a fascinating division in his work that leads to what may not be a positive valuation of history, but of humanity, at another level. Céline's narrator oscillates between displaying his lack of control over his own situation and inability to create a satisfying life for himself, on the one hand, and exuding a self-confident capacity for describing the social world and the human, in general. This split may be seen as expressing a profound admiration for the very existence of a complex social world, for which his hopes for a new and better version in America were crushed, but which in a generalized and distant view, is of value amidst the chaos and pain. In contrast to this, the life and deeds of individuals are always pathetic and miserable. In this connection, it is worth noting how the links between enchantment and war have played out in many other ways. Whereas Céline is essentially a pessimist, and sees little value in what war has to bring, there was a discourse about chivalry in the memorial culture surrounding the war, on both sides of the conflict (Goebel 2007, 188). Ernst Jünger, in particular, is a figure as divisive as Céline, who described the effects of enchantment in a number of ways in his classic, *Storm of Steel*. Such experiences of enchantment may be linked to a newfound feeling for one's homeland, and a conviction of wanting to fight for it, but also to the experience of the wasteland of the landscape created by the war as 'dark and fantastic' (Jünger 2004, 39). But while Céline will have none of this, and struggles to find a new way of being human. In a late interview, when asked, whether he likes boats, he replies:

> Oh, yes! Yes! I love watching them. Watching them come and go. That and the jetty, and me, I'm happy. They steam, they go away, they come back, it's none of your business, eh? No one asks you anything! Yes, and you read the local paper, *Le Petit Havrais*, and … and that's it. That's all. Oh, I'd live my life over differently. (Céline 1964)

To conclude this part, it is remarkable how Woolf, Williams, and Céline, very different and original writers in their own ways, relate to the long history of mankind as a backdrop for their works, as is the particular way each presents the divides between individual and collective, between hopes for enchantment and realizations of the uselessness of such hopes. The way that Woolf addresses evolutionary time, in *A Sketch of the Past*, corresponds to the hope for some sort of transcendence that is also expressed in *Orlando* and *Jacob's Room,* making her relevant in a discussion of the new human. In the same vein, Williams' *Spring and All* revolves around the idea of a new beginning in the long history of evolution, which is counterbalanced by an acute awareness of the ordinary phenomena of the everyday, undercutting hopes for something genuinely new, but instead creating an opportunity for a new sensitivity to the ways in which the past and the absent may be felt in the present. Finally, Céline expresses a desire for the possibility of being renewed, and for the discovery of a new beginning for the human species. Cynical about almost everything, in the rhetoric of *Journey to the End of the Night* there is a distinct fascination with the larger spectacle of human existence, but as Woolf also learns, it cannot be attained by the individual, much as he or she may try to engage with the social world.

Their fascination with evolutionary thought sets these writers apart from a number of canonized authors contemporary with Woolf, Williams and Céline, and each generated a distinct dynamic in their works by exploring the possibility of re-enchanting the world through this view of the process of evolution, which becomes a secular agent that provides cohesion and dynamics, without promising or demanding anything else. However, the evolutionary mindset and the visions of the long history of humanity are still confronted by individual existence, and the disparity between the continuity of the collective and the time-bound existence of the individual, hence the reliance on autobiography that lies at the core of Woolf's and Céline's works, a genre that ultimately also greatly influenced much of Williams' work.

For Woolf, Williams and Céline, the hope of experiencing the world as a new human, or the coming of a new human, are mostly poetic projects that should be taken seriously as such, but not as much more. This contrasts with the political changes that followed in the decades to come, when the new human became a societal project, which, in turn, is reflected in the literature dealing with these tumultuous changes.

Part Three

The Grand Projects

In the following chapters, the perspective on the new human moves from the idea of a modernization of human consciousness that would occur gradually and without overarching control, to the twentieth century's attempts to actively change people, by changing societies and cultures. Such attempts are not without precursors, as the idea of the absence of a human nature and the discovery of the high degree of human plasticity have their roots in the Enlightenment, which went on to have political consequences during the French revolution. What is unique to the twentieth century is the extent to which the rhetoric of the new human was used in different political contexts, in order to mobilize political action, and to legitimize these actions with reference to its goals, and not its means.

The efforts to create a new human through societal changes, which, in turn, would shape individuals, are tragically significant, as in many cases the changes came at immense cost to populations forced to take part in these projects, where the changes were legitimized and propelled by the rhetoric of a new human and a modernized society.

The idea of a new human in a new society was just one significant way of promoting change. Ideas of purification and the use of nationalism and a mythical past as the underlying justifications for change produced other disastrous results, with German fascism – which drew heavily upon a number of sources for its iconography and theories of purity – being the overshadowing case in point. This is in distinct contrast to the invention of the idea of multiculturalism that may be ascribed to Lenin, whose project did not stop at the borders of the nation, but was part of a worldwide struggle for revolution (Jenkins 2011).

The three following chapters are devoted to literary responses to different kinds of changes: from the ambiguous effects of European colonialism on

African tribal culture, as described in the work of Chinua Achebe, to the totalitarian attempts at cultural revolution in China, with both the Great Leap Forward of the 1950s, and the Cultural Revolution of the 1960s, as described by Mo Yan, to the attempts to westernize Turkish culture and nationality as an ongoing project and conflict that profoundly influences the work of Orhan Pamuk. Before entering into these analyses, the impact of the new human in both historical projects and in popular representation will to be further elaborated.

The most significant projects carried out by totalitarian regimes in the twentieth century are at the centre of societal change carried out to create a new human, but it is important to emphasize that there is an undercurrent of cult groups that have undertaken similar projects, and that the idea of the cult that creates a new human, distinct from the rest of humanity, has a strong place in popular culture. Finally, there are also societal changes that have not been carried out with a declared attempt to create a new human, but rather a Western human, although the impact of this change in scale is comparable to the changes envisioned within the political attempts to change a culture.

Soon after the Russian revolution, one of its leading figures, Leon Trotsky, wrote that it was important for the new society to not only gain control of psychic states, but that 'even purely physiological life will become subject to collective experiments' (Cheng 2008, 3). In *Creating the 'New Man'*, Yinghong Cheng also refers to a pamphlet that announces that the Soviet Union has become the homeland for a new and higher order of Homo sapiens, that is, Homo Sovieticus. Of this it is said that it is took the human millions of years to attain the form of Homo sapiens, but only 60 years be cleansed of all impurities, and give rise to a new biological species. The propagandist rhetoric of achieving such goals should not be taken at face value, yet some of the key elements in the statement are of interest, in connection with the thinking about the new human.

It is significant that for Trotsky, the mind and body of the individual are not seen as a limit for society's right to effect changes, but rather as integral parts of a process of change that is about to take place (Hellbeck 2006, 5). Even more extreme is the notion that the mission to create a new human had actually been accomplished, not just through the revolutionary speed through which it was supposed to take place, but also in the use of a forceful, and in many ways troubling conception of evolution as having created a number of impurities that have now been deliberately done away with. On the one hand, cultural development and civilization are praised, and are compatible with the ideals of enlightenment, while the descriptions of getting rid of impurities conjures up the rhetoric that is most associated with fascist ideology (Cheng 2008, 3).

The distinctions that are implied by such descriptions have multiple dimensions. They indicate a 'before' and an 'after', with two different sets of values that dominate these eras, and there is the triumphant conviction that the project may be carried out, or has been carried out, just as the rhetoric takes part in legitimizing change. Perhaps most significant is the idea that the process of evolution has taken a turn from being uncontrolled to being reflective and deliberate, whereby a metalevel that directs the process is implicitly established, transforming a natural evolution to an intellectual and willed process. Cheng emphasizes that this rhetoric was not only used in the Soviet Union, but that Fidel Castro also promoted the idea of a new Cuban as a result of the revolution, and that it would be a new human who would create new movements, in a process that had otherwise been arrested for two or three millennia (Cheng 2008, 3).

In the general public debate and in history lessons, the societal changes that were planned and took place in the Soviet Union, China, Cuba and Cambodia, for example, are the dominant issues, and the visions of creating a new human are secondary. One reason for this might be that the project of creating a new human was not successful, whereas the societal changes were apparent, often with very tangible negative results, in terms of the industrial and economic policies that were implemented. Nevertheless, the ambitions for change that were formulated are historically interesting.

The promotion of a less selfish human being is still being put on the agenda today – by Julian Savulescu for example (Persson and Savulescu 2008) – and it is difficult to not sympathize with visions of more generous, active, and creative humans, and also acknowledge that there is still ample potential for developing those sides of humanity. On the other hand, history provides example after example that indicates that plans for rapid and decisive changes to humans have rarely been sustainable. Cultural changes happen all the time, and some occur through deliberate effort and planning, but few have had the ambition to change the entire human identity and culturally induced behavior to an extent that it makes sense to speak of a new human.

Even failed plans for the creation of a new human entail making decisions about detailed questions of human existence. For example, Cheng describes how theories of future sexuality have varied. Alexandra Kollontai was among those who envisioned a new Soviet woman living in a sexually liberated society in which having sexual relations would be of no greater consequence than having a drink of water, not dissimilar to life in *Brave New World* (Cheng 2008, 38). But such proposals, which were openly discussed in the first years following the revolution, were later silenced, by Lenin, among others, and the official policy for this area eventually focused on sublimation to, and at times comically single-minded concern for the needs of society:

> In another drama, named *Where the Pine Trees Rustle*, a girl is waiting to rendezvous with her boyfriend and wondering why he wants to date her at this time. Suddenly she realizes the only possible explanation: he must anxiously want to tell her about his new production process. (Cheng 2008, 39)

The New Soviet Man was also studied in the West, not only as an ideological import, but also in an open-minded attempt to understand the common problems and values of East and West, and how individualism and collectivity were being balanced (Alt and Alt 1964, 294).

In China, Mao Zedong's adaptation of Marxist thought broke with the traditionally vague or absent conceptions in Chinese thinking of a specific human nature, by promoting the idea that not only was there a human nature, but it was a product of society and class divisions (Blair 2010, 252). Therefore, the idea of an unchangeable human nature was also an ideology that served the bourgeoisie well, according to Mao, but that would change after a revolution:

> Is there such a thing as human nature? Of course there is. But there is only human nature in the concrete, no human nature in the abstract. In class society there is only human nature of a class character; there is no human nature above classes. We uphold the human nature of the proletariat and of the masses of the people, while the landlord and bourgeois classes uphold the human nature of their own classes, only they do not say so but make it out to be the only human nature in existence. The human nature boosted by certain petty-bourgeois intellectuals is also divorced from or opposed to the masses; what they call human nature is in essence nothing but bourgeois individualism, and so, in their eyes, proletarian human nature is contrary to human nature. (Mao Zedong 1996, 478)

Che Guevara was one of the most significant political figures to use the rhetoric of the new human. As a global cultural icon, the legend of Che has survived, owing much to the iconic photo of the simultaneously determined and dreamy Guevara, which was originally a snapshot taken at a demonstration in Havana, but is now reproduced out of context on t-shirts and many other surfaces.[64] Part of the loss of context in the memorial culture surrounding Guevara involves his ideology of the creation of a 'new man and woman'. In 'Socialism and Man in Cuba', of 1965, he reiterates views he had expressed since the revolution, regarding the necessity of educating people to become new humans who will work for the new society, and put aside their own interests. Guevara also emphasizes that new technology will be central to this development, although he does not imply that there will be a biotechnological change, but instead, that technology will facilitate new modes of production. He also makes sure to state that there will be struggles and mistakes on the road to accomplishing a developing vision of a new human identity. He concludes by stating that freedom is the goal, but that the road is:

> long and in part unknown. We recognize our limitations. We will make the human being of the twenty-first century — we, ourselves. / We will forge ourselves in daily action, creating a new man with a new technology. (Guevara 2009, 27)

In *The New Man in Cuba: Culture and Identity in the Revolution*, Ana Serra shows how the vision of a new human was also a subject of Cuban fiction in the 1960s and 1970s, often balancing between promoting the idea of a change in humanity and criticism of such projects (Serra 2007, 6). Serra also notes how popular authors of crime fiction, such as Leonardo Padura, subtly, and sometimes not so subtly parody the rhetoric of the revolutionary visions of a new man and woman, giving voice to criticism of this project of changing identity: 'You ever hear talk of Che's New Man?' / 'What's that? Where can you buy one?' (Padura 2005, 70)

Edmundo Desnoes situates the torn Cuban identity between hopes for new future and the loss of identity at the centre of his fascination with the historical situation in Cuba:

> 'I have been and in many ways I still am a colonial of Western literature,' Desnoes confesses in his 1967 essay. 'I still feel torn between an image of man as a meaningless creature, with only his pleasure, his anguish and his day-to-day existence and the intuition that man can be different, transcendent, that the new man is possible'. If in Desnoes' novel the 'new man' proves elusive to Malabre, and Cuba's assault on history stumbles in its enthusiasm, *Memories of Underdevelopment* probes with fierce detachment their yearning for identity and respect. (Schaller 2009, 94)

Yingdong Cheng's conclusions regarding the three countries with which his book deals, and their relation to the world around them emphasizes that the 'communist new man' was a goal claimed by all communist countries, but only in China and Cuba was the vision seen as an immediate goal (Cheng 2008, 223). Cheng also notes how deeply rooted the hopes for reshaping human beings

are, and that the experiments in the communist nations resonated significantly with Western intellectuals who found their societies alienating and in
a cultural crisis, in the years following the depression of the 1930s, stretching
into the 1960s. Furthermore, the decolonization of the 1960s made leaders of
new nations look for inspiration for modeling their own nations' futures. Thus,
Cheng concludes that, 'the implication and impact of creating a communist new
man, therefore, went far beyond the communist movement itself and constituted a world historical phenomenon'. (Cheng 2008, 223)

It is quite significant that literature was unusually high on the agenda for
several key figures in the history of radical societal change, guided by one idea
or another of human change. Leon Trotsky was a more than capable literary
critic, and Mao Zedong expressed great interest in literature, and devised a
whole programme for the creation of a Chinese literature. Pol Pot was a lecturer
in French literature and history, and Che Guevara was prolific in his writing,
going back to his diaries of his travels in South America as a young student.
This pattern seems to be more than coincidental, and is also a testament to
the influence the medium of literature once held as means of moving culture
in a new direction, an influence that is not as clear nowadays. The connection
between political leaders' deep interest in literature and the idea of a new human
could also be seen as reflecting literature's capacity to create fictive worlds that
are possible to control, undisturbed by reality. As such, literary modes can be
deceptive, and ultimately part of a dangerous construction of ethical perspectives and political directions.

Even if the political projects implementing an ideology of the new human
were limited, with varying intensities, to three or four countries, including
Cambodia, it is important to note a number of other rhetorical underpinnings
of social visions. Two examples are connected to oppressed minorities seeking
to establish a new self-understanding and pride. 'The New Negro' of 1920s
America became a central vision for changing African-American culture in a
way that would free the population of the mentality imposed by slavery (Locke
1997), whereas 'the new Jew' signified a new ability to live as the majority in the
state of Israel, and to not let former times' assimilations and attitudes of subser-
vience and defenselessness be parts of the new culture (Almog 2000, 4).

The idea of the new human brought into the world through a profound
cultural shift was embodied in many different ways in the twentieth century;
some with disastrous results, others not quite worthy of the status of radical
changes, even though they were envisioned as such. The differences are also
significant, particularly between ideas of changing the culture of a population

based on a reflection of its specificity with respect to the rest of the world, and changing humans as a reaction to both the historical conditions of the population, and its general properties, generated by evolution. However, if changes of such magnitude are headed for disaster in real life, and seem improbable even in fiction, then the idea of the cult that might provide a new beginning has held significant fascination for the literature and popular culture of the twentieth century.

Cults, often religious, are a very real part of the world, and even if they are secluded, they are present in culture through fiction, in literature or film. A paradigmatic vision of the desire to separate oneself from the rest of humanity and start anew is Jules Verne's *Twenty Thousands Leagues Under the Sea*, of 1869. It has a charismatic leader, Captain Nemo, with a plan for a new mode of being that contrasts with the present state of civilization. Around him is an organization of people who participate in the project, mostly because of what is expected to come, rather than what actually occurs over the course of the narrative. However, it is also significant that not everything from the old world is rejected; in Verne's fiction, this is evident in Nemo's library, which bears witness to the fact that human civilization is fantastic, but has run off the rails. A reversal of this plot situation is also significant, for example, in Ray Bradbury's *Fahrenheit 451* and Aldous Huxley's *Brave New World*, where the proponents of humanity's heritage are those who live at the edge of a totalitarian, future society, and hold out hope for getting humanity back on track.

Popular culture's fascination with cult movements, most notably in film, has also been given significant scope. The James Bond series was, and often remains centreed on the evil genius who sets out to create a new world order, most significantly in *The Spy Who Loved Me*, where the plan of the villain, Stromberg, is to rebuild civilization under water, after the superpowers have mutually destroyed each other in an atomic Armageddon. The first film adaptation, *Dr No*, portrays the desire to leave the rest of the world behind, and abandon humanity, and *Moonraker* plays with the idea of destroying humanity apart from a select few, who will eventually establish a new beginning for humanity and repopulate the Earth.

The nuclear Armageddon that became a risk after the Second World War is, in many fictional instances, combined with the idea of a new beginning. Stanley Kubrick's *Dr Strangelove Or: How I Stopped Worrying and Learned to Love the Bomb* satirically presents Dr Strangelove's elaborate plan to save humanity, under specific conditions, with the selection of a limited number of powerful men and an abundance of attractive women to weather the aftermath of the bomb in mines, and recreate the population anew. A more somber version of the change in humanity that might be brought about by an atomic disaster is presented in Claude Marker's short film, *La Jetée*, which was also the inspiration for Terry Gilliam's *12 Monkeys*.

The cult plays a significant role in Kubrick's films. In his adaptation of Anthony Burgess's *A Clockwork Orange*, the arbitrary use of violence unites a group of young men,[65] whereas *Eyes Wide Shut* reveals an secret, erotic, upper-class society. Most significantly, *2001: A Space Odyssey* opens with scenes that lead to a killing among early hominids, and in a famous shot, a bone used for the killing transforms into a spaceship via a match cut, whereby the evolution of humanity is captured in its extremes. At the same time, the film also presents a departure from humanity, both by leaving behind the Earth and all traces of human history, and, over the course of the film, through the growing dominance of the spaceship's computer, HAL, whose artificial intelligence has not become less relevant to an understanding of what could happen since Kubrick's movie came out during computing's infancy.

The fascination with such scenarios appears across media, in both popular and niche genres. Usually, a clear-cut utopia is not promised, but more often, there is a warning against a possible future, although this criticism does not validate the norms and conditions of the present world. Real world cults have occasionally made headlines, but arguably, the greatest impact of cults could be said to be in the realm of cultural imaginings.

One of the historical movements with the most profound impact on all continents was European colonization. A large part of this history is one of atrocities, with millions falling victim to persecution, unjust wars, disease, and a general disrespect for the indigenous culture. Over 30 million indigenous people lost their lives in North America, probably even more in South America, and the effects of colonization and the African slave trade, and the prolonged domination of India and China also led to immense changes in societies that fought unequal battles against foreign powers. The events preceding 1900 are not at the centre of this work, but are mentioned as significant examples of the connection between violence and cultural change, and the destruction of cultures that are not thought of as equal in value to that of the colonizers. In the literature considered here, however, the emphasis is on the internal changes to a culture, or influences coming from the outside that do not annihilate existing cultures, but initiate more complex processes of cultural change.

The transformation of African tribal societies is at the centre of the chapter on Chinua Achebe's *Things Fall Apart*, of 1958, as they were driven to change by the two-fold pressure of missionary movements and the introduction of Western administration, law and power. The long-term effects of this change can hardly be underestimated, particularly in terms of religion.

Cultural change, or hopes for a change, may also occur as less direct colonization, such as that which gained momentum in Turkey following the First World War, where the goal set by Kemal Atatürk was to make Turkey a European nation. This led to a significant cultural shift, which was not, however, a seamless transition, but instead created tensions that still influence Turkish society, and which are at the heart of Orhan Pamuk's portrait of Istanbul.

Finally, Mo Yan depicts the effects of change on China, where both the Great Leap Forward and the Cultural Revolution were determined attempts to change Chinese society and culture, and where the underlying ideology of the creation a new human resulted in a number of complex clashes with the resistance of individuals.

Thus, three types of societal change are explored here, through their expression in literature: colonization, non-totalitarian cultural evolution, and totalitarian cultural revolution.

8

Chinua Achebe

In *Things Fall Apart*, Chinua Achebe's account of the transformation of a traditional African village with its own system of religion into a colonized and gradually Christianized society, could be described as depicting the creation of a new human through profound cultural change, as a result of colonization. No one is left undisturbed, as old traditions and mindsets are altered. Achebe makes this very visible in the themes of the novel, supported by his sophisti-cated choice of form, which is at the centre of the analyzes in this chapter. As Simon Gikandi notes, Achebe 'seems to be making a case for the absolute and inescapable linkage between being and voice' (Gikandi 1991, 32). At the end of this chapter, Ben Okri's *Starbook* is presented as a counter-narrative to Achebe's, with respect to universalism of theme and in form.

Cultural colonization

One of the main reasons *Things Fall Apart* is regarded as a modern classic is probably connected to Achebe's facetted presentation of the process of coloni-zation, as it took place in West Africa at the end of the nineteenth century. Achebe's short novel successfully presents both a compelling representation of the inner lives of the members of the colonized tribal village, and a criticism of the violence that was integral to these small, tribal societies.

The overall scale of the changes is enormous, and Achebe's economical style carefully captures the key events in a gradual process of transformation. From the portrayal of an isolated society, where few or none had seen a European man, different phases of colonization occur along two main tracks: the establishment of missionary outposts and their complicated relations with a community whose religion is incompatible with the monotheistic religion they preach, and the brute force of the new administrative and judicial systems that loom in the background, but strike with overwhelming force when they deem it necessary. The missionaries want to change people, whereas the colonizers want to exploit the country. Together, they put immense pressure on village culture. Or, as Robert Wren puts it: 'Trade, government, and religion came together and in its way religion was the greatest of the three' (Wren 1980, 17).

Taken together, the cultural changes are on a scale that eradicates the conditions for a certain way of life. This eventually leads to the suicide of the protagonist, Okonkwo, who refuses to adapt to the new conditions; his defiance is symbolized by his unsuccessful attempt to start an uprising, when everyone else has given up such resistance, and his own son had converted to Christianity. In many ways, he stands as a 'last man' of the culture that was portrayed at the beginning of the novel, and whose rituals, religion and sovereignty are lost or altered in a radical transformative process.

The balance of viewpoints, instead of deciding for or against the Africans or the Westerners, makes *Things Fall Apart* a work open to interpretation, and the meeting of cultures is supported by its formal expression. The novel both borrows European literary references, and includes Igbo in the original. The reader's position becomes complex, as Achebe inspires both sympathy for and antipathy to the villagers and the colonizers alike. The novel further supports this duality by combining formal traits that, for the Western reader, create a high degree of recognition of European literary culture, and alienation from an African culture held together by rituals, a unique mythology, and its own language.

Violence, which in many ways is not culturally relative, plays a central role in the novel, and it is an element that Achebe uses to go beyond an uncompromising defense of the tribal culture, but instead establishes the reasons why the missionaries might succeed. Achebe uses violence sparingly, but in many ways, its subdued presence in the novel makes its normality even more frightening than if it were exceptional. Okonkwo, with whom the reader generally is led to sympathize because of his courage, will, and strength, as well as the care he takes of his wives and sons, is also one of the primary agents of violence, even if the beatings he delivers are only mentioned briefly, they are not to be mistaken as an integral part of the way life is lived in the village:

> Okonkwo knew she was not speaking the truth. He walked back to his *obi* to await Ojiugo's return. And when she returned he beat her very heavily. In his

anger he had forgotten that it was the Week of Peace. His first two wives ran out in great alarm pleading with him that it was the sacred week. But Okonkwo was not the man to stop beating somebody half-way through, not even for fear of a goddess. (Achebe 1994, 29f.)

There is one central scene in which the violence is excruciating, and framed in detail. Okonkwo's foster son, Ikemefune, is led to believe that he will be returned to his mother, but actually, he is murdered because allegedly, spirits have said that this must be done. Significantly, Achebe slows the narrative, and significantly shifts his point of view to that of Ikemefune, who, unaware of what is about to happen, is longing to see his mother, and worries about her wellbeing. He tries to distract himself from these thoughts with an old rhyme equivalent to those 'eeny-meeny-miny-moe / catch a tiger by its toe' rhymes that are found in most cultures, and which he uses to determine whether his mother is well, or at least to comfort himself. But shortly after he has calmed himself, he is again worried by being unable to sense Okonkwo around him, when he is suddenly attacked, and cries for help from the man he considers to be like a father to him. The point of view changes again, as Okonkwo rushes forward and cuts down Ikemefune, in order to not be perceived as weak (Achebe 1994, 61). With this episode, Achebe creates an unbearably touching moment, but the scene is also important with respect to its representation of universalism, and the collective and individual. First, Achebe subtly discloses how Ikemefune's emotional life is structured in a universally recognizable way, with dependence on, and trust of adults at its centre, with the transcultural, linguistic phenomenon of a nursery rhyme adding its own layer. This is emphasized by the detail of the Igbo phrases used in the book being translated in an appendix, with the exception of the phrases used in the song Ikemefune sings. The effect of letting rhythm and childish superstition carry the message of universality seems far stronger than if Achebe had included the meaning (or lack of meaning) of the words.

The other significant element of this scene is the display of how Okonkwo acts on norms that he cannot completely comprehend, but which he trusts and sets above individuals and personal feelings. Nowhere in the book is the conflict between cultural loyalty and acceptance of tradition, and the universality of the individual cry portrayed more sharply than in this scene, reminiscent of the biblical story of Abraham and Isaac, but with a tragic outcome. This conflict runs throughout the novel, with Okonkwo at its centree, unable to get behind the symbols of his own culture because of the many taboos intrinsic to the hierarchical order, with judges and medicine men whose masked appearance he cannot decode. On the other hand, the organization of the colonial forces is also alien to him, and impossible to fight due to the way ideas of power and conflict have been instilled in him, throughout his upbringing.

Cultural meetings in the text

Achebe has made a number of choices in the form of his novel that emphasize the meeting of cultures. This is evident in its language, its narrative structure, the models on which it builds, and its title.

The novel is written in English, but also contains a careful and economical use of Igbo that provides a sense of authenticity and estrangement, which is used so sparingly that the context makes it possible to understand what is going on. It seems clear that the use of Igbo is intended as more than a rudimentary element, but on the other hand, it raises no doubts about whether or not *Things Fall Apart* is written in English. Achebe's defense of his use of English in 'The African Writer and the English Language' stresses the hope for authentic expression, even if it is in the vernacular of the colonizers:

> I do not see any signs of sterility anywhere here. What I do see is a new voice coming out of Africa, speaking of African experience in a worldwide language. So my answer to the question *Can an African ever learn English well enough to be able to use it effectively* in *creative writing?* is certainly yes. If on the other hand you ask. *Can he ever learn to use it like a native speaker?* I should say, I hope not. It is neither necessary nor desirable for him to be able to do so. The price a world language must be prepared to pay is submission to many different kinds of use. The African writer should aim to use English in a way that brings out his message best without altering the language to the extent that its value as a medium of international exchange will be lost. He should aim at fashioning an English which is at once universal and able to carry his peculiar experience. (Achebe 1975, 100)

The novel's overarching narrative structure is very clear, with a number of central scenes that drive the narrative from the steady state of the village to the exile of Okonkwo, to his fall, at the end. But it is perhaps easy to overlook a number of chapters and passages that in many ways do not contribute to the clear-cut narrative, but instead provide an anthropological discourse, describing the culture, rather than dramatic events. These include descriptions of sporting events, life in Okonkwo's family, his love of telling stories of old tribal warriors, and descriptions of the masked elders of the tribe. All these provide a background for understanding the abnormal events that change this society, but they also provide the novel with an oscillating sense of timelessness and rapid change.

The narrative also contributes to the description of the meeting between African and Western cultures by relying on, or referring to Western model narratives. The tripartite structure of the novel follows Okonkwo at home, in exile, and returning home, employing a well-known model from the nineteenth century *Bildungsroman*. The links to the genre are also made clear in the opening, where Okonkwo's difference from what he considers to be his lazy father is made very distinct, while during the novel, it becomes clear that Okonkwo is unable to develop an independent identity and to reintegrate it with the tribe, just as he is incapable of adjusting to the intruding culture. Thus, the novel is in keeping with the novel of disillusionment that Georg Lukács described in *The Theory of the Novel*, where there is neither an affirmation of the individual's ability to distance himself from the dominant culture, nor an embracing of its values (Lukács 1971, 112).

Related to the inclusion of a European genre, another principle of narrative composition is deployed, a central component of Greek tragedy, namely the hero's fatal flaw, or *hamartia*. In Okonkwo's case, it is not the shooting accident that sends him into exile, which is an almost innocent mishap compared to his inability to figure out what an overwhelming force he is facing, still drawing on his experiences of tribal warfare and wrestling matches. This eventually leads him to extend a hopeless conflict, using the means with which he is familiar, but which are inadequate in this situation. In general, Okonkwo's lack of insight is a recurrent theme, and it is made clear on several occasions that despite his strength and abilities as a leader, he is not a part of the assembly of the elders, and he is incapable of seeing through the theatrical elements of the masked appearance of the leaders of the tribe. Instead, he is described as bound to the rituals and norms that have been handed down from generation to generation, and in which he himself takes a very active part in carrying forward. In contrast to Okonkwo's relative lack of insight into his society, there are several characters who have a much more reflective stance, including his son, Nwoye, who ends up breaking with his father and converting to Christianity, and his friend Obeierika, who demonstrates his understanding of the possibility of change, and of the world outside the tribal communities (Achebe 1994, 152).

The role of religion is also significant as a focus of cultural change. The dialogues between Africans and missionaries present the missionaries' strategy as both empathic, taking the African world view into account, and also including strong proclamations of what is true and false within the framework of Christianity. Thus, the missionaries use the Socratic method to have the Africans relate that they do have a god that is stronger than the rest, and this information is used to explain that the Christian god is like that, but without the minor deities (Achebe 1994, 179).

The ability to improvise and use empathy as a way of exerting power is also central to Stephen Greenblatt's reading of *Othello* in 'The Improvisation of Power', where he singles out these two traits as Western strategies when colonizing other cultures (Greenblatt 1980, 229). The cultural change is not merely forced, even though the use of physical power takes place both in the historical material Greenblatt investigates and in Achebe's novel, but it is established through a dialectical process, where the colonizer uses elements of the local culture as part of his strategy to effect a change in the culture. Simon Gikandi also mentions this as a way of producing new idols in a culture (Gikandi 1987, 156).

Achebe's accounts of colonial violence are significant, without being dominant. One of the key elements is the bureaucratic organization of violence, which is much different from what the tribal people are used to. Arrests, imprisonment and randomly executed humiliations occur in a fashion unfamiliar and undecipherable to Okonkwo. His friends' attempts to convince him that resistance is fruitless fail to convince him that it is no use killing single representatives of the colonizers, as they will only be replaced by others. Okonkwo is in many ways a 'last man' with a tragic fate, but he is also part of a complex transformation. Achebe takes great care in describing how the villages had highly elaborate societal functions and organizations to deal with justice and create a sense of community, as well as a nuanced language that developed in accordance with the local conditions, and not as a formal language that has been imposed on the people.

While the magnitude of the societal changes that Achebe recounts is unquestionably vast, it is not a given that the rhetoric of the new human applies to this scenario. After all, African culture lives on alongside colonialism, Christianity, and the modernization of the culture, and even if the intrusion from without brings a revolutionary speed in the change of culture, compared to stability it used to have, cultural evolution is not unprecedented. Still, the distance between the world views, the ability to live life the way it used to be lived, and, looking ahead in colonial history, the subordination of the original language to the language of the colonizer, the idea of a new human created by the cultural impact of a changing society would be an apt description. One could also demonstrate the point negatively, by focusing on Okonkwo as a last man in a society where everybody else has submitted to the winds of change, and adapted to the new circumstances.

Ambivalence is a central part of *Things Fall Apart*, and the insistence on also rendering habitual and religious violence from the perspective of the victims is the closest one can get to a position from which it is possible to critique a historical condition that cannot be relativized or excused with reference to how the culture at large has evolved. An important part of the equation is that the status quo is neither rosy nor uncomplicated.

Strikingly, Achebe's novel ends by giving voice to the British Commissioner, who fantasizes about his planned book on the region, which will be entitled 'The Pacification of the Primitive Tribes of the lower Niger' (Achebe 1994, 209). With this change of perspective, which is quite important, given how carefully Achebe uses points of view, the narrative retracts from its confused and local observations of change, turning to the grand perspective of a representative of the colonizing force. In a mock-ironic fashion, the Commissioner gradually downplays how little space the case of this particular village should take up in his book, deciding on just a paragraph, which contrasts sharply with the richness of detail that the preceding story has provided. The title of the projected book demonstrates how plans for changes to a culture, fully intended or not, were vast and far-reaching, and by ending his novel on this note, Achebe underscores how central to his novel is the idea of creating a new human by means of societal changes.

Ben Okri's counter-narrative

Throughout his authorship, most notably in his prize-winning *The Famished Road*, Ben Okri has depicted modern Nigeria with literary techniques that incorporate spiritual elements in the narrative akin to what is generally referred to as 'magical realism'. In his 2007 work, *Starbook*, he goes even further in creating a narrative that in many ways is detached from being recognizable in time and space, and which hints at a supernatural, spiritual conception of the world, while confronting history. Rather than a plot-driven novel, the book reads as a meditation on Africa and universal being. Rosemary Gray notes that:

> Okri aims to educate both the mind and the spirit through complex theophanic or revelation myths. He prompts us to look at ourselves honestly and critically,

to examine our inner motives, to be self-reflective, to go beyond. His is a world composed not of self and external beings, but, as Larue insists, of personalities and divine beings. (Gray 2013, 140)

There is no doubt that *Starbook* is about Africa, as it uses iconic historical scenes to emphasize this, most notably with descriptions of the slave trade that refer to jointly held memories of how this occurred. But the dominant mode of the book is that of the fable, where princes, princesses, artists and so on, are used as generic figures. The absence of proper names is also striking, with sometimes more than 100 pages between instances of these, whereby Okri deliberately avoids naming that which might identify the characters as African. If Achebe's project could be said to depict and capture the particular elements of an African culture undergoing a process of transformation, then Okri's project is to identify the universal nature of the stories he tells, as is clearly stated at the end of *Starbook* (Okri 2007, 421f.). In the same way that Achebe used both African and Western elements in his novel to find his way between cultures, the reservoir of literary forms applied in *Starbook* removes that distance and strangeness that remain in Achebe's novel. The story could be about desires and deeds from any culture, even if the underlying reference is to Africa.

Okri differs radically from Achebe in another key area. Where Achebe presents violence as an integral part of the tribal cultures, in a way that makes it possible to be critical of old and new alike, the dominant cultural phenomenon in Okri's novel is art, and the way it strives for enchantment. A very large part of the book references tribes of artists, the importance of art, and the act of creating things that are of no particular practical use. This trait inscribes itself within a discourse of aesthetics, a topic that is usually grounded in a European perspective, but here reflects an African universe that, owing to the setting of the fable, and the references to the long historical past, cannot be seen as an imposed way of looking at the world, but a self-developed, albeit universal, mode of looking at the world. Furthermore, African art has been represented richly in Western culture, particularly in the creation, and uses of masks and other kinds of ornamentation that have been produced by generation after generation in Africa. Okri repeatedly returns to the production of art (e.g. Okri 2007, 157), so that there is no doubt that this is to be taken seriously as a narrative of a sophisticated culture with an abundance of resources that make it possible for the universal fascination with the creation of beautiful objects thrive. From this perspective, Okri's book may be seen as both a supplement to the much more concrete and harsh realism of Achebe, and a counter-narrative to the perception of Africa as a continent in which violence is something that has been subdued by an external, civilizing force (paradoxically, partly through the use of violent force).

Okri's overall message is one of timeless universalism that makes it impossible to imply the scheme of 'a last' and 'a new' in the African situation, but instead emphasizes how the stories that are used to sum up what is important in life does not differ much from one era to another. That does not mean that everything is beyond good and bad, but Okri's perspective is different from Achebe's, whose narrative is much more historically situated. In the end, the two books present different angles on universalism and tradition, each in ways that pay respect to local traditions, but with different ways of emphasizing changes.

The question of universal dignity is at stake in both books. Both authors are clearly defenders of human dignity, but they have different takes on what historical changes mean, and in this context, the extent to which it is possible to speak of a new human. To a large degree, Achebe's novel argues for the fact that profound changes can take place, but it is carefully presented, so that the underlying idea of human universalisms is never at stake, although the changes may be of such a magnitude that almost everything is changed.

The balance between a universalism that is indifferent to differences, and the value of specific traits in the cultural history of a people is bound to be a persistent issue everywhere, as ethical conflicts arise from differences. In Okri's and Achebe's narratives, the balance between respect for a cultural heritage and its specific expressions is played out against the often conflicting ideas of universal values, positively expressed by Okri, whose focus is on the arts, and negatively by Achebe, whose focus is on violence, and the right to be protected from this.

Both *Things Fall Apart* and *Starbook* reveal how the past is a valuable backdrop to one's identity, even if the past is not something that may be used as a model for the present. But as Achebe captures a transformation that shows that no culture is pure and uncontaminated by others, by demonstrating the ability to adapt and to experience the simultaneity of different cultural impulses, he also presents the picture of an unhappy and unresolved conflict between cultures. Difference is always a condition of cultural change, but ultimately, the tension that Achebe presents is untenable. By paying tribute to the traditional culture, but also welcoming some of the change colonization brought with it, Achebe's position suggests a necessary sequestering of memories as a passive backdrop that provides identity and traditions that shape everyday life.

From the perspective of the early twenty-first century, narratives of Africa as underdeveloped are being challenged by a rising middle class, the rapid adoption of cell phones, which transform communication on the continent, and the ever growing importance of the internet. It may be asked whether the latter are no more than media and means of communication, or whether these media are parts of a process of universalization, in which the whole world must almost simultaneously adapt to new symbolic universes and ways of relating to the world's information. This is also a transformation that occurs without being entirely deliberate, but has profound side-effects that resonate all the way to the levels of cognitive change and societal transformation. The last chapter in Okri's novel is entitled 'The Alchemy of All Things', and expresses the belief that transformation is the condition of life, but does not necessarily mean a loss of the longer history:

> All is not lost. Greater times are yet to be born. In the midst of the low tide of things, when all seems bleak, a gentle voice whispers in the air that the spirits of creativity wander the land, awaiting an invocation and the commanding force of masters to harness their powers again to noble tasks and luminous art unimagined. (Okri 2007, 421)

9

Mo Yan

In Nobel laureate Gao Xingjian's novel, *One Man's Bible*, the situation during the Cultural Revolution is mockingly presented in a mimicry of the official rhetoric:

> It was a tailor-made new society, brand new and shiny, in which everyone was a glorious worker. People were organized into work units so that they could serve the people, even the barefoot peasants who worked in the fields and the bathhouse workers who pared the calluses from people's feet. Outstanding workers were selected as model workers and commended in the newspapers. There were no idlers, begging and prostitution were banned, and grain was allocated according to the number of mouths to be fed so that not a single bowl of rice would be wasted. The sense of personal gain was eradicated and everyone relied upon a wage or salary. Everything was the shared property of society, including the workers who were rigorously managed so that they would be perfect. There was no escape for the bad, and those not executed were sent to prison or to a farm to be reformed through labor. Red flags fluttered everywhere and, although it was only the first stage, a human ideal of a heavenly kingdom had come into being. (Gao Xingjian 2003, 141)

A little later, the ideas of new humans and perfection are invoked: 'New people were also created. A perfect model, an ordinary soldier called Lei Feng, who grew up as an orphan under the five-star red flag not knowing what it was to be an individual, selflessly saved others and sacrificed his own life'. (Gao Xingjian 2003, 141f.). This is not how things went, and from his position as an exiled writer, Gao Xingjian enjoys the freedom of writing whatever he wants about the tumultuous projects that shaped the lives of several generations.

For a decade, Mo Yan was pronounced China's most legitimate, not-exiled candidate for the Nobel Prize in literature,[66] and in 2012, as this study was being completed, he was awarded the prize, sparking controversy over his involvement with a regime that censors all kinds of communication, including the works of writers.[67] In his work, Mo Yan presents many facets of the radical changes that have taken place since his birth in 1955, including the Great Leap Forward and the Cultural Revolution. While revealing how radical the grand projects were, he also shows how humans find ways to adapt without losing their dignity. His use of fables enhances this impression, while also revealing a longing for a supernatural enchantment of the world.

In recent decades, some of the most influential Chinese authors in the West have been exiled writers such as Jung Chang and Gao Xingjian. Mo Yan has remained in China, and was still a young man when censorship eased its grip on literary activity in the late 1970s, and gradually made it more possible to criticize past events. However, one exception to this is Chairman Mao, about whom Mo Yan does not write critically, even though his work looks back on the often catastrophic nature of the famine of the late 1950s, and the political terror of the 1960s. These were two very different kinds of attempts to change everything overnight, each with its particularly disastrous results.[68] But the catastrophes represented in his works, and the visions of a new human are parts of central experiences where the official ideology was to make such a radical developments happen, yet without being able to succeed in this endeavor.

Mo Yan's works are written about the margins of the dramatic changes, often with the perspective of the little man caught up in the broad events of history. He shows the people's resilience in the face of the grand schemes, while also using supernatural elements and generational memories to counter the official, future-oriented narrative of change and progress. This is apparent in his major novel, *Life and Death are Wearing Me Out*, where the protagonist is reborn as different animals, while living through the history of China since the beginning of the People's Republic (Mo Yan 2006, 9). Thus, the question of being fully human is very originally tied up between societal pressures to become a new kind of citizen, and escaping into the freedom of fiction to create the fantasy of being other species. The centrality of this theme becomes apparent in the final chapter of the novel, where the only short piece of dialogue is 'Starting tonight, we can be human again...' (Mo Yan 2006, 538).

In the preface of *Shifu, You'll Do Anything for a Laugh*, Mo Yan has written of his own childhood, and how it was marked by hunger during the Great Leap Forward (Mo Yan 2001, xii). He uses the perspective of the child or a juvenile in several stories, which gives a perspective with a looser affiliation to political considerations, from which he can more straightforwardly write about what it is to be thrown into a world one cannot completely comprehend. The stories of *Shifu, You'll Do Anything for a Laugh* will be central to my analysis of the strategies Mo Yan has used to portray human existence as more complex and uncontrollable than a strictly future-oriented ideology would like to think.

Hunger and magic

While Mo Yan may be criticized for not writing freely about the issues he takes up, being subject to Chinese censorship and a member of the Communist party, there are elements in his work that make his descriptions of some of the most traumatic years of recent Chinese history distinctive. His use of fables and different points of view, and the inclusion of supernatural, or at least inexplicable events, clearly distances his stories from the dominant paradigm of realism by which generations of authors in China had to abide. This approach makes it possible for Mo Yan to write about these periods of history in a way that captures the reasons everything did not end in a total collapse or deeply inhumane conditions, but instead, human needs and desires, from the hunger of the child, to the hormonal teenager, to the elderly worker who cannot learn new tricks, combined to resist the visions of change of the party in power. In stories such as 'Iron Child' and 'Love Story', Mo Yan both chronicles the magnitude of the changes that went through society in the 1950s and 1960s, and shows how human needs derailed and blurred these plans.

'Iron Child' starts out as a realist story of a childhood, where the narrator tells of being placed in a camp for children whose parents are working on a large railroad construction project. The opening lines relate the facts of the project, and the number of workers involved, before turning to the child's perspective of the miserable conditions in the camp, with dull and meager food, elderly and neglectful nannies, and children who all miss their parents. Suddenly, one day, all the children are released, because the work on the railroad has ended, but they not are returned to their parents. The protagonist asks to be taken home, as he does not know where he lives, but he is rejected by one of the old nannies. Shortly after, he drinks from stagnant water where a frog and a snake have been fighting, and the story takes a turn from the realist mode to the fantastic. The protagonist meets a boy who can eat iron, and who teaches him to eat iron, too. They live in danger of being discovered by the railroad workers, and show great courage and recklessness, for example, by chewing their way through a gun they have stolen from one of the workers. In the end they are caught, but the reader is left to speculate as to whether this was a hallucination, or whether the events should be taken at face value within the framework of the narrative. Mo Yan himself has commented on the ability to eat iron, referring to some of his friends who later became electricians, able to chew through wires, because as children they had gained practice in chewing almost anything (Mo Yan 2001, xiii).

'Iron Child' delivers a harsh critique of the cost of such grand projects of modernization, and the lack of basic care that was its consequence. The harsh and dehumanizing treatment of the children, as though they were animals, leads them to an existence on the edges of society, but at the same time, Mo Yan introduces a fantastic element to the story, and lets the boys appear transhuman in their ability to process metals, and to transcend normal human abilities, to accommodate to new situations:

> Hunger began to gnaw at me that night. Iron Child picked up a rusty iron bar and told me to eat it. I said I'm a human, how can I eat iron? Iron Child asked why a human can't eat iron. I'm a human and I can eat it. Just watch if you don't believe me. (Mo Yan 2001, 104)

Whereupon he eats the iron, and the protagonist soon picks up the trick and enters the borderland of humanity. Mo Yan very directly addresses the limits of the human, both by depicting the treatment of people that would otherwise be reserved for animals, and by a leap into something that transcends ordinary human capacities.

In 'Love Story', the scene moves to the time of the Cultural Revolution, and the effects it has on a small farm collective. The young Junior gradually falls in love with the slightly older and charismatic deported city girl, He Liping. At the middle of the narrative, He Liping puts on a dazzling show of her skill with the spear before the villagers, where she demonstrates both virtuosic and erotic mastery of the spear in her 'nine-stage plum-blossom'. To Junior, at the end of the dance she looks like 'a column of red smoke' (Mo Yan 2001, 131). But for He Liping the dance has consequences, since, according to the party committee, she is a former member of the bourgeoisie, the black classes, and therefore not worthy of performing with the spear (Mo Yan 2001, 132). Only the reddest of the red should do that, and thereafter, He Liping must live in the village in shame. Ironically, this gives Junior a chance to approach her, and at the end of the story she ends up carrying his twins.

As in 'Iron Child', Mo Yan designates two ways of obtaining relief from the pressure of the system. One is by revealing how ordinary, fundamental needs, in this case sex and romance, instead of hunger, are strong human forces, no matter where and how humans are situated, and that they find ways to satisfy their needs. The inclusion of He Liping is just as important, as a figure who is able to do something extraordinary, and who has an enchanting effect on the protagonist. Junior, who initially does not have a grand overview of the societal situation in which he lives, is further shaken in his world view by seeing the woman perform something that to him seems preternatural. The combination of fundamental needs and enchanted moments presents a dual critique of the grand projects that are at the centre of these stories. On the one hand, they remind us that humans are complex beings with strong fundamental needs that are not easily transformed, and thus can make even sophisticated plans fail. On the other hand, the inclusion of moments of enchantment and super-natural elements goes in the other direction, and hints that there may be more to the universe than what societal change can bring about with its unifying and controlling tendencies.

This thematic combination is also used in the title story, *Shifu, You'll Do Anything for a Laugh*, which is set in the present-day transformation of Chinese society. The protagonist, Shifu, is an elderly worker who is laid off in what begins as a social realist encounter with the disillusioning new era of capitalism. Shifu soon finds new ways of making it through life, as he rents a little shack where locals can carry out their sexual affairs. The story takes another turn by becoming a ghost story, as two of the visitors mysteriously disappear in such a way that the reader, along with Shifu and his nephew from the police, is left wondering how this could have happened, and the story offers no resolution as to whether this is merely fantasy (Mo Yan 2001, 58). But whereas the Great Leap Forward and the Cultural Revolution are events that one can firmly situate in the past, the current transformation of China is open-ended, and the mysterious element Mo Yan deploys seem less enchanting.

Human and not human

Animals play a significant role in Mo Yan's fiction. In *Life and Death are Wearing Me Out*, the narrative is structured around a series of reincarnations of the protagonist, who is allowed to escape hell in the forms of various animals, again with supernatural elements included alongside an emphasis on the mundane. The limits of humanity are tested in a number of stories in *Shifu, You'll Do Anything for a Laugh*, and also help to nuance a universe that has political projects at its centre. 'Man and Beast' excels in describing nature as experienced by the protagonist, 'Granddad', in his march through the landscape of postwar China, and how contact with other people becomes increasingly frightening to him. Descriptions of masses, numbering in the hundreds of thousands, of the new 'iron society' are contrasted with the loner who walks the mountains, yet is also bewildered by the direction he should take. Encounters with a fox are described in ways that are unlikely and preternatural, but never doubted within the context of the story.

The conclusion of 'Man and Beast' is typically perplexing, as Mo Yan tells of a strong and bewildering liaison with a Japanese woman presented in the introduction, which is said to have not involved intercourse, therefore the furry baby to which she gives birth could not be Granddad's son (Mo Yan 2001, 81). The idea of what is human is contested retroactively, by emphasizing bonds between humans and animals in a way that both criticizes the politically new human, and also makes room in the fiction for a biologically new human that is half human, half animal, and in many ways stands in contrast to ideas of progress, yet originates from an intense and enchanted relationship with nature.

'Soaring' takes a similar approach to 'Man and Beast', but with an absurdist twist, as the young woman, Yanyan, seeks refuge in a tree and refuses to come down, despite her family's prayers:

> 'Yanyan,' Hong Xi shouted, 'you're still human, aren't you? If there's an ounce of humanity left in you, you'll come down from there'. (Mo Yan 2001, 94)

The story evolves into a discussion of practical ethics, and whether it would be legal to shoot Yanyan down:

> In your arms, she's your wife, but perched atop a tree, she's some kind of strange bird. (Mo Yan 2001, 95)

With this, a policeman starts shooting arrows, and kills her. As she lies on the ground, Mo Yan describes two reactions from the bystanders. They want to know whether she dead, and whether she has feathers (Mo Yan 2001, 96). The lack of realism, which, in the context of Chinese literature since 1949, is noteworthy in itself, is not as important as the reflection on the relationship between humans and animals that these stories present, a theme that has become revitalized in connection with discourses on the posthuman, and cyborg fantasies.

The lack of human solidarity and universal respect for human beings is a related topic that is central to 'The Cure', which was written with reference to probably the greatest figure in Chinese literature of the first half of the twentieth century, Lu Xun, and his famous story, 'Medicine'. As in several

stories by Lu Xun, such as 'Diary of a Madman', 'The Cure' touches on cannibalism, and the lures and taboos associated with eating one's own species (Lu
Xun 2009, 31). 'The Cure' thematizes the question of capital punishment in
dialogues that demonstrate people's ability to describe others to suit their own
purposes. Similar to 'Iron Child', the story opens with a dry statement, in this
case, that there were so many executions that year in a city by the Jiao River,
attendance had to be made mandatory, in order to secure a crowd, thereby also
portraying the normalization of violence (Mo Yan 2001, 113). The narrator's
father awakens his child early, to take her to the execution, and while going
there, they talk about the condemned in a way that oscillates between superstition and cynicism. Both father and daughter believe in spirits, and that they
can feel the unjustly treated spirits in the air (Mo Yan 2001, 114), but on the
other hand, the father rejects the notion that those who will be executed are
being treated unfairly, as they are 'dogs that feed on the dead', and he hopes that
the condemned are young, because, as he cryptically says, 'Young people have
young bodies. Better results'. (Mo Yan 2001, 115). The scene is followed by a
description of dogs running around and creating a nervous atmosphere, before
the arrival of the condemned. The narrator sees that one of these is the landlord,
Ma Kuisan, who is the last person she would have imagined being executed. But
before she has time to ask, her father begins to comment, as though they were at
a sports match, while the condemned and their wives vainly beg for their lives,
and are met with insults and rejections. The officials call the condemned 'dogs',
whereby they echo the father's rhetoric, which stands out as a common way of
dehumanizing others, and, within the novel, is reinforced by the negative role
of the real dogs (Mo Yan 2001, 116).

Mo Yan describes the shot corpses in detail, and the narrator reveals how she
wets herself, as people begin to drift off. However, they do not leave, and her
father takes her to the corpses, and asks her whether she has forgotten that they
came to find a cure for her grandmother. Regarding the proceeding of cutting
up the still warm bodies, Mo Yan is again very explicit, describing how the gall
bladders are removed, and the narrator says that nothing made sense, although
everything seemed familiar (Mo Yan 2001, 121). The father is not untouched by
extracting the organs of the newly deceased, but he becomes more and more
comfortable, and in the end, removing a gall bladder is like cutting loose an
apricot. As they leave the square to go home with their harvest, the dogs are all
over the corpses. At home, the miracle man Luo Dashan is waiting beside the
grandmother, and he recommends that they use either pig or goat bile to cure
her cataract. But instead, they empty the human gall bladder into a drinking

bowl, which does not fool the grandmother, even though the father tries to convince her that it is from an animal. However, the girl cannot hold back the truth, which has fatal consequences:

> Unable to stop myself, I blurted out, 'Grandma, it's human gall, it's from Ma Kuisan and Luan Fengshan. Daddy scooped out their bladders!' / With a shriek, Grandma fell backward onto the brick bed, dead as a stone. (Mo Yan 2001, 125)

In this story, the many negotiations of the permissible and the forbidden create the central tension in the story, and the tragic but also comical ending sheds an ironic light on the efforts to find the cure, as well as more than suggesting that the line that the son was willing to cross remains taboo for the grandmother. The similarity to Lu Xun's 'Medicine' is obvious, and the differences Mo Yan has built into his story only reinforce the connection and the perspective Mo Yan wants to present. Instead of a son, Mo Yan has a daughter helping her father to save her grandmother's failing vision. Instead of finding a way to produce boys, the medicine is meant to cure failing eyesight, and instead of concealing the truth, it is eventually brought out. Furthermore, Lu Xun is not very explicit about the physical details of how the men are executed, or how their blood is taken from them, but lets a middle man provide the blood in a bun (Lu Xun 2009, 38). The theme of cannibalism recurs in *The Republic of Wine*, with very explicit references to the work of Lu Xun (Mo Yan 2000, 55), but also as a brutal commentary on those party members that took more care of their own interests than the common wellbeing of the people, and to show how it is possible to cross thresholds where other humans are no longer regarded as human (Mo Yan 2000, 241).

Mo Yan returns to his own story in *Life and Death are Wearing Me Out*, mocking the author Mo Yan for writing this untruthful story (Mo Yan 2008, 8), but continuing to link stories of the early years after the founding of the People's Republic, and stories of reincarnation and superstition, thereby making a case for the right to take enchantment and the mysterious seriously, and as having value. The insistence on not drawing clear borders between humans and animals works as a critique of the hope of changing society without showing respect for a traditional perspective on humans and animals.

Grand projects and lengthy evolutions

Mo Yan's story, 'Abandoned', thematizes the long, cruel tradition of abandoning infants to die of exposure. The story is essentially a commentary on the difference between the responsibility individuals may feel for each other, and the care a societal organization is able to provide, with a clear preference for the importance of the former (Mo Yan 2001, 174). At the same time, the story presents its views on how it is possible to determine how a village is structured, and what gives it meaning and beauty:

> The complex and colorful life of a farming village is like a great work of literature, one that's hard to finish and even harder to understand. That thought always reminds me of the shallow, insipid business of writing. What strange new discovery was waiting for me this time? (Mo Yan 2001, 159)

Here, Mo Yan explicitly formulates a sense of social life as impenetrable to a simple analysis that could serve as an eventual plan for creating a perfect society. However, by comparing society to literature, Mo Yan adds to the idea of beauty in a way that is akin to Martin Seel's considerations of how society and aesthetics are linked, but are impossible to formulate (Seel 2009, 236). Comparisons between unlike elements may be deceiving or seductive, but the similarity Mo Yan suggests is striking in its positing of a value that cannot be easily spelled out or broken down into a series of elements describing what life in a community should be about. The rapid changes brought about from without are also the central theme of Mo Yan's novel, *The Garlic Ballads*, in which the farmers in the ironically named 'Paradise County' are pushed into producing much more garlic than it is possible to sell, eventually leading to rotting fields of worthless crops (Mo Yan 2006).

While promoting the idea of a poetics of societal life that favours evolution over revolution, Mo Yan is not a conservative who cannot see change as a benefit, but is merely skeptical of how change will come about. The difference between societal actions and the cultural outlook of individual minds is stated clearly:

> And yet, here, in this place, where the land is blanketed with yellow flowers, the issue is much more complex than that. Doctors and the Township Government can work in concert to force sterilization upon men and women of childbearing age, but where might we find a wonder drug capable of uprooting and eliminating the petrified notions that cleave to the brains of people in my hometown? (Mo Yan 2001, 189)

The irony is hard to overlook, as the 'wonder drug' would 'cure' the compassion that is central to the story. Just as significant in this perspective, Mo Yan's volume of short stories concludes by suggesting the idea that human nature could be altered biologically. This should also to be seen against the background of the many suggestions in the book of how thin a layer is the idea of human nature, and how influenced people are by the extended histories of their societies.

The perspective of cultural evolution is also addressed in a criticism at the end of 'Abandoned', with its presentation of various methods for controlling people. Birth control of various kinds, and 'male and female sterilization' have cut down on the number of children that are set out to die, but, as Mo Yan states, unwanted babies, particularly girls, are still the underlying reason for control. Only the means that have changed, not the ends. The actuality of Mo Yan's story persists, as some regions in China have a huge and unnatural mismatch between male and female births, which clearly indicates that a form of liberal eugenics is taking place.[69]

Mo Yan's authorship engages with a series of societal changes with an underlying humanist, but also fatalist approach, which provides the individual with relatively little room for avoiding the forces of the changing currents in society, whether they are the planned projects of the 1950s and 1960s, or the new dynamics of a market economy in the 1990s and 2000s. However, within the acceptance of such framing conditions, his work provides a series of responses, from an insistence on the power of fundamental human needs, to superstition and supernatural elements. Most clearly, the importance of cultural heritage and the complex organism of the small society provide an argument for the enchanting effects of evolutionary phenomena, set across the rapid changes proposed by revolutionary plans.

Mo Yan could be criticized for not taking a clearer stance against the inhumane consequences of the grand visions and projects that were carried out during the reign of Mao Zedong. However, as Shelley W. Chan points out, it is difficult to situate Mo Yan as a conformist just because he is not in radical opposition to the government, and his stances on violence and corruption are clear (Chan 2011, 154, 225ff.). But it is also possible to question the value of uncompromising criticism, by asking how it is even possible that Chinese society, with all its problems, has been able to open itself to the rest of the world in a radical societal transformation, over the past 30 years. The dream of a new socialist human is gone, and has been replaced with a Western orientation that is essentially more liberal, while societal control is still high. However, the idea of a new human permeates Mo Yan's writings, from his historical looks backward, to the present-day fantasies of possible changes, from the strange creatures that could arise between human and animals, to the social engineering that makes its mark, but always at a cost and never as planned, to modern issues related to the transformation of the human body. Mo Yan's critique of these issues is embedded in distinctive characteristics of literature: imagination and narrative.

10

Orhan Pamuk

In his part autobiography, part portrait of a city, *Istanbul: Memories and the City*, of 2006, Orhan Pamuk provides a thorough description of how Turkish society has been changed, and finds itself between Ottoman and Western cultures. In an ongoing dialogue with history, Pamuk shows not only how society influences humans, but also the subtle ways a city may leave traces of something with which one cannot identify. To identify with the city and still find it full of strangeness is a fundamental paradox Pamuk explores. This is also deeply existential, as convictions of what makes humans human is conveyed in a series of descriptions of the city that suggest imperfection, such as melancholy, nostalgia, amnesia and palimpsests, a fascination with which Pamuk has not only put into words, but also given a space, with the opening of a museum in Istanbul.

Orhan Pamuk has repeatedly emphasized that Turkey was never a colony, and that he should not be grouped with postcolonial authors (Pamuk 2005, 217). In many ways, the process of cultural change in Turkey during the twentieth century is more remarkable than the colonial use of power, and no less influenced by Western culture. The forces unleashed by the founder of modern Turkey, Kemal Atatürk, urging and enforcing a westernization of Turkish society, created a central divide that permeates Pamuk's works. Atatürk's determination to change the culture, and his conviction that 'civilization' meant Western civilization, marks the foundation of non-totalitarian, but highly influential and significant attempt to bring about a vision of a new Turkish culture. This process of change not only comprised the establishment of a secular state in a very religious country and introduced Western traditions to the judicial system, but also extended to a ban on certain kinds of clothing, in an attempt to further the process of westernization (Zürcher 2004, 187ff.).

One of the most significant changes following the plans for westernization influenced literature very directly, with the shift from the Arabic to the Roman character set, in 1928. It was one of the most visible and influential manifestations of the break with the Ottoman past and the embracing of Western culture. As David Damrosch has pointed out, there are many historical examples of such changes in writing systems, usually with significant consequences for literature and culture, as well as for the collective memory (Damrosch 2007, 195). Some of the effects may be positive, and lead to a revitalization of the culture, or, as has been described in the case of African colonization, it has united people who otherwise lacked a common language. Renewed literary activity may also prompt an impulse to collect memories, yet the loss of access to older sources will gradually result in a loss of collective memory, as the writing of the past becomes inaccessible to new generations. In this way, the change of linguistic cultures constitutes a significant element in the attempt to make a culture change on the scale of the creation of a new people.

The transformation of Turkish culture cannot be said to be complete, but continues to involve a cultural rupture that manifests at many levels, from national politics, to the signals and memories to which interior design in private homes gives rise. Born in 1952, Pamuk grew up somewhat distanced from the first attempts to change Turkish culture, much as Chinua Achebe was a second or third generation witness to the initial influences from without. Even though all cultures change, few involve the kind of shift that took place in Turkey.

The change in a people and the memory of a city

In *Istanbul*, Pamuk considers how the influence of the Ottoman Empire was still felt, despite the efforts to westernize Turkish society:

> Still, the melancholy of this dying culture was all around us. Great as the desire to Westernise and modernize may have been, the more desperate wish, it seemed, was to be rid of all the bitter memories of the fallen empire: rather as a spurned lover throws away his lost beloved's clothes, possessions and photographs. But as nothing, Western or local, came to fill the void, the great drive to Westernise amounted mostly to the erasure of the past; the effect on culture was reductive and stunting, leading families like mine, otherwise glad of Republican progress, to furnish their houses like museums. (Pamuk 2005, 27)

Pamuk characterizes the effect on his childhood of a culture that had been pushed into a vacuum as calling for dreamy escapes from a state of melancholy, escape that, for the young Orhan, primarily took the form of daydreaming and strolls with his mother, which took them outside their museum-like home. Pamuk depicts another element in the cultural change, related to his family's lukewarm religiousness:

> So rather than see it as a system by which God spoke to us through prophets, books and laws, we reduced religion to a strange and sometimes amusing set of rules on which the lower classes depended; having stripped religion of its power, we were able to accept it into our home, as a strange sort of background music to accompany our oscillations between East and West. (Pamuk 2005, 163f.)

However, the young Pamuk's experiences of the religious people he met do not match the ridicule of these same people that predominates in the Pamuk building, where the rationale is that religion is an obstruction to Westernization (Pamuk 2005, 163). The preference for the West was such an important part of his identity that he looked down on those who were not oriented toward the West, no matter how successful they might otherwise be. Later, he came to revise those views, recognizing that tradition and religion are not just simple phenomena, but carriers of a refined history.

Pamuk also makes sure to not describe Turkish identity prior to Western influence as an eternal, monolithic unity, as he devotes a chapter to the conquering of Constantinople in 1453 as a decisive event in the city's long history, where its identity was radically altered in the years that followed (Pamuk 2005, 155). Yet, the desire to be attached to something greater is a declared need, although it has changed throughout his life.[70] Pamuk describes himself as a person with religious longings, but without any belief that fulfills this desire. It is a need about which he had to keep silent in his secular home, and during puberty, thoughts of sex replaced the thoughts of a divine being. His pain came not from being

> far from God but from everyone around me, from the collective spirit of the city. Even so, whenever I am in a crowd, on a ship, on a bridge, and come face to face with an old woman in a white scarf, a shiver still passes through me. (Pamuk 2005, 169)

This desire to be able to connect with something akin to a collective spirit is, as has been demonstrated in Williams' and Woolf's analyses, to hold out hope for a re-enchantment of the world, but also to experience the disappointment of having again run into a dead end, once the credibility of religion was exhausted.

Pamuk instead turns to the concept of *hüzün*, one of the few Turkish terms that he instructed his translators to keep in the original, while insisting that most other terms that may not have exact equivalents in other languages be translated. *Hüzün* means 'melancholy' (Pamuk 2005, 81), but by insisting on not translating the term, and instead explaining its effects and its specificity, Pamuk makes the case for a site- and culturally-specific view of an emotion that is fundamental to Istanbul. This is particularly important, as he traces the roots of *hüzün* back to the Ottoman Empire, and finds something that connects the people of the present to the people of the past, and which has withstood the attempts to orient the culture toward the West. *Hüzün* is also to be found in Sufi poetry, and thus is not an invention of modernity or of Westernization, but more profoundly connected with the place (Pamuk 2005, 93). Pamuk leaves little doubt that the term is essential for him:

> But what I am trying to describe now is not the melancholy of Istanbul, but the *hüzün* in which we see ourselves reflected, the *hüzün* we absorb with pride and share as a community. To feel this *hüzün* is to see the scenes, evoke the memories, in which the city itself becomes the very illustration, the very essence, of *hüzün*. (Pamuk 2005, 84)

After this passage, Pamuk goes on for four pages in a Whitmanesque naming of all the things that can cause this emotion, as if to overload the reader with possible ways of thinking about what can evoke this emotion. He further argues that the ruins of past empires have a particular beauty for the inhabitants of the city, which can be difficult for foreigners (Pamuk's example is Dostoyevsky) to comprehend. The imperfect beauty that arises from the complex life of a city is closely related to the melancholic emotion.

Pamuk also compares *hüzün* with the *tristesse* mentioned in the works of Michel de Montaigne. Whereas Montaigne saw the melancholic feeling as standing in the way of self-realization, Pamuk not only finds beauty in the feeling, but also the capacity to create a bond among people. Again, this contrasts with the solitary *tristesse* Montaigne describes (Pamuk 2005, 94f.). Memory is not just a question of personal feelings, but to a high degree, also of the political game of people's identity and their collective memory. Pamuk faced a trial for insulting the Turkish state, because of remarks concerning the killing of Armenians and Kurds during the First World War, in what is internationally regarded as one of the first modern genocides. The charges were eventually dropped, probably due in part to widespread international outcry, but the process did significantly influence Pamuk and his relationship to his country (Pamuk 2009, 274). In this instance, the right to collective memories revealed itself as part of culture, as well as of politics.

Pamuk broadens his analysis of the conditions of cultural change to include large parts of the world that are undergoing rapid change due to developments in the economy, not least, China and India. According to Pamuk, the structure of cultural change is initiated by newly rich groups – which must legitimize their power and wealth – occurs in a bizarre, two-step process. First, through westernization, those in power claim that there is vital knowledge to be gained through this process of transformation. When a counter-reaction occurs, in the form of the criticism that local traditions are being neglected, the response is intolerant nationalism (Pamuk 2009, 275). He refers to other writers, such as V. S. Naipaul and Kenzaburo Oe, who have described how the postcolonial era has been marked by a tendency to suppress the crimes of the past, as well as minorities, in a paradoxical attempt to both participate in the international economy, and to steer countries toward a democracy-hostile nationalism (Pamuk 2009, 239f.). However, Pamuk does not regard the West, particularly in light of the wars started after 11 September 2001, as the obvious role-model for change toward democracy in the non-Western world.

The enforced cultural change initiated by the wealthy who were behind the founding and modernization of the Turkish State, did not have support of the poor, and their resistance was met with 'legal threats, prohibitions and military repression. The result was that the revolution was left half finished'. (Pamuk 2007, 221) In Pamuk's view, the humiliation and powerlessness of not being heard are the main reasons for terrorism, not the traditional explanations, such as Islamism, or a war between East and West. The self-congratulatory behavior of the West and its lack of understanding are the primary reasons for the anger, and even in literature, there is little hope for seeing things as they are:

> It is a great shame that the Western world pays so little attention to the overwhelming sense of humiliation felt by most people in the world, a humiliation that those people have tried to overcome without losing their reason or their way of life or succumbing to terrorism, ultra-nationalism, or religious fundamentalism. Magical-realist works sentimentalize their silliness and their poverty, while travel writers in search of the exotic are blind to their troubled private world, where indignities are suffered day in and day out with compassion and pained smiles. (Pamuk 2007, 220)

Pamuk's analysis has global perspectives, but it also carries with it a paradoxical element with regard to the never-colonized Turkey, which, although it had been humiliated in wars, nevertheless chose to Westernize (Pamuk 2005, 218). Pamuk also expresses his belief in the role of the novel in understanding radical cultural changes (Pamuk 2011, 59). Of the rapid expansion of the middle classes in China and India, he writes: '[...] I do not think we shall truly understand the people who have been part of this transformation until we have seen their private lives reflected in novels'. (Pamuk 2007, 239) Pamuk is not a neutral observer who gives voice to his opinion, but that does not detract from his insistence that the novel as a form is unique in its ability to portray different points of narration, both individual and collective, to combine reflection and narration, and to include observations and descriptions of emotions over a prolonged period of time, are all qualities that no other widely available form of expression possesses.

Palimpsest and nostalgia

Pamuk's writing is very much an investigation of how human identity is tied to places and their histories. One of the paradoxes of this affiliation is that a distant and alienating world takes part in shaping individuals who ultimately cannot identify with the world of yesterday. This is very clear when Pamuk writes of the summer houses rich Ottomans built, and which remain as witnesses of a culture that is several generations removed from Pamuk's own, and which expressed a way of living and of organizing society that no longer exists. For Pamuk, this feeling of the layers of the city, what Andreas Huyssen termed 'urban palimpsests', creates remarkable effects (Huyssen 2003, 84). It is not of question of identifying with the past or distancing oneself from it, but accepting that it is present in the same space as the present, as a reminder that others have lived here and lived differently, that they formed the city and contributed to its imperfect beauty, and that one's own imprint will also be strange to someone who experiences the place as their own. This feeling is melancholic in its engagement with a double absence: both that which has disappeared, and that which will disappear over time. But the melancholy is also connected with an experience of intensity; not in a dramatic sense, but in a sense of something that is larger than the present and the tangible, and helps to reinforce the experience of the city as an organism that lives its own life. This is not just the comfort of a condition shared by all individuals whose tininess contrasts with the enduring life of the city, but also a way of creating enchantment through a sense of conti-nuity in the city.

Pamuk pursues many strategies for conjuring up such sensations. Words are well-suited to conceptualizing, to describing repetitions and contractions, but as other memory-oriented writers, such as W. G. Sebald, have done, in *Istanbul* he makes use of photography and illustrations as integral and significant parts of the book. The photographs often interact with scenery described, as well as having their surplus of meanings and ability to create a presence that is different from, and often stronger than what the words describe.[71] As Esra Santesso remarks, the photographs perfect the mood of the narrator, rather than his memory (Santesso 2011, 157). The photographs are also records of palimpsests, with their disclosure of how sites that still exist looked in the past, now either slightly altered, so that one feels as though nearly nothing has changed, or dramatically changed, creating the feeling that the past really was very different.

In a commentary on the photographer Ara Güler's pictures, Pamuk writes that they are witnesses to Istanbul of the 1950s, and that everyone who knew that time will be 'drunk with memories' (Pamuk 2005, 335). Such effects of photographs are, by all accounts of the relatively few works of literature that use photography as integral parts of the works, also experienced by readers who have not lived in the historical environment depicted. Even if the photographs are artistic representations with a language of their own, they are mimetic, while narratives always leave room for doubting the accuracy of the story, of recounting with a viewpoint.

When combined, text and images create a sophisticated interplay, where each medium has its own way of creating presence, and distance to the past. Some pictures show scenes that look as though they could occur today, such as one of Orhan's mother holding him on a balcony (Pamuk 2005, 5). Others show empty streets, taken with a technique that reveals its temporal distance through the medium itself, or people at social gatherings or in crowded streets, who do not match the impression of how life plays out today (Pamuk 2005, 197f.). On the other hand, a narrative is often capable of representing past events and routines of the everyday in ways in which superficial appearances are not at the centre, as the story cuts to the heart of things still recognizable today: a quarrel between parents, playful fights with a brother, or the long, boring hours of a Sunday.

Pamuk's historicization and musealization of Istanbul creates a sense that there have been people here who were the last of their kind, and this feeling is transferred to Pamuk's own time as a central condition. Pamuk suggests that his situation is arguably more exposed, because his memory-oriented relation to the city removes focus from his own time, whereas the people of the past seem, whether or not this is completely correct, to him to have lived more in the present. Thus, Pamuk is unable to present himself as part of an active and self-confident culture that is only now gaining its full momentum, but instead, he appears as someone living in a gap in time. This is far from the strong-willed project of modernization and westernization, and it is difficult to see a clear trend toward the future in Pamuk's writing, as new dreams of change exist at the risk of devaluing the past. Implicitly, however, his own narrative of broken dreams, abandoned projects, and eventually, his transformation into a writer, points to a certain optimism regarding how the past remains valuable, even if new identities emerge. Thus, the ending of *Istanbul* mimics Marcel Proust's description of his alter ego's transformation into a writer, with the young Pamuk declaring to his mother that he does not want to become an artist, but a writer (Pamuk 2005, 333).

By describing Istanbul as a bearer of melancholy and loss in a process that has changed down through the centuries, Pamuk is nevertheless able to connect to the past, which is both tragic, because the mental distance to those who were cannot be overcome, and inevitable, because change is a fundamental condition. The central role of the Bosphorus underlines this point, bearing in mind Heraclites' dictum that one cannot bathe twice in the same river. It is significant that the Bosphorus has a certain attraction as the location that binds the city together, and gives it an identity of being in constant motion, while the river is also something out of time, a guarantee of something constant that others must also have experienced in the same way, even if that is also an illusion, as the traffic on the river, of which Pamuk was an ardent observer, is not the same anymore (Pamuk 2005, 220). The Bosphorus is also an essential for presenting *hüzün*, as Pamuk mentions at the very end of his description of this pivotal term, thereby emphasizing the connection between a place in nature and the seemingly unchanging heart of the people (Pamuk 2005, 95). Pamuk is certainly not the first to employ the motif of nature binding generations together in the mind of the poet – Giuseppe Ungaretti has done this with his long poem, 'Rivers' (Ungaretti 1994, 73) – but the recurrent use of the Bosphorus is remarkable throughout Pamuk's authorship, as few other writers have insisted on a sublime representative of the collective life of a city throughout the ages, without ignoring the dialectics between what has changed and what seems unchanged.

Hopes for a new life

Early in *Istanbul*, Pamuk evokes a number of kinships and inspirations in literature, most notably to the migrant writers, Joseph Conrad, Vladimir Nabokov and V. S. Naipaul (Pamuk 2005, 6). Pamuk is not a migrant, and he instead insists that his fate and that of Istanbul are linked together, yet his is an existence almost as searching and rootless as any these seminal, migrant writers experienced.

The significance of openings of novels should not be overstated, yet they often reveal sentiments that are of the utmost importance to the author. The first sentences of Pamuk's *The New Life* contains a hyperbolic description of change:

> I read a book one day and my whole life was changed. Even on the first page I was so affected by the book's intensity I felt my body sever itself and pull away from the chair where I sat reading the book that lay before on the table. But even though I felt my body dissociating, my entire being remained so concertedly at the table that the book worked its influence not only on my soul but on every aspect of my identity. (Pamuk 1997, 3)

The desire to be profoundly altered, which is also a theme in the works of Céline, presents itself here as something that could happen by being influenced or seduced by a work of art. It is also reminiscent of a romantic dream of how an individual might be able to see itself as new; not through an involvement with general culture, but through a single encounter with a work that also has a unique signature.

My Name is Red also has changing identity at its core, as the different chapters have new narrators, including a dog, in Chapter 3 (Pamuk 2010, 19). However, the main tension that Pamuk explores throughout this work is that of the cultural dynamics of Turkish society, between East and West. The opening chapter of *The Black Book* carefully displays Turkish roots, specific Turkish words, and places and habits, and how travels to Europe and Africa, films from Hollywood, and magazines from France are integral parts of the milieu of the life of the Istanbul characters in Pamuk's international breakthrough. Chapter Two sets a distinctly different tone, by introducing the all-important view of the Bosphorus that is a transhistorical part of the history of Istanbul. It is not unchanged, but it gives rise to remembrance of other times:

> As this new civilization grows up amid mussel-encrusted Byzantine treasures, tin and silver knives and forks, thousand-year-old wine corks and soda bottles, and the sharp-nosed wrecks of galleons, I can also imagine its denizens drawing fuel for their lamps and stoves from a dilapidated Romanian oil tanker whose propeller has become lodged in the mud. (Pamuk 2006, 17)

The theme of being someone else and hoping for enchantment is also clearly marked at the beginning of *Istanbul*, where Pamuk writes of 'succumbing to enchantment' and writing 'as if my life were something that happened to someone else' (Pamuk 2005, 8). But Pamuk also corrects himself, saying that there is little conviction in such epics, and that the myths of the past will not prepare the way for a brighter future. Instead, 'the innocence of objects', which is also the title of the work Pamuk published about his museum, presents a vision of how to relate to a past in which what was given is preserved in all its contingency, demonstrating a certain resistance to all ideas of a common direction in culture. *Istanbul* renders the double complexity of not only figuring out how to shape an individual identity, but doing so in a society that is not at ease with the direction it is taking. Ian Almond has argued that Pamuk's narrators never find any delight in the lack of depth in the world, and struggle with the need for a metaphysics:

> One could say, however, that the most important question in books such as *The Black Book* and *The New Life* is not so much one of self-identity, but rather of meaning itself: are we ever able to fall in love with the thing itself? Or will we always need a deferred horizon—a Messiah, a true love, a political coup, a promised state of future happiness—to imbue the things around us with secondary meanings? (Almond 2003, 86).

It is not surprising that Pamuk shies away from presenting his own ideas for what Turkish culture should become, or how it should evolve, given that such attempts to figure out a plan go against the existential chord of his work. However, in his Norton lectures, *The Naive and the Sentimental Novelist*, Pamuk expresses hope for a future in which the values of the novel and the ability to touch people outside of one's own nation will stand stronger, as something the novel does and can continue to do. Pamuk rightly points out that the novel has influenced literature all over the world, and brought the tradition of writing novels to national literatures in which the genre was not dominant. At the level of its content, Pamuk notes that the novel conveys that the world has no natural centre, but that the search for something essential is part of the long tradition of the novel. In this regard, Pamuk draws on Lukács and his theories of how the novel provides a link between the soul and an outer world, even if it can never perfectly match the world (Pamuk 2011, 155; Lukács 1971, 113).

The central value Pamuk ends up defending is akin to what Kwame Anthony Appiah calls 'rooted cosmopolitanism', which is an argument for a third way, between ideas of local authenticity and global belonging, which ultimately is also not belonging (Appiah 2005, 222). To Pamuk, the idea of speaking for humankind as such is not possible, even if he shares with others the inherent desire to do so. However, the hope that the novel can bring with it a certain way of looking at the world is a decisive hope for a different future, and also one in which the exchange of ideas and templates for figuring out how to describe human identity play larger roles than grand schemes for social engineering. The fundamental capacity of the novel to transform itself while maintaining a core identity resonates well with the perspective on life that Pamuk presents. In many ways, transformation and nostalgia are interlinked, and Pamuk's hope for the novel as an engine of transformation is a genuine hope for the way that literature may have an impact that stands for the opposite of the grand projects of change.

Istanbul, with its elaborate description of how foreign writers have been influenced by, and influence cultural life in Turkey, and Istanbul in particular, also reveals how relatively little influence high culture has had, and how effective political programmes are, for better or for worse, when it comes to setting new directions, reforming institutions, languages and civil rights. For all the feelings attached to a lost past, there is nothing about Pamuk that indicates that he would rather have lived under Ottoman rule. The same could be claimed with some probability of Achebe and tribal Africa, and of Mo Yan and imperial China.

To conclude these chapters on the vision of the new human achieved through societal changes, it is clear that, for all the differences between the events in what was to become Chinua Achebe's Nigeria, Mo Yan's China, and Orhan Pamuk's Turkey, particularly the loss of life as a consequence of the grand projects, there is a persistent impression of the ambiguity that has been imposed on these cultures. The projects for change were not brought to completion, not least because of their miscalculation of the difficulty of reshaping the complex fabric of culture according one's own wishes. Instead, the authors give voice and literary form to the feeling of being stuck by a sense of displacement between a tradition that no longer seems viable, and a future-oriented project that seemed doomed from the outset, owing to its insensitive treatment of tradition.

Living in the aftermath of experiments that never lived up to their promises has created a breach in collective identities, but the conditions these authors portray also demonstrate that the cultural fabric, and the complexity of human societies and cultures are like living entities that cannot be changed without resistance, because of the need for a connection to a larger historical framework. This does not mean that all change is for the worse, as all three authors also take the trouble to demonstrate, since violence in culture, and social control of individuals come at a high price, and Western influences on technology and production have, in the long run, created opportunities.

Instead, they all seem to advocate the joy that should be taken in being part of evolving and imperfect cultures, each with its own distinctive tone. But as Mo Yan subtly forecasts, the central question of the new human has moved from societal changes to human biology.

Part Four

The Final Frontier

Change to the human body is the ultimate, and probably most unsettling frontier in the history of possible human change. Science fiction has a long tradition, particularly associated with the golden age of the genre in the 1950s and 1960s, of describing evolving human beings, and using biological and technological changes as narrative vehicles. H. G. Wells and Olaf Stapledon were early adopters of such ideas, while less genre-specific and more mainstream literature have paid minor attention to the subject. However, with the accelerating advances in technology, ideas of physical changes to humanity have also made their way into mainstream literature.

The first chapter in this part discusses central strategies and contributions to science fiction, and analyzes of a selection of writers, including Wells, Stapledon, Philip K. Dick, Margaret Atwood and Thomas Pynchon amongst other. This is followed by two chapters on the works of Don DeLillo and Michel Houellebecq, which analyze the different ways they have integrated the idea of the new human into their otherwise non-science fiction works, demonstrating how the lure of physical changes to human bodies also influences societies and human mindsets.

11

Literature as Lab

While science fiction has been, and is rich and imaginative when presenting future new life, not all future existence implies a change to human biology. The fascination with space travel does not need to be supplemented with altered bodies, just as advanced technology that brings people further from the Earth is a theme that does not hold the fascination it once did.[72] Post-apocalyptic literature representing returns to more primitive ways of living is also not necessarily associated with describing changes in human biology. However, there are numerous other ways in which human biology might acquire new properties. These range from ongoing evolution, to increased man-machine interaction, and changes to the genetic code, either through technology or owing to inter-species breeding, including with aliens, which would allow humans to explore hitherto unknown domains, such as the ability to communicate telepathically.

The sudden rise and brief history of the terms 'posthuman' and 'transhuman'[73] are remarkably easy to observe in a comprehensive work of reference, such as John Clute's and Peter Nicholls' *The Encyclopaedia of Science Fiction*. Neither term was present in the 1999 edition, but there is now an extensive entry for 'posthuman' in the online edition.[74] However, even if the most-used term presently defining the field is missing, for a long time there has been a keen awareness of the central themes that also govern the debate on the posthuman: the attraction of immortality, the ongoing evolution of humanity, the idea of genetic engineering, uploading minds to free them from flesh, the possibility of mutations and much more. Even so, a significant part of science fiction does not thematize a trans- or posthuman condition, as is also evident in other recent works of reference of the genre, such as Blackwell's *A Companion to Science Fiction*, where terms such as 'posthuman' and 'transhuman' only play a minor role.

In his seminal collection of essays, *Archaeologies of the Future: The Desire Called Utopia and Other Science Fiction*, Fredric Jameson includes a number of works that are related to a posthuman agenda. While making some references to the idea of posthumanism, his focus is on the societal consequences of changes, but his study demonstrates stimulating overlaps between societal and biological changes. However, it is telling that the impulse of human change is mostly connected with aliens. It is the non-human, rather than the posthuman, that interests Jameson, as is political allegory, rather than the straightforward imagining how the human body might be transformed (Jameson 2005, 106).

The general surge of interest in the posthuman is more apparent in *The Wesleyan Anthology of Science Fiction*, where the thematic ordering of classic short stories and extracts from novels places a significant emphasis on concepts of evolution, the posthuman, and artificial intelligence. Classic themes such as the post-apocalypse and alien encounters are also present, but its shift toward posthuman discourses is noticeable, when compared with other recent encyclopedic works. The shift in interest away from space travel, for example, also influences the selection of past works. The selection from the almost required corpus of Jules Verne is from *Journey to the Centre of the Earth*, in which the focus on evolution is obvious, and quite different from the technical achievements of moon travel, for example. The anthology also includes Nathaniel Hawthorne's 'Rappaccini's Daughter', which chronicles the acquisition of new properties through contact with plants, in this case, that of becoming poisonous.

In *Technophobia! Science Fiction Visions of Posthuman Technology*, Daniel Dinello analyzes many of the varieties of visions of transcendence that literature, and film and television, in particular, have presented. His analysis centres on the two dominant ways of imagining transcendence, either through machinery or biological engineering. In addition to this basic distinction, Dinello provides a number of clarifying subcategories that cover various imagined uses of technology. There are the various kinds of uses of machines that can produce hybrid cyborgs or independent androids with humanoid connections, but there is also the idea of intelligence that is detached from the physical world, and takes place in computers. On the other hand, there are a number of ways biotechnology can influence humans, from what Dinello calls 'engineered flesh' to the intrusions of nanotechnology (Dinello 2005, 223ff.). Dinello also argues that science fiction is at its best when it is political, projecting a dark future and urging the creation of a better one (Dinello 2005, 275). He thereby underscores the trouble with imagining a positive posthuman future, and the artistic difficulties of creating stories that 'merely' tell of a world where incremental progress has taken place without compromising human dignity. One remarkable aspect of the fiction that Dinello's book covers, is how effective and influential visual imagery has been, and is in general culture, in representations of the future, for example, in the *Star Trek* series. In this respect, it is also very telling that Ridley Scott's *Blade Runner* has become a more significant cultural reference than its literary source, Philip K. Dick's *Do Androids Dream of Electric Sheep?*, or that Arthur C. Clarke's legacy is so bound up with his interaction with Stanley Kubrick.

The limits of science fiction are not always easy to draw, and the genre is also used and addressed by mainstream fiction. Kurt Vonnegut's fictive author, Kilgore Trout, from *Slaughterhouse-Five* and a number of other novels is said to be modeled on Philip K. Dick and Robert Heinlein, kindly suggesting that they were perhaps not the greatest writers, but that their ideas could carry their work. The descriptions of Trout's work bluntly underscore the discrepancy between the wealth of ideas and the quality of the writing: 'His prose was frightful. Only his ideas were good' (Vonnegut 1969, 110). Nevertheless, Vonnegut also sympathizes with Trout, affirming the values arising from scientific insight, particularly in a prognosis of the growing importance of Darwinism:

> On Tralfamadore, says Billy Pilgrim, there isn't much interest in Jesus Christ. The Earthling figure who is most engaging to the Tralfamadorian mind, he says, is Charles Darwin–who taught that those who die are meant to die, that corpses are improvements. So it goes. / The same general idea appears in *The Big Board* by Kilgore Trout. The flying saucer creatures who capture Trout's hero ask him about Darwin. So it goes. (Vonnegut 1969, 154)

The posthuman theme is not only thriving in the critical perspective of contemporary science fiction studies, but also in new fiction, as reflected in an increase in recent titles directly addressing concepts of the posthuman, for example in the novels of David Simpson, entitled *Sub-Human, Post-Human* and *Trans-Human*. In M. Darusha Wehm's *Beautiful Red* (2007), the epilogue describes the reflections of a being with artificial intelligence who, among other things, considers its gradual acquisition of self-consciousness and, later on, its superiority over humans:

> With great power comes great responsibility. I learned this quotation and recognized its truth when learning all of humanity's history. And I have great power. I am the living, breathing everywherenet; Gaia for humanity's virtual life. But I do not know my own strength. I can only hope that I will learn. (Wehm 2007, 194)

While this triumphant rhetoric combined with doubts about self-understanding marks the end of a fascinating narrative, there is also something essentially unfulfilled about this non-ending. The situation in *Beautiful Red* is a classic scenario that is also found in the fiction of Arthur C. Clarke, Philip K. Dick, and William Gibson, where artificial intelligence exceeds that of humans (Clarke 2002, 126). Wehm's narrative is also used to display a lack this intelligence feels. In a balanced way, Wehm depicts the sense of purposelessness the machine intelligence seems to experience, while suggesting that the evolution of feelings in such creations or systems seems no less likely than the development of consciousness in humans. The strength and beauty of evolution is put forth as a principle that also rejects all ideas of a final and constant condition, and instead accentuates the interrelation between lived life and changing structures.[75] But like Wehm, William Gibson holds on to a belief that something valuable will be lost, no matter how sophisticated an artificial intelligence becomes. In *Neuromancer,* Gibson accentuates the role of the body:

> It was a vast thing, beyond knowing, a sea of information coded in spiral pheromone, infinite intricacy that only the body, in its strong blind way, could ever read. (Gibson 1984, 232)

On the other hand, Gibson also frequently refers to the burden of 'meat', and to the 'meat-puppets' that are not 'jacked in' to the matrix (Gibson 1984, 142). The paradox of improvable humanity and human existence as the highest value is rendered very concretely in displays of the different ways in which life may be lived and valued.

In the *Routledge Companion History of Science Fiction*, Veronica Hollinger aptly uses the term 'post-singularity' to designate fiction that describes a world after artificial intelligence has surpassed human intelligence, along with other technological developments that could radically reshape the world. Thomas Pynchon notes that the convergence of 'artificial intelligence, molecular biology and robotics' will bring about enormous changes (Pynchon 1984). However, part of this scenario also includes the possibility of multiple humanities (Hollinger 2009, 268ff.). Essentially, anything is up for grabs in such visions of the future, and the lack of limitations is a freedom that works counter to the persuasiveness of the genre, but at its best, science fiction also finds ways to push the imagination to the limits of the possibly imaginable, while maintaining a fruitful tension between humans and new humans. In the remainder of this chapter, three significant kinds of human change in science fiction will be examined: mutation, replication and engineering.

Mutations, slow and fast

Like Olaf Stapledon's work, H. G. Wells' *The Time Machine*, of 1895, is not set in an immediate future, but more than 8,000 years from our time. Significant evolution by natural selection is thus more than credible, particularly given what else is known about the speed of the evolution of humanoids. As in many other stories of future worlds, there is a significant gap between the long time-span it addresses, and the concurrent lack of technological development. Rapid technological development is something that we have come to take for granted, and it is difficult to describe future worlds credibly, without reflecting on how its new technology might have emerged.

Wells shrewdly uses expectations of what this future world could be, to depict a utopia in which human culture has tamed nature. True to his socialist convictions, his tale is one of renewed class division, but this time it is so severe that the subservient Morlocks have evolved differently from the dominant Elois. The Morlocks live beneath the surface of the Earth, a condition that drives the evolution of their group differently from that of those who still literally enjoy the light of day.

By including both a vision of what the world could have become and what it has become, Wells does not merely succumb to a dystopian vision. Instead, hopes and desires for what humanity could have become are a large part of the prolonged overture to the real encounter with the world, almost 1,000,000 years from now. But ultimately, Wells' story is pessimistic, suggesting that the strong will always outmaneuver the weak, and create inhuman conditions for them:

> The great triumph of Humanity I had dreamed of took a different shape in my mind. It had been no such triumph of moral education and general co-operation as I had imagined. Instead, I saw a real aristocracy, armed with a perfected science and working to a logical conclusion the industrial system of to-day. Its triumph had not been simply a triumph over Nature, but a triumph over Nature and the fellow-man. This, I must warn you, was my theory at the time. I had no convenient cicerone in the pattern of the Utopian books. My explanation may be absolutely wrong. I still think it is the most plausible one. But even on this supposition the balanced civilization that was at last attained must have long since passed its zenith, and was now far fallen into decay. The too-perfect security of the Upper-worlders had led them to a slow movement of degeneration, to a general dwindling in size, strength, and intelligence. That I could see clearly enough already. What had happened to the Under-grounders I did not yet suspect; but from what I had seen of the Morlocks—that, by the by,

was the name by which these creatures were called—I could imagine that the modification of the human type was even far more profound than among the 'Eloi', the beautiful race that I already knew. (Wells 1965, 53)

The defining trait of Wells' narrative is the revelation of how living conditions could lead to speciation. This is also what renews interest in the story, as it takes the vision of unequal physical development seriously, as something that would disturb the idea of a single humanity. In our world there may be an unequal distribution of height, and childhood damage to the development to both physical and cognitive capacities through malnutrition, but the idea of different strands of humanity is not relevant. However, with the growing pace of technological inventions, and a plethora of ways of selecting, developing and maintaining humans, the possibility of radically different kinds of conditions for different segments of humanity cannot be easily written off. There is no moral justification for letting this situation occur, nor is there for Wells. His 'revenge' consists of describing a fatal decay among the dominant class:

> The two species that had resulted from the evolution of man were sliding down towards, or had already arrived at, an altogether new relationship. The Eloi, like the Carolingian kings, had decayed to a mere beautiful futility. They still possessed the earth on sufferance: since the Morlocks, subterranean for innumerable generations, had come at last to find the daylit surface intolerable. And the Morlocks made their garments, I inferred, and maintained them in their habitual needs, perhaps through the survival of an old habit of service. They did it as a standing horse paws with his foot, or as a man enjoys killing animals in sport: because ancient and departed necessities had impressed it on the organism. But, clearly, the old order was already in part reversed. The Nemesis of the delicate ones was creeping on apace. Ages ago, thousands of generations ago, man had thrust his brother man out of the ease and the sunshine. (Wells 1965, 60)

While Wells' story chronicles an almost too slow evolutionary trajectory, Edmond Hamilton's 'The Man Who Evolved', of 1931, very directly addresses the further evolution of humanity, and imagines that it could be accelerated. The dubious idea that cosmic rays are the driver of evolution is a central plot device, even if the science behind this is non-existent, just as evolution is never individual, but takes generation after generation to happen. But as a desire and a thought experiment, the story is thought-provoking. Hamilton lets his protagonist, Pollard, make a projected leap over 50,000,000 years of evolution, by voluntary subjecting himself to cosmic rays. He triumphantly boasts how he has made a leap into the distant future, and become a bigger, stronger, smarter and more beautiful individual (Hamilton 2010, 87). Eventually the story turns into a grotesque, horrifying tale of a man who becomes all brain, once again denying an unproblematic outcome to development. The irony of Hamilton's story is that Pollard ends up as protoplasm, thus taking him back to the beginning of evolution:

> From the earth's bosom had risen the first crude organisms. Then sea-creature and land-creature and mammal and ape to man; and from man it would rise the future through all the forms we had seen that night. There would be super-men, bodiless heads, pure brains; only to be changed by the last mutation of all into the protoplasm from which first it had sprung! (Hamilton 2010, 94)

The class aspect of uneven development with which Wells is concerned is also taken up by Octavia E. Butler in her late twentieth century trilogy, *Lilith's Brood*, where alien intervention leads to the transformation of some humans. The capacities of the aliens are immense and awe-inspiring to humans: 'We're in the hands of people who manipulate DNA as naturally as we manipulate pencils and paintbrushes'. (Butler 2000, 167). Just as Wells' story is very much about his contemporary historical situation, Paul Youngquist remarks that Butler's novels could be read allegorically, substituting spaceships with slave ships (Youngquist 2011, 21). Like Wells and others, Butler also hints that class hierarchy would lead to human extinction, thereby giving the aliens a moral right to intervene (Smith 2009, 555).

Butler's novel portrays a dystopian and post-apocalyptic universe, in which the societal order is different from that we know. The sense of strangeness is supported by the writing, which, unlike the fiction of Stapledon, Wells and Huxley, does not give a larger and authoritative perspective on the present state of the world. Additionally, there is a sense of the loss of cultural complexity, and a world that is difficult to navigate, yet bears traces of a valuable past:

> There was immense newness. Life in more varieties than I could possibly have imagined–unique units of life, most never seen on Earth. Generations of memory to be examined, memorized, and either preserved alive in stasis or allowed to live their natural span and die. Those that I could re-create from my own genetic material, I did not have to maintain alive. (Butler 2000, 693)

Theodora Goss and John Paul Riquelme argue that, in contrast to Mary Shelley's *Frankenstein*, Butler introduces posthuman offspring that are the result of encounters between humans and aliens. They see this as part of a larger strategy of challenging counterparts, including male and female, animal and plant, machine and human. This differs from Shelley's approach, as:

> [t]he goal is not the elevating of the human to superhuman status at the top of a hierarchy, as in *Frankenstein*, but rather the survival of the human and the alien, primarily in mixed forms. It is important in this regard that the death of the individual does not disappear in the posthuman world. (Goss and Riquelme 2007, 555)

Yet, for all the breaking down of barriers, the story of Lilith begins with the loss of her husband and son, and Butler's novels are marred by the absence of human presence. On the other hand, Lilith cannot help but be fascinated by the powers of the aliens, and their ability to make changes in her. The inclination to insist on the human as having the highest value is challenged by the many instances of the alien's sensitivity, just as the creation in *Frankenstein* displays superior reasoning and sensitivity. At the same time, Lilith experiences coldness and exclusion from other humans, who are distrustful of her relations with the aliens (Hollinger 2009, 130). Nevertheless, the desire to hear human voices and to interact with other humans is deeply rooted in Lilith (Butler 2000, 60). Inevitably, the social aspect of human existence comes to the fore, even more so, when the limits of biology are less stringent than they are in the world outside of fiction.

Replicated

Human replication is another central topic with roots in Romantic representations of doubles, and the eerie perspective of not being a singular and unique individual. This might be said to not lead to a posthuman condition, as replication does not offer new features, but it certainly creates a new situation, as it is evident in Huxley's *Brave New World*. In addition, human replication and the creation of artificial humanoids through robotic means, as described by Isaac Asimov and Philip K. Dick, provides a different take on a situation in which humans reproduce themselves by using technology, rather than natural means. From the changes technology can precipitate, and the presence of humanoid robots, to the replication of human minds, the theme of replication has been explored in numerous works, either in fully developed universes, or as fragments of a future that could come into being.[76]

One of the more surprising recent literary contributions to biotechnologically informed literature has come from Kazuo Ishiguro, who made his name with *The Remains of the Day*, depicting the English upper-classes in the 1930s, a world quite apart from ideas of cloning. *Never Let Me Go* is a novel that, using the same calm, subdued and realistic style of narration as Ishiguro's other novels, and with a sense of life lived in a setting out of time from modern life, addresses questions of cloning and its possible inhumane consequences. The novel is set in the 1990s, a small provocation to its readers, implying that these things have already happened, rather than warning of a future scenario. Kathy and her peers live in isolation in small cottages in the countryside, after having been raised at boarding schools. Gradually, it is revealed that they are clones of older people, and that their purpose in life is to be used as spare parts, donating their organs to the often 30-years-older originals. Kathy develops a tender relationship with another clone, Tommy, but they are heartbreakingly aware that they will enter a phase where pain and the slow evaporation of life will be their fate, and their lack of resistance to this only enhances the affective appeal of the novel, as Anne Whitehead has also noted (Ishiguro 2005, 208; Whitehead 2011, 78f.).

The simple imperative of not treating humans as means, but their being their own ends is embodied in Ishiguro's narrative, which further uses dramatic irony by letting it be known that Kathy is not quite aware of what is at stake for her, but in way that leaves the reader in no doubt. The ability of literature to establish empathy with fictional characters is effectively displayed in the pages of *Never Let Me Go*, which portray a world that apart from cloning has no connection to highly technological future scenarios.

Through simple means, Ishiguro draws attention to a scenario that, in various ways is already part of reality. The sorting of embryos to create suitable donors takes place, although the respect for the newborns' lives have been preserved, but this has still given rise to discussions of when the balance between means and ends tips. Animals have been cloned, and there is no reason to think that human cloning could not eventually occur, whether authorized or covert.[77] However, regarding the need for human body parts, there have been attempts to grow human organs in other species, under artificial conditions or even being printed, which might even make the dystopian visions in Ishiguro's fiction superfluous. Finally, the theft of and trade in organs is a phenomenon that brings focus to a world where, for many reasons, some people's wellbeing is valued less than others', even by themselves.

What Ishiguro recounts is not technically unlikely. The interest is not so much in the techniques, but the social organization, which the reader also never fully comprehends, but sees through Kathy and her views on the normalcy of her situation. Here, there is a direct line between this scenario and the normalcy of class division as perceived by the characters in *The Remains of the Day*, as well as in the fiction of H. G. Wells, and many other visions of the future.

What makes *Never Let Me Go* a particularly moving novel is the accentuation of the code of bravery that exists among the clones, and that is upheld through euphemisms such as 'carer' and 'donor' (Ishiguro 2005, 4). The reader's hopes that Kathy may be able to understand the system and revolt against it are unsatisfied, and the novel is instead a display of how given conditions can produce a sense of what is normal and unavoidable. Thus, the parallels to other fiction by Ishiguro are obvious, as is the familiarity with the universes described in classics of the genre by George Orwell and Aldous Huxley. What sets Ishiguro apart is the lack of drama and of plot twists, which intensifies the sense of fatality and hopelessness.

Taking a much different approach to replication, Philip K. Dick's classic, *Do Androids Dream of Electric Sheep?* chronicles the existence of artificial life that is almost indistinguishable from the human, thereby drawing very efficiently on the emotional discomfort of being unable to recognize oneself in the other. Paranoia is one of the consequences of living in a society where one can never be sure of whether one is interacting with another human, or a machine. Among the many sophisticated layers in his novel, Dick highlights an appreciation of the natural, including animals, which have become scarce in the universe he describes (Dick 1999, 28). The android bounty hunter, Rick Deckard, mentions his curiosity about finding uncontrolled nature:

> I've never found a live, wild animal. It must be a fantastic experience to look down and see something living scuttling along. (Dick 1999, 188)

In the novel, androids gradually become less and less distinguishable from humans, and Dick finds multiple ways of tacitly posing the question of what difference it makes to be a human, particularly if it is impossible to discern humans from machines, and for the machines themselves to comprehend that they are not human (Dick 1999, 106). Human purposelessness ends up being a positive quality, as, in contrast to androids, they have not been created for a purpose.

In *What is Enlightenment?*, Immanuel Kant urges governments to treat 'man, who is more than a machine, in a manner appropriate to his dignity' (Kant 1991, 60). This dignity is now under pressure, thanks to ideas of designer children and other kinds of interventions in the conventional means of reproducing, which may marginalize the idea of the individual being its own end. In this situation, art could be an important reminder of the value of purposelessness.[78]

Thomas Pynchon's incredibly complex *Gravity's Rainbow*, often read in light of its setting during the Second World War, is also rife with speculation and desires regarding what might happen.[79] The fascination with rockets, in particular the German V2, developed by the eventual head of the American space programme, Werner von Braun, places new technologies at the centre of the novel's universe. What is even more telling, four decades after the novel's initial publication, are the kinds of visions that are conjured up:

> Maybe there *is* a Machine to take us away, take us completely, suck us out through the electrodes out of the skull 'n' into the Machine and live there forever with all the other souls it's got stored there. *It* could decide who it would suck out, a-and when. Dope never gave *you* immortality. *You* hadda come back, every time, into a dying hunk of smelly *meat*! But *We* can live forever, in a clean, honest, purified Electroworld- (Pynchon 1973, 699)

This idea of achieving immortality through a replication of the mind recurs in much of the fiction about humanity's liberation from the body, toward a regime in which systems and information become more important. In *Gravity's Rainbow*, Pynchon includes a strange tale of 'Byron the Bulb', which mixes the features of human personality with the material industrial product, which happens to be immortal (Pynchon 1973, 648). Eventually, Byron begins to communicate with other electrical appliances on the Grid, but he is 'condemned to go on forever, knowing the truth and powerless to change anything' (Pynchon 1973, 654). Elsewhere, the predictions for the information age, and how all interests will move toward information, are spun into a wealth of references to the material world, and the hunt for precious possessions, which counters the bold predictions of the reign of information (Pynchon 1973, 258).

The most significant character in the novel, Tyrone Slothrop, is not a conventional protagonist, but a transformative figure who, at one point, is caught in the Zone, an allegory of a postwar landscape, as well as a vision of a new way of existing, where the question of what counts as human is at stake (Pynchon 1973, 302). Pynchon utilizes elements from the Second World War's industrial production, and inhumane warfare and expulsion, as settings for a meditation on a posthuman way of existing. The erotic attraction of war and machinery is emphatic (Pynchon 1973, 306), including at the end of the novel, when the sex-slave Gottfried is launched in a rocket, symbolizing the marriage of man and machine (Pynchon 1973, 774). While history and landscapes are part of the setting, a sense of a new mode of existence makes everything in the Zone ambiguous. Early in the novel, Slothrop is called 'The New Mark in Town'

(Pynchon 1973, 259), and given Pynchon's penchant for puns and jests (such as 'Post-A4 humanity'), it is hardly a stretch to think of his adventures and transformative nature in the context of either the new or the last human.

Modified

Olaf Stapledon's novel, *Last and First Men*, was in many ways ahead of its time, in its description of human change. Like Aldous Huxley's far more famous *Brave New World*, Stapledon imagines a world government, following a disastrous war in Europe little more than a decade preceding the start of the novel. But whereas Huxley focuses on the stability and control that is achieved in his fictional universe (Huxley 2005, 48), Stapledon plays out a number of scenarios over a much longer time-span, to be counted in millions of years, and with much more ambitious, but also unrealistic, developments.

The enormous time-span that Stapledon covers, which Fredric Jameson dismisses as childish, has some noticeable effects (Jameson 2005, 126). On the one hand, it seems naïve to think that the processes chronicled would take so long, considering how human culture has developed over the past millennia. But the long time-span also serves as a reminder of how long processes on Earth normally take, and how historical time is almost nothing, compared to the time nature keeps. Stapledon was well aware that he was not writing an accurate account or the best guess about the future, and labels his otherwise well-informed and learned novel 'a myth' (Stapledon 1930, vi). Read as such, the many different ways of organizing the future of humanity and the perils that it could meet form a survey of what could enchant human lives and bring value into it. The role of the aesthetic is particularly pronounced among the 'Third Men', whereas the highly intelligent 'Fourth Men' struggle with their lack of emotions (Stapledon 1930, 232). Some cultures are overwhelmed by the fear of dying, even though they have very long lives; others develop frivolous sexualities, and in between there are eras of sharp decline and despair. As such, this is a myth of things to which humans could aspire, but which only shows that there are more parts to the equation of a good life than bigger brains, stronger muscles, and longer lives.

From the beginning, *Last and First Men* is fascinated by the relationship between individual and collective, using the differences between American individualism and Chinese collectivity as vehicles for presenting a conflict that persists throughout the novel, whereas European culture is wiped out very early, in wars carried out with poisonous gas and biochemical warfare (Stapledon 1930, 41). Later, the Earth is invaded by Martians that have the ability to communicate with one another as though through some kind of telepathy, and – very apt, given the current metaphor for data storage – sharing knowledge in a sort of cloud (Stapledon 1930, 161). Humans acquire some of these features, and also the ability to communicate with the past, which explains how the narrator of the book is actually two individuals living in different times. Although man–machine integration should not be ruled out as being able to provide something like this, what is more interesting is the desire for, or mythical musing about the possibility of connecting individual minds to something collective. Here, this theme, which is also very much at the centree of Virginia Woolf's writings, is developed in a fantasy in which the sense of self and sense of collective are brought together in a very concrete way. The recurrence of this throughout the novel, and the use of the effect to create an unlikely but fascinating narrator, underscore the significance of the theme as one of the ways that a re-enchantment of the world could take place, even if the way Stapledon describes it is tragically beyond reach.

The idea of telepathy is more of a belief in unexplored natural powers than a subject of science fiction, such as that which Stapledon presents in his vision of the Martians. Theodore Sturgeon also uses the idea of sharing minds in his 1953 novel, *More than Human*, where such powers are bestowed on a new branch of humanity, *Homo Gestalt* (Sturgeon 1998, 212). But the idea of brain-machine aided telepathy is something that is imagined as within reach. Freeman Dyson has written about this possibility, even extending it to communicating with other species.[80] For Dyson, this could make the world a better place, as we 'will feel in our flesh the community of life to which we belong' (Dyson 2009, 147).[81]

Just as the general idea of the posthuman is more pervasive than other scenarios envisioning the future that do not involve changes to the idea of human identity, the subject of telepathy presents a vision that alters the idea of selfhood. As much as literature may express the desirability of being able to access other minds and share the world, the idea of the loss of selfhood and clear borders between individual minds and the world is almost unimaginable. The enchantment of breaking through to a new form of being in the world is alluring in theory, but difficult to describe in a concrete scenario, without presenting a number of less desirable side-effects, as it will also be evident in the analysis of Michel Houellebecq's work.

Stapledon's later and more acclaimed novel, *Star Maker*, addresses the exploration of space and the discovery of other, advanced civilizations living far away.

Again, the time scales are enormous, which increases focus on the framework Stapledon presents, rather than on narratives with subjects, something that the novel straightforwardly admits, while arguing that there are thousands of worlds to be described. A significant trait of Stapledon's world is that aliens are essentially humanoid, having passed through phases similar to those on Earth, but have a number of unusual features, such having wings that enable flight, a previously-explored motif (Stapledon 1937, 91ff.). The fascination with improved communication within groups, which was a strong theme in *First and Last Men*, recurs in *Star Maker*, leading to the phenomena of 'world spirits' (Stapledon 1937, 209).

While very inventive at the levels of technology and biological evolution, Stapledon is simultaneously deeply rooted in a diagnosis of his time as one of political change, and of a spiritual crisis of the human race (Stapledon 1937, 84). Stapledon's works are very open to interpretation, and it is telling that Fredric Jameson focuses on the societal consequences of human change, rather than taking seriously the desire to be a physically different being (Jameson 2005, 126).

There are a number of contemporary writers who deal with issues similar to those Stapledon addressed early on. In *Oryx and Crake*, part of a trilogy that also includes *The Year of the Flood* and *MaddAddam*, Margaret Atwood has written in a very different way about engineering posthumans, which is telling of the present state of wariness regarding what might actually be in store for humanity. As in the novels of Octavia Butler, this novel conjures up a confusing, post-apocalyptic landscape, which the protagonists have difficulty navigating. This is very different from the grand scale and historical authority presented in Stapledon and others' works. As Ralph Pordzik notes: 'Natural environment, the human body, and cultural production are intrinsically connected, each evolving in response to another's position or activity in a complex network of relationships'. (Pordzik 2012, 155). Atwood's literary strategy underscores this, and produces a sense of a decentred humanity, far from the position of being in control of its own development.

The idea of producing a new and improved form of human is central to *Oryx and Crake*, as the geneticist, Crake, tries to implement a plan that will kill off the old humans and replace them with more benevolent and environmentally conscious ones. Eventually, Crake is killed, and the project is not brought to completion. As in many other works of fiction, the perfect plan is not allowed to be carried out, and the bewildered humans prove their resilience. The desire for immortality is addressed, but is also taken in the direction Huxley (and Don

DeLillo) envisioned, namely, suggesting that mortality is not overcome, but anxiety about death is:

> 'Immortality,' said Crake, 'is a concept. If you take "mortality" as being, not death, but the foreknowledge of it and the fear of it, then "immortality" is the absence of such fear. Babies are immortal'. (Atwood 2003, 356)

Atwood's novel is both explicitly and implicitly intertextual, with quotations from Jonathan Swift's *Gulliver's Travels*, and Virginia Woolf's *To the Lighthouse*. A pandemic that kills almost the entire population of the Earth evokes Mary Shelley's work, just as Crake is another incarnation of a Frankenstein-like, mad scientist. The theme Shelley took up is still vibrant, but the distance between fiction and possible future has become eerily smaller. Thus, the open ending of Atwood's novel is also a reflection of an uncertain future for humanity, rather than a possible return to a stable present.

The golden age of science fiction is past, which may be regarded as either paradoxical or logical, as the increase in technological sophistication has increased dramatically since the 1950s, and in many respects far exceeds what writers then thought possible. William Gibson lets his aptly named character, Bigend, explain the new situation:

> [...] we have no idea, now, of who or what the inhabitants of our future might be. In that sense we have no future. Not in the sense that our grandparents had a future, or though they did. Fully imagined cultural futures were the luxury of another day, one in which 'now' was of some greater duration. For us, of course, things can change so abruptly, so violently, so profoundly, that futures like our grandparents' have insufficient 'now' to stand on. We have no future because our present is too volatile. (Gibson 2003, 57)

Nevertheless, science fiction continues to generate projections and narratives that are closely linked to our fears and desires, and to do so by presenting concrete consequences of changed living conditions. Some of these, such as the quest for immortality, which has a much longer history than this genre, have been around for a long time, but have experienced a renewed interest,[82] whereas other aspirations, such as certain forms of telepathic connectedness, tell of other kinds of desires, which also resonate with today's use of new social media.

12

Don DeLillo

The literary public largely associates Don DeLillo's work with recent American history and culture, in novels such as *Libra, Underworld* and *Falling Man*, which give his impressions of the assassination of John F. Kennedy, the Cold War and the attack on the USA on 11 September 2001, respectively. At times, DeLillo's novels have also uncannily predicted events to come. Besides the coincidental detail of the cover of *Underworld* depicting the World Trade Centre with a silhouette of a bird that could be perceived as an airplane, novelist Richard Powers has noted in a foreword to *White Noise* that in this work, completed shortly before the Indian Bhopal disaster of December 1984, DeLillo takes up toxic catastrophes (Powers 2009). Such correlations may have no epistemological status, but they do cast a certain aura around his works.

The fact that DeLillo also writes about biotechnology and cyberculture as two key phenomena that affect humans is sometimes overlooked. He combines this interest with descriptions of how the search for memories and for a languageless, physical existence interacts with those elements. In this context, two of his strongest works, *The Names* and *White Noise*, present a wide range of determined cults, the desire to cope with human mortality, and the emptiness of contemporary culture. The influence of the digital age is already remarkable in his early works, and it is later sustained even more emphatically in the shorter and less accomplished novels, *The Body Artist* and *Cosmopolis*.

The fascination with materiality is also highly significant in DeLillo's 2010 novel, *Point Omega*, which explicitly thematizes the desire to end human consciousness, here in the words of the mysterious Richard Elster:

> We want to be the dead matter we used to be. We're the last billionth of a
> second in the evolution of matter. When I was a student I looked for radical
> ideas. Scientists, theologians, I read the work of mystics through the centuries,

> I was a hungry mind, a pure mind. I filled notebooks with my visions of world
> philosophy. Look at us today. We keep inventing folk tales of the end. Animal
> diseases spreading, transmittable cancers. What else? (DeLillo 2010, 50f.)

The dialogue then turns to climate change, asteroids and famine as possible
apocalyptic scenarios. But Elster rejects them as uninteresting, and calls for
thinking further, as he attempts to sketch out principles of evolution and
annihilation, and of the collective thought that exists outside of the individual,
as a collective hive mind (DeLillo 2010, 52). After this, the possibilities of
transcending biology and the coming omega point, which gives the novel its
title, are addressed. Elster asks:

> … Do we have to be human forever? Consciousness is exhausted. Back now to
> inorganic matter. This is what we want. We want to be stones in a field. (DeLillo
> 2010, 52f.)

At the end of the novel, the film director, Jim Finley, reflects on what Elster has
taught him, in a passage that, in telling of the mix of earthly presence and mystic
imagination also draws on the Jesuit philosopher Pierre Teilhard de Chardin's
idea of an endpoint of the universe, the Omega Point, where everything comes
together (McGrath 2011, 195):

> We drove in silence behind a motorboat being towed by a black pickup. I
> thought of his remarks about matter and being, those long nights on the
> deck, half smashed, he and I, transcendence, paroxysm, the end of human
> consciousness. It seemed so much dead echo now. Point omega. A million years
> away. The omega point has narrowed, here and now, to the point of a knife as
> it enters a body. All the man's grand themes funneled down to local grief, one
> body, out there somewhere, or not. (DeLillo 2010, 98)

This chapter discusses the importance of technology to the new human in
DeLillo's work, followed by an analysis of the fascination with cults in his novels,
and their hopes for a new human. Finally, there is also the more curious, but
significant, presence of young persons who suggest the possibility of a break in
human cognitive capacity.

Biotechnology

DeLillo's funniest and most accessible novel, *White Noise*, is also his most
somber. The novel revolves around university professor Jack Gladney's life

as a husband, father and academic in a small and peaceful town. It is a fast-paced narrative, divided into mostly short chapters, with the exception of one forty-page-long chapter that tells of an evacuation after a toxic spill. This strange and surreal event comes to haunt Jack, and reinforces his thoughts of disease and death. The satire in the novel has many sources and targets, such as Gladney's role as the head of a centre for Hitler studies, and the comments of his annoyingly clever son, Heinrich. When asked whether he wants to visit his mother during the summer, Heinrich's answer is devoid of any faith in human subjectivity:

> Who knows what I want to do? Who know what anyone wants to do? How can you be sure about something like that? Isn't it all a question of brain chemistry, signals going back and forth, electrical energy in the cortex? How do you know whether something is really what you want to do or just some kind of nerve impulse in the brain? (DeLillo 1985, 45)

Heinrich is a pessimist, who sees no probability of progress for humanity. We live in a world that we barely understand, which he demonstrates by asking his father to explain how a radio works, receiving only vague and uninformed answers about radio waves, and sarcastically answering back: 'They travel through the air. What, like birds?' (DeLillo 1985, 148). The idea that we are people of the Stone Age equipped with airplanes and potato chips in plastic bags is also entertained, as a reminder that all the equipment around us does not make us that different from people of the past (DeLillo 1985, 147).

However, beneath the humorous portraits of modern family life and its immersion in modern consumerism, death is the lens through which everything is seen. In a dialogue with his colleague, a caricature of a postmodernist academic named Murray J. Siskind, the possible reconciliatory features of death are discussed, and Siskind excels in a comically upbeat form that dismisses the possibility of there being anything good to say about death (DeLillo 1985, 283). Death is also the pivotal theme in Jack's relationship with his wife, Babette. They confirm to one another that each wants to die first, because they cannot imagine life without each other. But Gladney admits to himself that he is lying. He does not want to die, even if it means being alone after the death of Babette. They also comfort each other with the notion that parents cannot die when they have small children, even though this thought is blatantly delusional, and they know it. Jack also has to acknowledge that his fascination with Hitler is a fascination with death, and of forces that somehow embraced death, rather than trying to push it away (DeLillo 1985, 287). But all these evasive strategies do not cure his anxiety about dying, which is only reinforced after the toxic spill, when the doctors only give vague but worrying indications regarding whether or not Gladney has been seriously harmed.

Besides the toxic spill in the middle of novel, the plot is driven by the discovery that Babette is more deeply concerned with death than Jack thought. At one point, Gladney wonders why Babette seems discreet and forgetful, and later, he discovers some mysterious pills called Dylar she is taking. He learns that she is part of an experiment with a drug intended to cure anxiety about dying and all thoughts of death. Gladney begins to spy on Babette, and discovers that an enigmatic scientist, Willie Mink, provides her with pills. An unfortunate side-effect of the pill is amnesia. Gladney seeks out Mink, and after a conversation on the nature of being and death, there is a gunfight that takes both men to the hospital (DeLillo 1985, 312). At the end of the novel Babette explains how far she was prepared to go to avoid thinking about death, as she recounts the possible risks:

> I could die. I could live but my brain would die. The left side of my brain could die but the right side could live. This would mean that the left side of my body would live but the right side would die. There were many grim specters. I could walk sideways but not forward. I could not distinguish words from things, so that if someone said 'speeding bullet,' I would fall to the floor and take cover. Mr Gray wanted me to know the risks. There were releases and other documents for me to sign. The firm had lawyers, priests. (DeLillo 1985, 193)

The pill, which, as far as is known, is not based on any existing product, is interesting for several reasons. It is significant that DeLillo does not introduce a wonder drug that solves all problems in a frictionless manner, or more radically, a drug that could prolong life indefinitely. The pill's manner of functioning is also in accordance with one of the other main themes of the book, namely, the blurring of the difference between signs and things, and that a symptom that is actually a sign for some other thing may be misunderstood as the thing itself. In this mode of thought, appearances and the perception of appearance are what matter, but DeLillo counters that with discourses that emphasize the inevitable confrontation with the material basis of the world.

Anthony Miccoli notes that the idea of being represented as information and not as one's body is central to the description of how Jack interacts with the medical system, after he may have been contaminated (Miccoli 2010, 106). The alienating experience of being reduced to a set of data, the deeper meaning of which the doctor is reluctant to disclose, is comical, but in several scenes this is also portrayed as deeply disturbing to Jack (DeLillo 1985, 277). In a broader perspective, the feeling of being not only one's body, but also the package of information stored in one's DNA, gives rise to a thought-provoking duality of modern existence: not between body and mind, but between flesh and code. Thus, representations of such underlying codes, in which DeLillo took an interest early on, become more significant to contemporary ideas of identity.[83]

David Cowart remarks that Jack and Babette never seek comfort in religion, as a consequence of the erosion in the twentieth century of the structures that used to provide a spiritual foundation for existence (Cowart 2003, 78). The hope that others may believe is addressed when Jack meets a nun at the hospital. But she bluntly reveals that she gives off the impression of believing to help others, giving up her life to help others deal with their non-belief (DeLillo 1985, 318f.).

The very end of the novel is set in the comforting scenery of a supermarket, of which DeLillo writes with implicit references to James Joyce's short story, 'The Dead'. Instead of the whiteness of the snow that covers all Ireland, reminding one of the small difference between the living and the dead (Joyce 1996, 224), DeLillo places Jack and his family among all the colourful goods, where almost everything one longs for is available:

> Everything we need that is not food or love is here in the tabloid racks. The tales of the supernatural and the extraterrestrial. The miracle vitamins, the cures for cancer, the remedies for obesity. The cults of the famous and the dead. (DeLillo 1985, 326)

No one has been transformed in the novel, but the threats to the integrity of the individual have been effectively displayed on many fronts, from the biological manipulation of the mind, to the dangers of the environment, and the mental changes propelled by our use of media. Yet, the dreams conveyed in the last sentences only serve to remind one of the pervasive desires for human change and the avoidance of death that are so central to the novel. The possible sources of such change are plentiful, but have little credibility.

Cyberspace and abstract systems

Media have been important in DeLillo's novels since early on, and the intro-duction of the internet to the public in the 1990s has left significant traces on the novels of an author who has made point of stating that he uses a typewriter, and uses a whole page for each paragraph, no matter how short it is, in order to get a feel for its rhythm (Begley 1995). In *Underworld*, the internet thematizes different kinds of presence and longing for presence, and it is a medium through which the exploration of the relationship between signs and things may be taken further. The novel ends with a description of an online search, where a whole page is used to build up to the word that is most longed for globally. It turns out to be 'Peace', which is the last word of the novel (DeLillo 1997, 827). A page before, the question is asked:

> Is cyberspace a thing within the world or is it the other way around? Which contains the other, and how can you tell for sure? (DeLillo 1997, 826)

The ideas here are characteristic of DeLillo's interest in signs, and at the same time express a rhetorical strategy of presenting such impossible and initially easily rejected questions with an almost mythical authority. The paragraph also expresses a fantasy of a totality of signs that could replace the world, not unlike that Jorge Luis Borges[84] depicts in stories such as 'Tlön, Uqbar, Orbis Tertius'. It would also be wrong to see one possibility or the other as univocally positive, whether the primacy of signs or things. Rather, both DeLillo and Borges provide descriptions of situations where each domain promises something that will be undermined by the other, but where the tension between them makes them significant: the signs and the things, the absent and the present, the endless and the finite. All these opposites influence human existence in ways that make existence complex, but also foster a longing for a resolution of these contrasts toward a settled state of being.

In DeLillo's subsequent, shorter novels, the internet is alluded to in relation to communication, to isolation, and to the idea of things themselves. In *The Body Artist*, the signature scenario is an isolated house on the American East Coast, where the artist, Lauren Hartke, is fascinated by a webcam showing an even more deserted road in Finland (DeLillo 2001, 38). In *Cosmopolis*, the central difference in the novel's universe lies between the tangible world represented by the protagonist Eric Packer's drive across Manhattan on a day of traffic jams, and the various kinds of information systems that keep him up to date on the exchange rates' abstract reflection of certain condition in the world, as well as the closed world of the exchange rates themselves. The other protagonist, Benno Levin, lives detached from technology, and ends up murdering Packer in what seems like an allegory of two ways of relating to the world: either as part of a networked society, where appearances are only a small part of what one has to consider, or a more simple life, oriented toward the immediately tangible (DeLillo 2003, 65). For his part, Packer is not only interested in streams of money, but also in poetry, abstract art and music, whereby he represents a recurrent triangle in DeLillo's work: the things themselves, the networks within which one orients oneself, and art, which are parts of the world, while not really taking part in the world. The defining trait of all three spheres is that none is able to establish communication among people to lift them out of their isolation, and instead, networks and art confirm the fundamental loneliness of people.

Merlin Donald has emphasized the development of mathematics as one of the most significant cultural events in human history, particularly as a clear marker of the dramatic evolution of cognitive properties resulting from exchanges between individuals and the cultures by which they are influenced (Donald 2002, 307). Don DeLillo's ambitious 1976 novel, *Ratner's Star*, is structured around the development of mathematics as a layer that supplements its more traditional plot. *Ratner's Star* is set in the future, and follows the young genius, Billy, who, at the age of 14, receives the first Nobel Prize in mathematics, which is presented to him in the USA, as Sweden is at war (DeLillo 1976, 4). Billy works on a project in which a group of scientists is trying to communicate with aliens, and his role in the project is to decode the messages they receive. Seen in light of DeLillo's later fascination with the internet, cyberspace, and the Omega Point, it is significant that in this novel, he includes a supercomputer – Space Brain – which is mapping the universe. Of his intentions with this novel, DeLillo has said:

> I was trying to produce a book that would be naked structure. The structure would be the book and vice versa. I wanted the book to become what it was about. Abstract structures and connective patterns. A piece of mathematics, in short. To do this I felt I had to reduce the importance of people. The people had to play a role subservient to pattern, form, and so on. This is difficult, of course, for all concerned, but I believed I was doing something new and was willing to take the risk. A book that is really all outline. My notes for the book interest me almost as much as the book does. This is an incriminating remark, but there you are. (DePietro 2005, 11)

The interest in mathematics should also be seen as an attempt to make the evolution of human intellectual capacity concrete, just as its inclusion in *The Names* does. One of the central paradoxes is that with mathematics, humans are able to transcend naturally given sensations, and imagine phenomena that cannot exist or be represented in the real world, such as multidimensional spaces. But the brain that is able to do all that is still a physical object, and parts of it have long evolutionary roots, including remnants of the primal brain that is on guard against external threats, and resists death (LeClair 1987, 140). *Ratner's Star* plays, often with great humor, with the distance between abstract thought and the world of the flesh, to which the same brain must relate. While DeLillo is obviously fascinated with the idea of a transformation into a new way of being that could be furthered by technology, he is equally critical of what that world might be like.

Weak protagonists and young geniuses

Ratner's Star recursively addresses how new knowledge will stratify society. At the very outset, it is made clear that only three or four persons in the world understand what Billy does, a motif that is repeated in *The Names*, when James Axton asks about the studies of his friend's son, Maitland, but is told that it is useless to ask. This gap between generations, embodied by the child genius as a marker of the ongoing evolution of human intelligence, also reveals a breakdown in communication between generations. Both *The Names* and *White Noise* include younger, highly articulate characters who seem to have deeper insights into the world than do their parents' generations; in *White Noise*, this is communicated with much sarcasm by the son, Heinrich. The novels also include very young children who have a rather undefinable spiritual approach to the world, which cannot be rendered in normal discourse. In *White Noise*, the three-year-old son, Wilder, is abnormally mute, and at the end of the novel, he drives his little tricycle out onto the expressway, in what seems to Jack Gladney an almost angelic incident (DeLillo 1985, 322). The last chapter of *The Names* is presented as an excerpt from the novel that Axton's nine-year-old son, Tap, has been writing. The story is set in a church, in the Mid-West most likely, from which a young boy runs out onto the prairie, because he cannot or will not speak in tongues, at which the rest of the congregation excels (DeLillo 1982, 339).

   In all DeLillo's novels, the generation gap makes more than a slight difference, but illustrates a radically different approach to the world that cannot be comprehended from the perspective of the older generation of main characters. The differences are related both to knowledge – with mathematics being almost a fetish in DeLillo's work, which carries with it all the other qualities of a purely cultural invention – and to the promise of a world view that generally sees more deeply than is normally possible. There is no definite idea of what these young men will evolve into, nor is any animosity expressed toward them, except when they fail to empathize with the older generation. From the perspective of the new human, it is significant that mathematics provides a sharp threshold of either 'getting it' or 'not getting it', which is different from just being a bit smarter and a bit more adept. Thus, the older generation has difficulty communicating with the emerging world, which is symbolized by the younger generation.

Ratner's Star demonstrates a particular ambivalence about the role of cultural memory. On the one hand, the novel's universe is a society where the attachment to national memories, habits and so on is being overshadowed by a more future-oriented and functional way of living, highlighted through Billy's point of view, and the plans to communicate with aliens. On the other hand, the novel is deeply historical in its respect for the progress that has been made in mathematics, and in its observation of how old habits and patterns still influence humans, and may even deliver keys to an understanding of communication with other planets. The sexagesimal system and its Mesopotamian roots is an example that inspires the search for other ways of decoding messages, in a chapter where the contemporary layman's understanding of numbers, the numerical systems of the Sumerians, and the riddle Billy is facing are brought together (DeLillo 1976, 239).

In *The Names*, mathematics is also used to demonstrate how human evolution proceeds in leaps, and detaches humans from the world. With a bizarre enthusiasm, a minor character, Charles Maitland, speaks of his son's studies in mathematics, after James has complained that the son himself does not want to talk about it. Maitland comforts him by saying this branch of mathematics is understood by hardly anybody, and that there are topics that his son cannot even discuss with his professors. Once again, James is presented as someone displaced, and Maitland situates this in a larger cultural framework:

> 'It doesn't bear on human experience, human progress, ordinary human language,' Charles said. ... 'It's interesting in itself, you see. It refers to itself and only to itself. It's the pure exercise of the mind. It's Rosicrucianism, druids in hoods. The formal balances, that's what counts. The patterns, the structures. It's the inner consistencies we have to search for. The symmetries, the harmonies, the mysteries, the whisperies. Good Christ, Axton, you can't expect the man to talk about these things'. (DeLillo 1982, 164)

DeLillo is by no means downplaying the satirical element in the scene through the enthusiasm with which a father defends his son's inability to communicate about how he is spending his time. But at the same time, this quotation is significant for its disclosure of DeLillo's fascination with something that is not connected to the world or dependent on the world, but has its own existence. Religious desire is also woven into the appraisal of mathematics, as are connections to esoteric mysticism, both unusual contexts for the otherwise rationally driven science of mathematics.

The rejection of human experience, progress and language contrast with Axton's experience at the Acropolis, at the end of the novel, where the collective development of languages is emphasized in an appraisal of their enchanting effect on a place Axton had thought of as solitary and utterly silent. This reveals how individual, collective and the search for higher meaning make themselves manifest. In the last chapter, the satirical mention of speaking in tongues by charismatic Christians is a clever staging of how an individual sense of a unique insight may be accepted by a collective, even if the content of the message cannot be communicated (DeLillo 1982, 338). On the other hand, the young Maitland does not seek a community that understands him, but excels at distancing himself from ordinary ways of thinking, in a way resembling Nietzsche's lonely overman on the mountaintop, liberated from the haphazard evolution of the rest of humanity. This position is effectively undermined by his remark that his stay at Berkeley makes it possible to study two of the contemporary world's wonders: pure mathematics and the state of California (DeLillo 1982, 163).

No identity but in things

The coupling of thought patterns and places is a recurrent theme in *The Names*. Axton meets a terrorist who vividly describes how the desert influences his mind (DeLillo 1982, 294). The cityscape of Athens plays a major role as a catalyst for Jack's emotions, as do the archaeological excavations, where the confrontation with artifacts of the past also marks a connection between abstract and often sublime thoughts, and the tangible objects. *The Names* is populated by individuals who constantly analyze themselves, a trait that recurs throughout DeLillo's work (DeLillo 1982, 167). Not only are his protagonists very self-reflective, they also speak very straightforwardly, in an almost Socratic manner, of the ontology of the world, as well as what research relates about the function of the brain (DeLillo 1982, 98). In *The Names*, this analytical concern emerges early, in the form of 27 'depravities' that Axton and his Canadian ex-wife have identified as characteristics describing him, with the twenty-seventh being an emphatic and ironic 'American' (DeLillo 1982, 27). In DeLillo's novels, the question of human identity contributes a fascinating dual perspective on the individual human, by letting the characters have an almost overly detached interest in their own subjectivity, as though it did not concern them directly, while at other times being very strongly and emotionally engaged with what they are doing with their lives. By pursuing this conflicting grasp of identity, DeLillo captures a particular mood in a postheroic age, where the ends of existence may be redefined, and where necessity and the narrow paths that have defined the conditions of most people throughout history have been supplanted by the feeling of a lack of necessity. In *The Names*, this condition is part of the reason for the setting, as Axton has the opportunity to be close to his ex-wife and their son in Greece. Here, Kathryn has found a way to create an unnecessary necessity as an excavator in a more than dubious archaeological project, but which fulfills her ambition of being in contact with a past time that eventually gives her comfort:

> She was digging to find things, to learn. Objects themselves. Tools, weapons, coins. Maybe objects are consoling. Old ones in particular, earth-textured, made by other-minded men. Objects are what we aren't, what we can't extend ourselves to be. Do people make things to define the boundaries of the self. Objects are the limits we desperately need. They show us who where we end. They dispel our sadness, temporarily. (DeLillo 1982, 133)

The problematic relation of the individual to its own individuality is a persistent theme of the novel, and Axton is particularly concerned by the lack of commitment to what he does, whereas some of the people with whom Kathryn surrounds herself, filmmakers and archaeologists, exude the determination to invest their lives in these identities, with a strength and focus that James does not possess. In essence, this lack of faith is also what scares him about the Acropolis at the beginning of the novel, but which takes a turn in the end, when he discovers it to be a place where languages are being spoken in what seems like a celebration of language itself.

National identities are used as a significant and amusing way of decoding stereotypes that eventually also reveal their limitations. The Swedes are lively, but suffer in the sun, while the English walk around in their unnecessary coats (DeLillo 1982, 231). Of the Americans, one of the minor characters, David Keller, says, 'Eerie people. Genetically engineered to play squash and work weekends' (DeLillo 1982, 67). Thus, James constantly sees patterns in the world that could help capture its essence, while he is unable to believe in it. In conversation, he is often intimidated by strong convictions about underlying, naturally given causes for the order of things, from people, to behavior in general, to postulates of deep-rooted instincts that may explain the fascination with murder. Only when James gets drunk does he take on this role as an aggressive and confident male, and makes a fool of himself, by insisting to a woman that she should say certain words in certain ways, because they were meant to be said so: 'Say legs. Seriously, I want you to. *Stockings*. Whisper it. The word is meant to be whispered'. (DeLillo 1982, 228).

The desire for mystical connections is an inherent element of many kinds of thought systems, including religions. The mystical or mysterious are also elements of conservative philosophies of life that emphasize the individual's inability to see through his or her present condition, and combine this with a desire to connect to something overarching that may be articulated through myths. This is different from being politically conservative, which DeLillo is not, but it entails a fundamental skepticism about being able to predict why certain things fascinate and influence life, here and now. DeLillo takes this skepticism to the heart of the themes in his books, whether they are the causes of terrorism, modern humans' inability to explain the world in which they live, or their desire to connect with objects from the past, a persistent theme in his works, most radically explored in *The Names*.

DeLillo's interest in symbolic systems and codes permeates a number of his works, and provides another source of strangeness. The highly ambitious *Ratner's Star* has the evolution of mathematics as its structuring principle, although it may be debated whether this is obvious in every aspect of the novel, *The Names* focuses on the history of writing systems, whereas *White Noise* is influenced by (and parodies) postmodernist theories of the simulacrum. Conversely, DeLillo also presents a number of characters who make the case for the non-symbolic, for the thing itself, as in *Point Omega*. This schism between identifying communicative systems and underlying meanings, as opposed to materiality itself, is not only a long running and still potent way of discussing different approaches to the world, but also concerns the way human identity is being altered because of the discovery, and more importantly, the sequencing of the human genome. If secularization has gradually put ideas of essentialist selfhood and dualisms in the shade – although in many respects these thrive as parts of everyday metaphysics – then the idea that humans are what they are as physical systems that can sustain life for a limited period of time, while the DNA represents a supplement to this identity, is a way of reintroducing a new essentialism, even if the whole process of building identity is much more culturally founded.

DeLillo does not have a grand vision of a trans- and posthuman reality, but nevertheless, in his work, future change is a defining element that circles around different ways in which humanity could be changed, triggered by different desires that are expressed in both the explicit reflections and the actions of the characters. Thus, it is possible to discern various types of desires in his novels. One relates to becoming one with nature or the universe, and ceasing to be a human, which is presented as an attractive possibility through hints at a broader cosmological understanding, where ideas of the non-trivial nature of the material world are accentuated, while human consciousness is described as exhausted (DeLillo 2010, 52f.). Another desire goes directly in the opposite direction, focusing on the ability of information to dominate and create its own world. This thought, which owes a great deal to Thomas Pynchon, is explored early on in *Ratner's Star*, and later, the idea of the increasing importance of information is taken up in various ways, and builds on the argument that information seems to lead its own life, detached from the control of human subjects, whose own capacity for self-inspection and control are undermined throughout the novels. The leap from the present time to the fantasy of a new order in which the world of information dominates may be posited as a not-impossible concept that, outside of literary fiction, resonates with the ideas of singularity, cyberspace and the Omega Point. Finally, in *White Noise*, DeLillo depicts how medicine could potentially be used to alter the human psyche, with the idea of a pill that would eliminate anxiety about death, effectively creating a new life condition that would be similar to that of Huxley's *Brave New World*. But DeLillo abandons the pill as an experiment with latent consequences, and focuses more on the consequences of technology on bodies and minds.

The fascination with codes, representations, and systems in DeLillo's work resonates with the way genetics has reinstated a new kind of dualism into the thinking about individuality, as discussed in Chapter Two. The individuality of the individual is not only defined by the mind and the physical body, which evolve over time, but also by the DNA, which is the most stable representation of individuality, but not of personality. In his later works, the erosion of personality is apparent, and one criticism of DeLillo's work has been that he is unable to create memorable characters (Tanner 2000, 214). Instead, descriptions of strategies of artistic representation predominate. These descriptions lead to abstraction, where art plays a central role, whether it is the performance artist of *Falling Man*, who re-enacts a person falling from the World Trade Centre, a 24-hour version of Hitchcock's *Psycho* in *Point Omega*, a webcam transmitting images from an empty road in Finland, in *The Body Artist*, or the numerous musings on currencies, stock values and much more, in *Cosmopolis*. Thus, DeLillo seeks the strange kind of enchantment that systems bring about, the ways in which processes seem to organize themselves, whether they involve waste, terrorism, or the entire universe. All kinds of fascination with systems exclude the individual, but in DeLillo's novels these formations and patterns seem to be worth admiring in a post-metaphysical world. Humor was once a very significant part of his writing, which provided a redeeming perspective on the pessimism inherent in the world of systems, but this aspect seems to be more and more compromised, as technology advances. Still, human experience remains at the centre of DeLillo's work, as he explains in an interview, commenting on what the novel can do:

'It is the form that allows a writer the greatest opportunity to explore human experience,' he says. 'For that reason, reading a novel is potentially a significant act. Because there are so many varieties of human experience, so many kinds of interaction between humans, and so many ways of creating patterns in the novel that can't be created in a short story, a play, a poem or a movie. The novel, simply, offers more opportunities for a reader to understand the world better, including the world of artistic creation. That sounds pretty grand, but I think it's true'. (DeLillo 2010)

13

Michel Houellebecq

Michel Houellebecq is a contemporary writer whose work is not considered science fiction, who has written very directly of the possible consequences of biotechnology to humankind. He is a controversial author in more ways than one, both with regard to his views as they are presented in his works and in public debate, and with regard to the question of whether he is a truly great writer, or lives off the controversy surrounding his works. What cannot be questioned is that he has a broad, international presence, and is one of the few contemporary French writers who is read throughout the world. With the award of the Goncourt Prize in 2010 for *The Map and the Territory*, his authorship also seems bound to have more staying power than was foreshadowed by the media sensationalism surrounding his first works.

Like Louis-Ferdinand Céline, Houellebecq has background in a practical academic education, in the case of Houellebecq, computer engineering, a field in which he also worked, before turning to writing full-time. This background has also added to his reputation as a literary outsider, just as his raw tone and broad sarcasm have underlined his kinship with Céline. He does not shy away from making judgments, often negative, about other writers in his novels, but also displays great reverence for the work of Aldous Huxley, whose literary stock is otherwise not the highest, despite the status of *Brave New World*.

In two of Houellebecq's more significant novels, *The Elementary Particles*[85] and *The Possibility of an Island*, a defining aspect of the plots is that they are partly, although not exclusively, narrated from a point in the future, when human living conditions have been radically changed. The epilogue to *The Elementary Particles* depicts a situation where UNESCO has propelled a genetic change in humankind, creating a gentler and more docile species, while the original human species has given up, and is slowing dying out. Given the novel's harsh criticism of our contemporary society, Houellebecq has his tongue firmly in his cheek when he has future humans declare the book a tribute to the human race.

This ambivalence also extends throughout the structure of *The Possibility of an Island*, where the chapters alternate between narration from the contemporary point of view of the comedian, Daniel, in the twentieth century, and the story of three of his clones, more than 20 generations later, each trying to come to terms with being put into the world to carry on the life of the original Daniel. The novel mercilessly criticizes life and society in the twentieth century, above all, the false and twisted relations among people, while also revealing how tedious and sad life could be in a future world with no purpose and no struggle. The novel ends with Daniel26 leaving his high-tech cell to join a tribe of uncloned humans who live in primitive conditions in the wilderness.

In the pages, Houellebecq's novels will be analyzed with an emphasis on the intricate dynamic between present and future, and between pessimism and hope, followed by an examination of how infinity and boredom are connected, and lastly, how evolution and imperfect beauty emerge as having value in the otherwise bleak universe of his novels. The chapter closes with an analysis of the idea of the new human in the work of Georges Perec, to put DeLillo's and Houellebecq's strategies into perspective.

A two-fold criticism of the present and the future

In Houellebecq's novels, the fundamental attitude toward life and culture is pessimistic and dissatisfied, and in his first three novels in particular, his protagonists are misanthropic figures who constantly vent their contempt for society and the brutality it engenders among people. Nevertheless, it is significant that these first novels, and to some extent, *The Possibility of an Island*, share a basic narrative structure that offers some sense of hope. The protagonist, named Michel in all three of his earliest novels, starts out disillusioned with his own life and with culture in general, not least with the idolization of youth and the pressure work exerts on people, forcing them to be inauthentic in their relations with others. But despite his great skepticism that this could happen, he falls in love with a woman who, like him, is imperfect and is facing middle age. This marks the beginning of a period during which Michel experiences a contemplative, rather than ecstatic, state, in which the experience of distance and alienation from others disappears. Thus, in the misanthropic coldness of his novelistic universe there are traces of a warmer and more romantic voice. However, in none of the novels do these happier times determine the conclusion, and in both *The Elementary Particles* and *Platform* the woman dies, respectively by suicide after having been paralyzed and confined to a wheelchair, and as a victim of a bomb attack on Bali. After this, Michel can return to despising the world, now even more than previously, having lost something that he had never thought possible to attain in the first place.

This specific and significant structure, which, in *The Possibility of an Island*, is emphasized by the clones' vague and helpless attempts to get in touch with one another through internet-like media, explores how the transformation of humanity into a posthuman condition is a loss, despite all humanity's flaws. This structure also nuances the commonly held view of Houellebecq as a cynic and narrow-minded critic of almost everything. Houellebecq's pessimism is positioned between two grand negatives, death and endless repetition in a world that is not worth inhabiting, followed by a fragment of life in which intimacy with another person generates so much meaning that something actually matters.

In *The Elementary Particles*, the narrator's relationship with the 40-year-old Christiane begins at a new age resort, New Borders, where Bruno experiences a connection quite different from those he is used to. Christiane is far from timid, not only with regard to the practice of sex, but also in conversation about it. She even talks about her own body's gradual deterioration in a way that is honest, almost clinical and which changes Bruno's views on sexuality and love:

> Just now, I could tell you didn't really like my pussy – it already looks a bit like an old woman's cunt. Increased collagen bonding and the breakdown of elastin during mitosis in older people means that human tissue gradually loses its suppleness and firmness. (Houellebecq 2001, 118)

Christiane goes on to talk of how her vulva was beautiful when she was a young woman, leaving Bruno speechless, but they tenderly fall asleep together. However, happiness is never a stable condition with Houellebecq, and over the course of a few pages in the second part of the novel, Christiane is paralyzed below the waist and unable to accept her new life as an invalid, and apparently commits suicide by letting her wheelchair roll down a flight of stairs (Houellebecq 2001, 239). This short passage of the novel also contains a reflection on how suicide is often an escape from a life in which the sum of physical joys is less than the sum of pain, and the narrator remarks that two intellectuals, Gilles Deleuze and Guy Debord, both took their own lives because they could not bear their physical decay.

Bruno's reaction to Christiane's paralysis and death is subdued and ambiguous. He shows tenderness by asking her to live with him in Paris, but his own doubts about whether he really wants this are also clearly stated (Houellebecq 2001, 238). In the same vein, he does not cry at the sight of her in her open coffin, but nevertheless he admits himself to a psychiatric hospital afterward (Houellebecq 2001, 241). After this, he returns to a world of sex without emotions, which prostitutes and lithium help provide.

The hope for a different life has a significant place in Houellebecq's novels, not just in the form of romantic love, but also through the creation of a different place outside of society. Cult movements and resorts play important roles in his fiction, as ways of trying out alternative lifestyles. The fascination with cults is far from positive, as Houellebecq also launches a harsh criticism of the nostalgia for the 1960s and 1970s, and showcases the bizarre ideas that could lead to new insights into reality. In *The Elementary Particles*, the new age resort, New Borders, is mocked through descriptions of less-than-convincing activities, such as 'Dance your job', and classes in painting with watercolours that might just as easily take place at a retirement home (Houellebecq 2001, 141). In *Platform*, the key difference is that the Michel of that novel is not just a passive and disgruntled guest at a resort (as is Bruno in *The Elementary Particles*), but opens a number of holiday resorts based on a swinger club model. Finally, the idea of leaving the world is foregrounded through the title of *The Possibility of an Island*, which one might assume references Aldous Huxley's novel, *Island*. In this novel, the idea of a segregated and controlled society is essential to the cult, the Elohimites, that organizes the cloning programme that is supposed to give Daniel and other members of the cult a sort of immortality (Houellebecq 2005, 91).

Houellebecq's use of Huxley's work reveals an elective affinity with an author who took up controversial issues in a survey of future scenarios, and who, rather than being canonized for his literary gifts, is acknowledged for presenting an array of provoking ideas. Yet, Bruno's monologue on Huxley is not without a disarming irony:

> He paused, dipped a shrimp into the chili sauce and then put down his chopsticks. 'Like his brother, Aldous was an optimist...' he said with something like disgust. 'The metaphysical mutation that gave rise to materialism and modern science in turn spawned two great trends: rationalism and individualism. Huxley's mistake was in having poorly evaluated the balance of power between these two. Specifically, he underestimated the growth of individualism brought about by an increased consciousness of death. Individualism gives rise

to freedom, the sense of self, the need to distinguish oneself and to be superior to other'. (Houellebecq 2001, 133)

Bruno continues to speak of the 'metaphysical mutation' as a source of unhappiness, because the desire it awakens can never be satisfied. In Bruno's account, the solution of all utopian thinkers, from Plato to Huxley, has been to reorganize society in a way that extinguishes desire and compensates for any suffering. This stands in stark contrast to the eroticized commercial society they live in, which increases the human desires, and devours their lives (Houellebecq 2001, 132f.). In this way, Bruno rejects two changes as insufficient. Both the 'metaphysical mutation' corresponding to the fascination with a change in consciousness that is the theme of the second part of this book, and the reorganization of society, which is the means for both the theories of the utopians and the societies that have been changed as described in the third part, are insufficient. But there is the hope that biology can deliver what it takes to make a utopian society come true. In the chapter that follows, Bruno's concerns regarding religion are put forward, while Michel is going about separating sex from reproduction, and by extension, his fascination with death and power, which leads him to the conclusion that a world that consisted of women only would be a slower developing, but happier place (Houellebecq 2001, 137).

While a number of authors are criticized in Houellebecq's novels, in an attempt to push them from the pedestals on which literary history has placed them, a revaluation of the work of Aldous Huxley is a significant element. In *The Elementary Particles*, chapter 10 is entitled 'Julian and Aldous' and is dedicated to a portrait and appraisal of the allegedly underestimated importance of Aldous Huxley in the twentieth century. By including Huxley's brother, Julian, who is correctly described in the novel as the first director of UNESCO and a member of a British society for eugenics, a mirror image of the relationship between the two brothers, Michel and Bruno, is created. The miserable but visionary Bruno lays out his vision for a project, which is carried out by UNESCO, as described in epilogue.

Bruno's interpretation of Huxley's work is that in many ways he was right, and that societies have been changed according to his ideas, with the exception of the division into castes (Houellebecq 2001, 153). But Huxley was right about science and technology leading the development, and that following breakthroughs in physics at the beginning of the twentieth century, biology would be the next significant field. Aldous Huxley also made this case in *Brave New World Revisited*, of 1963, where he compared his own visions favourably to those George Orwell presented in *Nineteen Eighty-Four* (Huxley 2005, 238).

In *The Possibility of an Island*, one of the central accusations is directed at the fixation on youth that predominates in society. Daniel24 reads a radical comparison, likening the treatment or perception of older people to a perpetual genocide, and comparing old people's homes to concentration camps, after the heat-wave of 2003 that led to the death of many, owing to dehydration. But the 'problem' is solved in subsequent decades, when active, voluntary euthanasia becomes more and more widespread (Houellebecq 2005, 61f.). When viewed in relation to the means of and hopes for biotechnology, the contrast between youth and old age clearly marks conflicting values that demand correction, according to the view of life as a process in which development is necessary, in order to avoid endless repetition. But such narratives cannot find real purchase, and are always in danger of being trumped by the simple oppositions between life and death, and youth and old age, which provide an argument for the use of narratives that reveal the hollowness of an abstract life in eternity.

While the world of the future plays an important role in *The Possibility of an Island*, as a result of the many cuts back and forth in time, the future of *Elementary Particles* is concentrated in the epilogue, which outlines a future in which a posthuman condition has become a reality.[86] In this case, it is revealed that Michel was central to the attempts to genetically engineer humans, and that this project was supported by world society, as mentioned by UNESCO. This contrasts with the secluded and selfish culture that is behind the cloning in *The Possibility of an Island*, although their results came more quickly than expected, because scientists all over the world had begun experimenting with genetic engineering (Houellebecq 2001, 262). Houellebecq provides a quasi-technical description of the biological engineering, which gives the exact date of the creation of the first new human as 27 March 2029, the twentieth anniversary of Michel's disappearance, an event that supersedes by far the interest in the first moon landing in 1969. The rhetoric surrounding this new human, as formulated by the driving force of the project, Hubczejak, is highly charged, providing ample opportunities for ironic readings:

> The creation of the first being, the first member of the new intelligent species made by man 'in his own image,' … humanity should be honored to be 'the first species in the universe to develop the conditions for its own replacement'. (Houellebecq 2001, 263)

The religious metaphor of creating in 'in his own image' is clearly intended, but at the same time, the idea of replacing and exceeding is radically different from creating in one's own image. These juxtaposed thoughts establish contrasting desires, which are, on the one hand, about confirming and reinforcing identity, and on the other hand, about progress and self-critique. A theological parallel to this situation is the biblical god creating humans in his image, but as imperfect beings. But when humans take on a promethean role, they do not seek an imperfect, but an improved image of themselves. So, without any other comparison, the posthuman being is more akin to the perfect god of whom humans see themselves as offspring. Such descriptions extend an invitation to consider the complex relationship between creator and perfection, suggesting that humans cannot free themselves from being weak and erring, which, to a large degree, is part of their identity. This is underscored further on the following page of the novel, where the narrator, clearly a new human, writes:

> We have even been known to refer to ourselves–with a certain humor–by the name they so long dreamed of: gods. (Houellebecq 2001, 263)

The end of the novel recounts the slow extinction of original humans, which happens without any conflict, even though the 'old humans' continue to exist 50 years after the creation of the new human. This resignation is anticipated a few chapters before, when, approaching the year 2000, humanity is described as tired and exhausted, which is the reason the new human is not met with greater resistance (Houellebecq 2001, 282).

Houellebecq's final point is that the new world must look like Paradise to the old humans, since egoistic behavior has been eliminated, and personal vanity does not mean much anymore. It is also clear, particularly when seen in light of *The Possibility of an Island*, that this condition is not fantastic, but rather dull and passionless. The affinities to *Brave New World* and its sterile and frictionless world are significant, along with the description of how an agency corresponding to a world government takes charge of the project of making the new human. The book ends with a tribute to humans that is both strong and puzzling:

> This species which, for the first time in history, was able to envision the possibility of its succession and, some years later, proved capable of bringing it about. As the last members of this race are extinguished, we think it just to render this last tribute to humanity, an homage which itself will one day disappear, buried beneath the sands of time. It is necessary that this tribute be made, if only once. This book is dedicated to mankind. (Houellebecq 2001, 264)

Self-identity above all

The defining trait of *The Possibility of an Island* is the boredom and repetition in the lives of the clones, whereby a recurrent criticism of utopias is foregrounded. A thoroughly controlled and protected life is not worth living, particularly if it supposed to be lived as a tribute to a person from the twentieth century. Technologically, cloning is possibly more within reach than the fantasies of radically changing the human genome, as is suggested in *Elementary Particles*.[87] From Houellebecq's perspective, with regard to narcissistic dreams of eternal life, cloning remains highly controversial, as well as strangely unsatisfying. In a short essay, 'Love Thy Clone', Houellebecq provokingly explains the reason he wants to be cloned as soon as possible:

> I don't like myself. I only feel a touch of sympathy, and even less respect, for myself; what's more, I don't interest myself much. As a teenager, then as a young man, I was full of myself; this is no longer the case. The mere prospect of having to recount a personal anecdote plunges me into boredom verging on catalepsy. When I absolutely have to, I just lie. / Paradoxically, however, I have never regretted reproducing. You could even say that I love my son and I love him more each time I recognise in him the trace of my own flaws. I see them displayed over time with an implacable determinism, and I rejoice. I rejoice immodestly at seeing there repeated, even made permanent, personal characteristics which have nothing particularly estimable about them; characteristics which are quite often worthy of contempt and have, in reality, the sole merit of being mine. Moreover, they are not even exactly my own; I fully realize some have been lifted straight from the personality of that vile cunt, my father. But, strangely enough, that takes nothing away from the joy I feel. This joy is more than selfishness; it is deeper, more indisputable. (Houellebecq 2003)

But in the end, self-identity trumps all other concerns, even if the value of this identity has no solid basis:

> On the other hand, what saddens me about my son is seeing him display (is it the influence of his mother? the different times we live in? pure individuality?) features of an autonomous personality, in which I cannot recognise myself and which remains utterly foreign to me. Far from marvelling at this, I realise that I will have left only an incomplete and faded image of myself. (Houellebecq 2003)

Houellebecq presents, rather calculatedly, an image of a narcissist, but he also cuts to the bone of what cloning could do for people, particularly emotionally, while questioning the narrative of unconditional love between parents and offspring, and the meaningfulness that is usually attached to knowing that one came from somewhere, and has a stake in younger lives and generations to come. No matter that the provocation is brought further than that in which Houellebecq actually believes, he pushes the hope for a conservation of a self-identity to its furthest extent, in a way that is difficult to distinguish from other kinds of hope for immortality, thereby turning the critique back onto Western civilization.

There is also a glaring difference between the world of the original Daniel and his successors when it comes to sex. The original Daniel has plenty, while at the same time criticizing how fundamental desires shape the world, whereas the later Daniels come off as docile and estranged from their physical desires (Houellebecq 2005, 245). In keeping with this, complete self-identification ceases to be possible, as the clones become more and more vaguely reminiscent of the original, just as the idea of paying tribute to a former life, instead of living one, results in Daniel26's eventual departure from the cloning programme. Identity as a palimpsest does not present itself as a viable model. The situation Houellebecq's clones face is a variation of what Kazuo Ishiguro portrayed in *Never Let Me Go*, where the clones are deprived of the option of figuring out their own way of living, but essentially are in this world because of a life already lived.

It is worth noting that boredom and imperfection are parts of the reflection on the advantages and limitations of a cloned existence. Here, abstract thoughts of immortality or eternity are deliberately countered by narratives that demonstrate that time is never abstract, but always needs to be filled by something that makes a difference. Life in nested boxes could also be seen as a commentary on modern existence, particularly life in those suburban dwellings to which Houellebecq paid much attention in his debut novel, *Whatever*,[88] as spaces where people live isolated lives and get along with various media as substitutes for actual human company. However, this is the perspective of an infinite existence in a space where nothing is supposed to happen except the upholding of the sense of a self. Again, this is in strong contrast to Aldous Huxley's descriptions of how the individual does not flirt with immortality or substitutes thereof, in a society that has gone in the opposite direction, and put a cap on human longevity, as in *Brave New World*, which chronicles a situation where the millennia-old concern of individual death has been done away with, and where death is not only accepted, but more and less programmed.

Houellebecq's portrait of contemporary society is one of struggle and a dehumanizing fight for a better life, which essentially cannot be achieved as long as the world is based on differences. His novels explore different ways of leaving these struggles behind, both personally, in the construction of cult societies, and in the creation of new humans. Ultimately, these attempts to find a place outside the normal human condition do not hold. However, coming to terms with evolution is not an option for Houellebecq's protagonists, even if the idea of evolution may be seen as enchanted. The final words of Charles Darwin's The Origin of Species reflects on the impression that there is an enchanted unity behind the diversity of nature:

> It is interesting to contemplate a tangled bank, clothed with many plants of many kinds, with birds singing on the bushes, with various insects flitting about, and with worms crawling through the damp earth, and to reflect that these elaborately constructed forms, so different from each other, and dependent upon each other in so complex a manner, have all been produced by laws acting around us. These laws, taken in the largest sense, being Growth with repro-duction; Inheritance which is almost implied by reproduction; Variability from the indirect and direct action of the conditions of life, and from use and disuse; a Ratio of Increase so high as to lead to a Struggle for Life, and as a consequence to Natural Selection, entailing Divergence of Character and the Extinction of less improved forms. (Darwin 1985: 459)

Darwin was well aware that this process was not optimal for every individual, and that there is a flip side to the coin of life. But nevertheless, Darwin insists on the grandeur of this perspective on a process that is capable of creating complex and beautiful organisms out of simple forms and simple laws:

> Thus, from the war of nature, from famine and death, the most exalted object which we are capable of conceiving, namely, the production of the higher animals, directly follows. There is grandeur in this view of life, with its several powers, having been originally breathed by the Creator into a few forms or into one; and that, whilst this planet has gone circling on according to the fixed law of gravity, from so simple a beginning endless forms most beautiful and most wonderful have been, and are being evolved. (Darwin 1985: 459f.)

This famous ending has been analyzed in detail by Richard Dawkins in *The Greatest Show on Earth*, and has been used by Franco Moretti in his literary studies (Dawkins 2009, Moretti 1996). All else being equal, this evolutionary aesthetics also presents a view of the beauty of the world that takes a long step away from the perspective of the individual, and sees nature as a unified system. It is exactly in this regard that the staging of actual situations for actual individuals is a central element of literature that will always fight a frictionless acceptance of this perspective. Houellebecq examines this conflict thoroughly, particularly in his shifts from general philosophical considerations to specific narratives of lived life. As described in a previous chapter, with regard to H. G. Wells' idea of a modern and perpetually evolving utopia, the utopia is always challenged by the ways in which the life of the individual differs from the ongoing structures of the collective. Eastern philosophies and religions have reconciled with the brute conditions of individual life to a much greater degree, and provide other images of circulation and rebirth to comfort the individual, while the individualism against which Houellebecq rages is firmly rooted in Western beliefs. There is essentially no reliable source of re-enchantment for Houellebecq, certainly not in the form of a new human, whether it is a clone or genetically modified offspring. But on the other hand, the anti-utopian stance is also a call for not thinking too hard about human potential, and accepting existing conditions.

Houellebecq's most recent novel, *The Map and the Territory*, is apocalyptic rather than posthuman in its perspective. A fascination with the industrial era is central to the work of the protagonist, the photographer Jed, and emphasizes the dehumanization of culture that is a consequence of technological development. The ending explicitly mentions the 'annihilation of the human species' (Houellebecq 2010, 269), and earlier in the novel, the practice of looking at maps is also connected with the ability to imagine the incomprehensible multitudes of lives being lived (Houellebecq 2010, 28). At other points in the novel there are speculations about how metals have shaped human history, and that the consequences of the era of polymers and plastics have not yet been comprehended. There is little optimism for this future, yet there is a sense of a decisive threshold, even if it is marked by the dominant forces of technology (Houellebecq 2010, 26). As in DeLillo's later work, there is a distinct fascination with art and human representations of non-human or dehumanized phenomena. The strange objects we create bear the impression of human intention, but ultimately, they also imply a world after humans, as does the reign of nature, after humans.[89]

Coda: Georges Perec

Georges Perec's magnum opus, *Life – A User's Manual*, was published four years before his death in 1982. For the better part of his life, Perec made his living at a neurophysiological laboratory, while as a writer he was a member of the scientifically oriented writer's group, OuLiPo (Ouvroir de littérature potentielle). Another very prominent member of OuLiPo, Italo Calvino, did not shy away from using and playing with the natural history of the world in his 'Cosmicomic' tales. Therefore, it is somewhat surprising how little biotechnology matters in Perec's works. Instead, the intersection of mathematics and language serves as a vehicle for various kinds of memory projects. Nevertheless, there are a number of indicators in the 99-chapter-long *Life – A User's Manual*, toward imagining new and improved humans. Chapter 58 portrays the life of the disabled widower, Oliver Gratiolet, and ends with a description of his two main projects. One is the creation of a novelistic hero who is a combination of a man of the world and a bit of a dandy, always perfectly well-dressed, charming and handsome. In contrast to this optimistic fiction of a perfect man, his other project is to prove that evolution is a failure, and that the human organism is a catalogue of weaknesses. The project is meticulously described over the length of a page, with a very detailed rebuttal of any idea of human perfection. After describing the problems caused by the spine, feet, muscles, hips and so on, the chapter concludes:

> Hands are frail, especially the little finger, which has no use, the stomach has no protection whatsoever, no more than the genitals do; the neck is rigid and limits rotation of the head, the teeth do not allow food to be grasped from the sides, the sense of smell is virtually nil, night vision is less than mediocre, hearing is very inadequate; man's hairless and unfurred body affords no protection against cold, and, in sum, of all the animals of creation, man, who is generally considered the ultimate fruit of evolution, is the most naked of all. (Perec 1992, 276)

This kind of thinking in Perec's work is aligned with his affection for projects and plans that may attain a certain purity and perfection, also with respect to humans, but he eventually reveals them as impossible and essentially idealistic models in an imperfect world.

The same sense of imperfection predominates the central narrative of *Life – A User's Manual*, which centres on the eccentric millionaire, Bartlebooth. He has set out to spend his life according to a simple plan: ten years will be spent learning to paint in watercolours, 20 will be spent making paintings of harbors, paintings that will be made into puzzles, on which he will spend another 20 years solving them. After this, the pieces will be glued together, and the paint will be removed, essentially leaving behind a life's effort with no traces. Around the story of Bartlebooth, numerous stories are told of the people who inhabit, or have inhabited a Parisian apartment building otherwise unrelated to the narrative, recounting their often ordinary, but still fascinating lives.

Bartlebooth's project is primarily a personal project designed to not leave behind any traces, and to pass the time. But there are also descriptions of projects that aim to change society. One of the more bizarre and potentially extreme is the description of the small cult, 'Shira name' or 'The Three Free Men'. As with all the chapters in this novel, this chapter begins with a description of a room in the building where the novel takes place, in this case, occupied by four members of a cult, who are engaged in some sort of meditation. The three novices must remain in an uncomfortable position, balancing on the edges of sharp metal cubes. If one of them fails to remain in the position for all six hours of the session, they will all be expelled. The plan of the cult is for each member to recruit three new members, and, with the logic familiar from multilevel marketing and chain letters, for the whole world to one day be taken over by the cult:

> Smautf has calculated that in 1978 there would be two thousand one hundred and eighty-seven new members of the sect of The Three Free Men, and, assuming none of the older disciples dies, a total of three thousand two hundred and seventy-seven keepers of the faith. Then things would go much faster: by 2017, the nineteenth generation would run to more than a thousand million people. In 2020, the entire planet, and well beyond, would have been converted. (Perec 1992, 13)

Perec's humor is notable in the presentation of the illogical excess – 'and well beyond' – in the less-than-convincing effects of the meditation. But despite the humor, there is also, in connection with Perec's general interest in the matter, a significant description of how global culture could be changed radically in a generation or two, whereby the creation of a new human would be accomplished. The cult functions as a generator of mystery. As in the work of Ian Fleming, Pynchon, DeLillo and Houellebecq, the cult that positions itself outside of society with the determined goal of establishing a new order, with little regard for the rest of society, fascinates with its will to exert power and realize pure visions, while at the same time being frightening, because of these same traits.

The humorous description of the cult members also reveals that in their case, the desire to take over the world is not driven by a particular vision with elaborate content, but primarily for its own sake, and for the possibility of exercising power. Thus, it stands in distinct contrast everything Bartlebooth does not wish his plan to amount to. The final chapter's tribute to the diversity of ordinary life may also be understood in relation to the idea of the cult and its unifying powers. Whereas all the way until the last chapter, each chapter of the book has taken its point of departure in a single room, and from there continued on to a story that was separate from most of the other stories, the final chapter presents simultaneous spaces, describing an abundance of things happening simultaneously in the building: dinners are being made, salesmen pass each other on the stairway, Bartlebooth sits with his puzzle, and, as though it were a mantra, 'It is the twenty-third of June nineteen seventy-five' is repeated six times, as the first sentence of each paragraph. At the end, it is stated that Bartlebooth has died over a puzzle that lacks an X-shaped piece, while holding a W-shaped piece in his hand (Perec 1992, 497).[90] The circumstance of his death, combined with the sudden and very noticeable simultaneity, and the many quotidian acts, gives the chapter a particular combination of serene loftiness and everyday normalcy. The death of Bartlebooth becomes a quiet and unspectacular death, and life will go on without him, but at the same time, it is the climax of a very long novel, where hundreds of pages about isolated rooms suddenly connect to the sublimity of experiencing an entire building bursting with life, which in turn is just a microcosm of the larger world. At the end of this very unconventional novel there is an elaborate index of all names in the novel, as well as a time table of events that puts major and minor characters into a different tale of strange and time-bound activities, each displaying its individual lack of perfection and deeper meaning, when put together, but also presenting a large and, maybe, beautiful canvas of human activity and desire.

Life – A User's Manual may be read as a monumental document about how individuals and collectives interact at different levels, as well as a work that discreetly argues about the future of mankind. There is a respect for and fascination with the minutiae and quotidian aspects of life, which also runs through the works of other authors analyzed in this study, particularly that of William Carlos Williams and Orhan Pamuk, whose interest in 'the innocence of objects' underscores this. The aesthetics of imperfection is connected to the idea of what it means to be human, and what produces value in human existence, just as DeLillo and Houellebecq each emphasizes human imperfection as a beautiful trait, in the face of a future in which promises of perfection loom.

Conclusion

This study of the new human and the posthuman in literature has two primary ambitions: one is to determine what literature can express about this topic in a way other kinds of discourse cannot substitute; the other is to establish how and to what degree this theme is important in literary history, and what literature, as an art form, has been able to accomplish because of the theme of the new human. I will conclude by summarizing the key points with regard to both these dimensions.

The lingering dilemma

The twentieth century was marked by some of the darkest hours in history, imposed by and on humanity through wars and tyranny, but a universal respect for human beings re-emerged, stronger and also embodied in international treaties. However, if history has any sense of irony, one expression of that might be that the technological possibility of evolving humans has come at a point in history when the principal values of humans and their rights is at their peak. The human condition was simpler, when all flaws, limited capacities and short lives were regarded an inevitable part of being human. Religious systems helped to keep meaninglessness at bay for millennia, but the secular existence of modern humans, given that they live in stable societies and do not have to struggle for existence, has proved to be surprisingly unproblematic at a metaphysical level. Now, the hope for change may take a number of forms, in what is not a pressing reality in the lives of individuals, but presents itself as a posthuman horizon, where the unity and the characteristics of humanity are at stake, for better or for worse. The key paradox and lingering dilemma is that the human represents both the highest and most absolute values, and is a being that is subject to improvement.

The options for improvement, and perhaps even perfection, are manifold at present, with new opportunities for creating incremental or significant change through new media environments, 'cyborgfication', and genetic engineering, which in turn place a heavier burden on ethics, increase the number of choices individuals and societies must make, and present them with greater risks, both individually and at a societal level. Many of the technologies that drive this are new, although, as has been argued throughout this book, the ideas of change and conditioning are not new, but previously expressed themselves through less powerful means.

One of the central insights on which the literature on the new human insists, and which permeates the visions of the posthuman in the literary works that have been analyzed in the preceding chapters, is that the human individual cannot be thought of as an independent entity, but is dependent on shared knowledge and capabilities, on existential values when communicating with other humans, and is part of the long narrative of evolution. These perspectives, so clearly articulated in Niklas Luhmann's theory, are neither mutually dependent nor universally present in the literature, but they add up to definitions of what it means to be human, through a certain family resemblance.[91] The media of literature and language particularly underscore a central aspect of human existence that both makes humans differ from other animals, and is central to producing a consciousness beyond what biology (at present) can explain. This makes literature particularly well-suited to countering reductions of the human condition to one particular aspect of its existence, regardless of whether it is the mind, body or social life.

Ideas of human perfection are addressed by literature in various significant ways. Insofar as literature variously demonstrates the absurdity of human existence apart from involvement with other people, and that the recognition of the other is central to generating meaning in existence, it follows that the idea of the lone superhuman never succeeds in a fictional setting. The 'perfect' human would instead be the human who is adapted to its time and its social environment. One of the most significant longings conveyed in the works analyzed is the hope of being able to connect with the collective, through some means of telepathic communication, or if not that, to experience a more profound connection to humans beyond those with whom we have close or intimate relationships. This is one area in which the medium of literature is unable to fulfill this longing, but, at least through its particular mode of enunciation, it comes closer any other medium to offering access to other minds.

Through its form, literature also includes inherent arguments for an aesthetics of imperfection that has revealed itself as prevailing and enduring throughout the twentieth century, and which leads to conclusions regarding what is valuable, in a manner that would be impossible to reach with classic logic. Literature and other arts provide representations of how the world may be seen as enchanted and beautiful, even against the backdrop of the looming meaninglessness, the tragic events of the world and the imperfections found all around. William Carlos Williams is one example of a prolific chronicler of this through his poetry, but the poetics of imperfection may be seen as a pervasive and positive element of the literature studied here and elsewhere.

There is another dimension of perfection that also comes up frequently, namely, immortality. The lure of immortality is just one, currently highly utopian, desire connected with posthuman fantasies. The desire for immortality is significant in the works of Virginia Woolf, Don DeLillo, Michel Houellebecq and many other representatives of what a human might aspire to. One example of this is José Saramago's *Death with Interruptions*, which explores the consequences of a sudden cessation of death among all people, a situation that eventually proves to be quite problematic (Saramago 2008). In no imminent scenario is this age-old longing a likely outcome of technological advances and inventions, but ideas of backups of the mind, anti-aging compounds and cloning as means of achieving some kind of immortality are recurrent topics in both fiction and real life projects. Again, literature provides investigations of scenarios that use narratives to show the effects of the endlessness of time and its potential boredom, or of the social isolation in an increasingly static society. And even if the prospects for indefinite life were more likely, ideas of what it might be like to live in such a world should be, and indeed are very forcefully questioned through fictional narratives. These are unsuccessful at conjuring up a desirable scenario where personal identity, the social environment and infinite time work together to produce a seamless, perfect state of being.

Maxwell Mehlman, among others, argues that dreams of immortality are quasi-religious elements of transhumanist visions that are not matched by technology, particularly the complexities of the fundamental workings of biology, which disclose new layers and uncontrollable elements, as science takes advantage of its knowledge (Mehlman 2012, 46).[92] A further interest in non-biological consciousness appears as a solution to some futurists, such as that Ray Kurzweil projects in *How to Create a Mind*, with scenarios that are ripe for further exploration by literature, but fundamentally also seem too distant from biological reality (Kurzweil 2012, 124). Despite all the trouble bodies create, it is hard to imagine a worthwhile life without them.[93]

Mortality, along with language, is an essential human characteristic that is difficult to imagine radically differently. It is easy to suggest that human life would be better without death, but it is far more difficult to imagine that kind of life and its conditions. Even if there were technical solutions to the death of consciousness and physical existence, the technological scenarios still fall short of the kind of immortality religions promise in vague terms (and which is also without the problems entailed by the possibility of a large meteor striking the Earth, or a new contraction of the Universe). Eternity is a very long time, and the idea of existence without temporality is even more absurd, as narratives demonstrate through their form. To repeat a point made earlier, literary discourse is distinguished from other discourses by putting subjects into a narrative where it is not a matter of whether this or that feature seems preferable in isolation – longer life, higher intelligence – but whether it is possible to tell actual stories of how it would be to live with this or that feature, in all its complexity.

This study has also tried to demonstrate how the literature of the twentieth and twenty-first centuries reveals a fascination with an enchanting dimension of evolution at several levels of human existence, be it body, mind, or culture. As the analyses of the works in the preceding three parts showed, there is great strength in the feeling of being connected to deep time in the history of human life and the existence of the universe, and to the collective development of habits, communicative systems and societies. The individual can never master or possess these, but only observe symptoms of them, while recognizing the larger whole behind it, as Virginia Woolf expressed clearly in her autobiographical writings (Woolf 2002, 84), or as Mo Yan and Orhan Pamuk each presents through intricate descriptions of the past that may still be felt as present.

When it comes to human change, the most significant difference between philosophy and literature is that philosophy may speak of improvements in a way that does account for how life would actually play out, were such changes to happen. Such discourse may be helpful when trying to cut to the root of ethical arguments, without succumbing to sentimental portrayals of how the world might feel under a given set of changed conditions. But when it comes to life, it is difficult to avoid the question of whether or not a life is worth living, in all its complexity of moments and sensations. This is where fiction presents a vision of what life feels like under certain conditions, and where ideas of improvements are challenged from a number of perspectives. In this study, the works analyzed from the perspective of change include significant strategies for responding to the idea of a new and better human. Ideas of perfection are part of their thinking, but are also abandoned. Instead, the most credible strategy of re-enchantment lies within the embrace of evolutionary dynamics, or in the imperfect but wondrous diversity and beauty that have been generated by nature and culture. However, this comes at the cost of rethinking individuality and collectivity, which ultimately cannot offer an unproblematic solution, apart from a stoic attitude toward the finite nature of life.

Evolution is or could be part of an enchanting narrative, which bears on an emotional aspect that literature thrives on. Arguably, evolution is also the most significant and appreciated grand narrative in Niklas Luhmann's otherwise not very emotionally laden theory (Luhmann 1997, 1138). Coupling evolution with enchantment requires an elaborate cultural memory, in order to give meaning to the process, which in turn may contribute to filling an existential need to bridge the gap between individual and collective.[94] John Richardson notes that even for Nietzsche's superman, memory and language were necessary for his freedom, in order to have something to select from (Richardson 2008, 95). However, a gap also remains, as there is no consolation for the individual in the evolutionary narrative (unless the quest for a posthuman immortality proves to be less of a mirage than that it seems at present). Evolutionary enchantment is also a non-utopian way of describing the world, which does not present an apocalyptic ending or a transformation to a final mode of being. All's well that transcends well, is the most that this narrative offers the individual.

Popular culture's current lack of interest in, or excitement about the future that awaits, four or five decades from now, apart from the serious issues of climatic change and reduction of natural resources, is very telling about the collective state of mind. After more than 100 years of Darwinian theory and general secularization, humanity must still come to terms with not being the end of history. Even more important is the lack of excitement about techno-logical advances, even if they do not alter the basics of the human condition. It was different just a generation ago, when ideas of the posthuman and the transhuman did not mean anything, but space travel did.[95]

The debates about how humanity will and should evolve will probably increase, as technology creates more new opportunities and more actions that could be taken, and there will be a number of issues on which most would agree that it would be immoral to not use technology, even if, for example, it alters the genetic code slightly, or involves further advances in man-machine interaction. Scholars with quite different positions, such as the mostly conservative Francis Fukuyama and the mostly liberal Julian Savulescu, agree on this (Fukuyama 2012, 165; Savulescu 2012, 201). The broader debate will address how far greater changes should be taken. In any case, human evolution still occurs, with or without conscious human decision, and it is worth remembering debates concerning evolutionary theory, in which proponents of theories of rapid rather than gradual changes, such as Stephen J. Gould, argued that rapid changes in humanity could certainly occur (Wells 2010, 12). Freeman Dyson even speaks of a 'Darwinian interlude' that will be supplanted by an era of culturally driven evolution (Dyson 2008, 6). In this situation, the persuasive, social, critical and imaginative traits of literature and other arts are distinct elements of determining directions for further evolution.[96]

Literary value

The works examined here are just a fraction of those that could have been included in this study, especially since the field of relevant works extends beyond clear-cut instances of changes in human biology, to the dimensions of consciousness and societal change. The patterns that have emerged from the analyses may reflect particular interests, but I believe that some of the conclusions regarding what literature can do with this topic are generally applicable. One central trait reveals a fascination with the various ways in which human change could or already has taken place, but the complexity of existence shows how difficult perfection might be. Instead, the pressure of thinking beyond the human leads to investigations into the finer web of values for which humanity lives.

William Carlos Williams, Virginia Woolf and Louis-Ferdinand Céline make their cases for what might be a more desirable way of existing, in terms of being less subordinate to the cultural patterns of the here and now, and being less estranged from other humans, while having a greater sense of the broader fabric of human culture and the universe as a whole. These three writers let their style and literary strategies reflect those desires, by challenging the relationship between subject and object, by destabilizing the unity of the narrative voice, and by writing very composite works, particularly in the case of Williams. Literature is one medium that can express and help to experience this sense of patterns that exist beyond the human mind,[97] but Céline in particular makes it clear that while there are glimpses of liberation, there is no credible future living up to those glimpses. Yet, it is significant that the hopes for individual transcendence become entangled with the social fabric.

Chinua Achebe, Mo Yan and Orhan Pamuk describe traumatic transitions in ways that show the resistance to grand schemes for new societies, while displaying ambivalence about the new and more complex cultural situations in which they find themselves. For better or worse, though, these new situations are also presented as preferable to what came before. Cultural memory, and often nostalgia, are central to the texts, without being dominant. Instead, they situate human existence in a broader time-frame, and warn against a clean break with the past. The physical experience of the objects of the world and their cultural semiotics, as well as the unchanged human body, provide resistance to the high hopes for changing for society.

An important difference between these three authors is that, while Achebe and Pamuk essentially write about one central conflict of transformation, cultural contact with the West, Mo Yan has no stable situation to refer to, but instead, a series of quite varied and very disruptive events, including the transformation of China into a post-socialist society, along with visions of a biotechnological age, when human change could take place by other means than natural selection. Still, the sense of how change has created hybrid identities is unmistakable in the work of all three writers, and it is accompanied by a sense of a loss of enchantment that the changes have brought about. The conversations with the past take the forms of inclusion of language, photography, old rituals, fairy tales and other ways of incorporating elements that express values that cannot be rationalized and measured, but which form parts of evolving cultures.

Science fiction also struggles to reach a positive posthuman vision, regardless of the kinds of change – realistic as well as unrealistic – it deals with. There is a decisive difference in style and plots between the early generation of writers who imagined physical changes in humans and the newer generation. Thomas Pynchon creates a complex universe entangled with projections regarding the reign of information, which William Gibson made predominant in his *Neuromancer* trilogy. Octavia Butler and Margaret Atwood invoke a post-apocalyptic atmosphere through their complex and opaque narratives, and the information about their new societies is more difficult to grasp than are more traditional ways of presenting an imagined future.

In the works of Don DeLillo and Michel Houellebecq, vivid explorations of current desires are combined with visions of a different future. Their scenarios do not present a perfect future either, but instead, nuanced reflections of how humans are trapped between several situations, none of which is completely desirable. Even then, in both authorships, the everyday, with all its faults, presents itself in various ways as more than desirable, when put into the perspective of future scenarios of radical change.

Houellebecq and DeLillo share a fascination with non-human representations in art works, in computer systems, and in other places where human inventiveness brings about something that estranges humans. This should be seen in connection with the failed hope of envisioning a transcendence of the human condition, and instead seeking refuge in visions of a world without humans. DeLillo and Houellebecq's visions of new states of mind and different conditions for physical existence are eventually chronicled in ways that create a choice between the end of human consciousness, or an acceptance of the imperfect ways in which humans now exist.

Taken together, the works analyzed reveal how literature responds to human change across a range of different modes, all converging on a shared interest in, and engagement with the great challenge of figuring out what it means to be human in a world where the human is both the highest one can aspire to, and something that could be improved. Literature has the capacity to give form to this dilemma, without trying to resolve it, instead showing the many emotions involved in hope for change, as well as for preservation of the status quo. In modern literature, the imperative of innovation furthers this dilemma, which was never as divisive as during High Modernism, when questions of on what the future should be built led to complex reconfigurations of the past.

The theme of the new human creates opportunities for new readings of, and observations about works in which the idea of the new human, or the representation of posthuman beings is not central, but that nevertheless contain elements that relate strongly to these themes. I have made the case for a number of such bodies of work, but would like to mention two others that have potential. One is that of Marcel Proust, where one finds reflections such as that below, which conveys a different sense now, about 100 years after being written. This passage from *In Search of Lost Time* follows a reflection on how other cultures need time to adjust to new artistic expression, which is:

> [...] like a sort of first isolated individual of a species which does not yet exist but is going to multiply in the future, an individual endowed with a kind of *sense* which the human race of his generation does not possess. (Proust 1998, 716)

The rhetoric for trying to describe the transformation of a culture could have been much different, and it need not have invoked 'species', which ups the ante from a merely cultural change, or the atmosphere of a new era or similar. But Proust wrote it as he did, and once it is contextualized in the frame of reference of the new human, it is difficult to not be drawn in by the bold coupling of ideas in his novel.

The work of Jorge Luis Borges, from the middle of the twentieth century, contains fascinating elements that are highly relevant to the current theme, although they cannot be claimed to provide a definitive key to his work. The consequences of having a complete memory, which might characterize an enhanced human or cyborg, is presented as devastating to the ability to live and think, in 'Funes, His Memory'. But Borges also addresses the idea of the new human directly in relation to Nazism, in an analysis that could be said to conflict with the otherwise conservative elements of Nazism, but which Borges interprets as following in 'Deutsche Requiem', from *The Aleph*, of 1949:

> Nazism is intrinsically a *moral* act, a stripping away of the old man, which is corrupt and depraved, in order to put on the new. (Borges 1999, 231)

The references to Nazism continue in 'A Weary Man's Utopia', but with other subtle reflections on how culture could be changed to do away with memories, politics, money and much else that is taken for granted. As in Huxley's work, death would not be tragic, but inevitable, and in this case, would occur as suicide (Borges 1999, 464f.). However, utopias are not the primary visions in Borges' writing; instead, the problem of becoming one with the universe without losing oneself is played out in a number of specific scenarios, thereby conveying a desire expressed by other authors analyzed in this study, most notably Virginia Woolf and Don DeLillo.

Literary history is rewritten time and again, adding new perspectives on the past that are inspired by changes in the present. A current vogue is to focus on how new media make book history relevant to the revision of past histories, just as societal changes were once the primary frame of reference for a new interest in the past. In recent years, globalization has been linked to an interest in world literature, and in expanding and reconfiguring literary canons that took over from postcolonial theory. Part of the interest in ecocriticism hinges on the impact of climate change, and resonates with posthumanism. Just as importantly, changes in fundamental life conditions could turn out to be essential to literary studies, as more literature takes on ethical problems arising from the use of new technologies.

A central point I tried to make in this study is that the many visions of the posthuman resonate with much older desires for a new human. In this respect, the task of literary criticism is to determine what orders in the long history of literature this may disturb, and look back and discover what produces stimulating readings under the new conditions, what interconnects over time and becomes modern again, on its own terms. An element of literary history that cannot be denied is the fascination of observing prophesies and ideas of the future that may not hit the nail on the head, but were at least onto something very important.

Literature will always find itself between desire and concern. It may express hope for new realities, new societies, but it must paint a complete picture of the human, and how body, mind and society constitute it, and in many ways, literature benefits as an art form when pushed to respond to various ideas about, and desires for a new human. Its formal vocabulary is expanded in new modes of narrative and poetry, such as those Woolf and Williams have explored, and in depictions of the universal in the local, as Achebe finds ways to present in his dual perspective on the present. This push toward new forms continues in the oscillations between the imagined future and problematic present, of which Houellebecq makes use, or in the sentences detached from human subjectivity, at which DeLillo excels.

The affective dimension of the motifs of the human and the new human plays a pivotal role in the works studied, regardless of the period they are from. The very idea that humanity is at stake, both as a species and as a privileged being, is an essential part of them. This theme raises the stakes in a way that is akin to what is seen in witness and trauma literature, in which mundane matters of achieving small social gains are put in a different perspective by a fundamental threat to the value of the human being. There will not necessarily be a posthuman future soon, but there surely is a posthuman horizon, and the investigations of the new human in literature are both a literary impulse and a way of facing the desires and anxieties attached to change in the present, as well as in the future. Fortunately, however, the human remains difficult to dethrone as the most incredible creature on Earth, a strange product of evolution that can perceive itself and its fellow humans as paradoxical, as Shakespeare does, in sonnet 130:

> I love to hear her speak, yet well I know
>> That music hath a far more pleasing sound;
> I grant I never saw a goddess go;
>> My mistress, when she walks, treads on the ground.
> And yet, by heaven, I think my love as rare
>> As any she belied with false compare.
> (Shakespeare 1996, 1241)

Bringing value to such a paradox through aesthetics is something literature has achieved again and again, by means of imperfect communication that embraces the complexity and changes in the human condition. If nothing else, the visions of the new human may bring about a re-enchantment of the human.

Notes

1 Posthuman and transhuman are not the same, but obviously related. See Chapter 3 for more on this.

2 There are numerous works dealing with the future of humanity and the impact of technology, such as those of Savulescu (2009), Mehlman (2009), Stock (2002), Brockman (2003), Buchanan (2011a and 2011b), Clark (2003) and Kurzweil (2005).

3 This shows very clearly in this Google ngram: http://books.google. com/ngrams/graph?content=posthuman&year_start=1800&year_ end=2000&corpus=0&smoothing=3 (Accessed on 15 January 2013).

4 Another new term is the 'Anthropocene age', which for geologists indicates that the earth is now influenced by human activity to such an extent that this constitutes an age of its own. This is different from the idea of the posthuman, but still important for recognizing how the human environment is constituted. See http://www.see. ed.ac.uk/~shs/Climate%20change/Geo-politics/Anthropocene%202.pdf (Accessed on 10 February 2013).

5 For a detailed discussion of the political dimension, see Rose (2007), Žižek (2010), Fukuyama (2002 and 2012) and Chan and Harris (2012). On religion and the posthuman, see Water (2006) and Sutton (2008).

6 Such as Vint (2007) and Pordzik (2012).

7 Thanks to Peter C. Kjærgaard for pointing this out.

8 See also Andy Mousley's edited volume, *Towards a New Literary Humanism*.

9 Bioethicist Leon Kass has tried to make the argument for human dignity central, while retaining an idea of the universe that encompasses the grandeur of things not human: 'If all truth is thought of to be merely human creation, there really is no engagement with the truth. If there is no truth beyond that which we have put there, then this project which was meant to produce a home for us against the partial inhospitalities of nature finally makes us strangers in the world and fully alienated from it. / We are home only with our own gadgets. That is not what the human soul longs for'. (Kass 2003, 5) Kass's rhetoric is highly charged, but it captures and diagnoses a central aspect of our time, when consumer society's fascination with new gadgets both demonstrates advanced technology, and flattens and simplifies existence by focusing on short term desires. The question of the posthuman elicits differing perspectives on the value of humanity and the idea of the human. On the one hand, 'the human' presents itself as something both

natural and dignified by its advanced evolution, whose value cannot be relativized, despite all the wrongdoing in the world. The ability to see oneself in the other, and to accept that the individual's value is dependent on acknowledging the value of others, despite any differences, in various ways underlies essential religious and ethical conceptions of the human.

10 For example, see Kwame Anthony Appiah's reflections on how future generations may look back on the present era: http://www.washingtonpost.com/wp-dyn/content/article/2010/09/24/AR2010092404113.html (Accessed on 3 March 2013).

11 And then again: It is likely that the creation of androids, robots that are indistinguishable from humans, is no longer a farfetched idea, and that they could be produced for many different uses, including keeping people company.

12 'Boundless Bodies: 'bio-art' in 2009—or the man with three ears' at http://arcade.stanford.edu/boundless-bodies-bio-art–2009-or-man-three-ears (Accessed on 20 August 2012).

13 Bruce Clarke, Ivan Callus and Stephan Herbrechter are other scholars that draw on Luhmann's work in relation to posthumanism. Luhmann's theory has its own blind spots (Borch 2011, 134ff.). Yet, the core of his theory remains relevant as a challenging contribution to philosophy and social theory, and not least for the way humans are defined.

14 This cycle of replacement is not simple, as Nicholas Wade explains: http://www.nytimes.com/2005/08/02/science/02cell.html?pagewanted=all (Accessed on 3 March 2013).

15 See also Marilyn Robinson's defence of the idea of the mind in *Absence of Mind*.

16 Tellingly, regarding the changing vocabularies of the social sciences and humanities, 'culture' is one of the most significant entries in Raymond Williams' *Keywords*: 'one of the two or three most complicated words in the English language'. (Williams 1976, 87). 'Identity' does not have its own entry, and is used less than a dozen times.

17 Tony Judt argues that 'identity' is a dangerous word that has not had a respectable use in our time (Judt 2010). He worriedly examines the attempts to initiate debates about national identity in France and the Netherlands, among other countries, in part because such attempts to define an identity presuppose an essentialism that has also been left to die on the philosophical battlefields, and in part because personal and collective self-descriptions cross all kinds of borders in the available vocabulary for describing identity. Judt calls those who live between national and collective constructions of identity 'the edge people' (Judt 2010). Overall, the essentialist terms in which nationalism could be expressed and described in public discourse throughout the better part of the twentieth century has gradually waned, and given way to a social constructivist approach, among which systems theory should also be included.

18 Artificial intelligence could eventually challenge this definition.

19 For example, see the chapter on Don DeLillo.

20 In a debate at Aarhus University on 7 May 2010, Fukuyama said that it was more important to help developing countries to solve their problems than to develop advanced technology, for example life-extending genetic engineering that would help relatively few, privileged people in the West. He was contradicted by Julian Savulescu, who correctly noted that many technologies began by being exclusive and for the privileged only, but within a few decades became widely available, even in developing countries. Two examples underscored this, one being the spread of cell phones, which, in about a decade, have revolutionized communication in Africa with the distribution of more than 400 million handsets; the other, that HIV treatments have been extensively distributed, despite initial research costs that patent holders wanted to earn back.

21 Bruno Latour's and Manuel Castells' network theory are other important examples of an understanding of the organization of modern societies that goes beyond the hierarchical.

22 Thanks to Jakob Arnoldi for pointing out that about half of the trades in contemporary stock markets are made by trade robots. See also: http://www.huffingtonpost.com/mark-gongloff/high-frequency-trading-gif_b_1751855.html (Accessed on 7 March 2013).

23 Artists such as Eduardo Kac, Stelarc and Natasha Vita-More are some of the most significant artists working in the field of biotechnology and art. Thanks to Pernille Leth-Espensen and Jacob Wamberg for introducing me to the work of these artists.

24 In some respects, this literature is more complicated than the witness literature of the Holocaust and other mass killings of the twentieth century, because the combination of building a new society while committing atrocities created situations that were very different from the determined, one-sided attempt to annihilate an ethnic group. On the importance of trauma in world literature, see Thomsen (2008).

25 See http://today.msnbc.msn.com/id/28892792/ns/today-today_pets_and_animals/t/couple-spend-clone-dead-dog/#.UESanbLN-z0 (Accessed on 3 September 2012).

26 See http://stelarc.org/?catID=20242 (Accessed on 3 September 2012).

27 To show that he has an open mind, Savulescu also mentions alien life forms (Savulescu 2009, 214).

28 See also Chris Stringer's account of how Homo sapiens ended up as the only hominoid today (2012).

29 As noted before, the cost of technology often falls quickly, e.g. cell phones in Africa, and important medications have become accessible, e.g. HIV medicine.

30 As one group already has, but with little of results for it. See: http://www.cbsnews.com/2100-500202_162-4961152.html (Accessed on 3 March 2013).

31 Huxley describes a process of providing insufficient oxygen to the fetuses as a
    primary technique for producing individuals who will serve without questioning
    their own rights. The interest in the ongoing evolution of humankind was also
    pronounced in his debut as a novelist, *Crome Yellow*: 'Where the great Erasmus
    Darwin and Miss Anna Seward, Swan of Lichfield, experimented—and, for all
    their scientific ardour, failed—our descendants will experiment and succeed.
    An impersonal generation will take the place of Nature's hideous system. In vast
    state incubators, rows upon rows of gravid bottles will supply the world with the
    population it requires. The family system will disappear; society, sapped at its very
    base, will have to find new foundations; and Eros, beautifully and irresponsibly
    free, will flit like a gay butterfly from flower to flower through a sunlit world'.
    (Huxley 1936, 28)
32 Aubrey de Grey is the most outspoken exponent of this modern search for the
    fountain of youth, for example in *Ending Aging: The Rejuvenation Breakthroughs
    That Could Reverse Human Aging in Our Lifetime.*
33 The seventeenth century French writer Cyrano de Bergerac's posthumously
    published *Voyages to the Moon and the Sun* remains an incredible foresighted work
    with its meeting between humans and aliens. This is also where de Bergerac and
    Shelley differ: one establishes a meeting with very different being, the other the
    creation of a new continuation of the human species.
34 The role of animals isalso on the agenda, and it is noteworthy that a prolific young
    author such as Jonathan Safran Foer has written a work of non-fiction concerned
    with the treatment of animals. Human-animal relations are also central to a
    number of Pixar movies; for example, *Ratatouille*, which is not only the title of the
    movie, but also the vegan meal that joins humans – embodied in a Parisian food
    critic – and rats in long-lasting bond.
35 I return to the work of Stapledon in Chapter 11.
36 See Chapter 4 in *Mapping World Literature*, on mass killing.
37 See Hammond's *The World in 2030*, and Kurzweil's *The Singularity is Near*.
38 A counterargument to this logic would be that the first increase has more to do
    with a better distribution of wealth and health care, and that the normal person
    should not expect to live much longer. On the other hand, the number of living
    centenarians has risen remarkably.
39 The structure of this thought is also central to Scientology, which both insists on
    a series of individual developments, which are more easily attained by paying, and
    the existence of entities similar to human souls, 'thetans', that are reborn again and
    again, whereby the static and the dynamic are brought together in an alluring way.
40 As documented in Shuzhuo Li (2007).
41 It is notable that Kant also speculated about the advancement of humanity,
    particularly with regard to the elimination of violence (Kant 1970, 177).

42 This topic is recurrent in the work of Don DeLillo. See the chapter on his work.

43 See http://www.darwinawards.com (Accessed on 21 November 2012).

44 See also Nikos Papastergiadis's thoughtful reflections on hybridity and eugenics (Papastergiadis 2000, 173ff.).

45 There is some irony in the fact that it was eventually revealed that Tiger Woods himself had done more than many to increase the genetic diversity of the human race.

46 John Harris argues for this technique in a commentary: http://www.guardian. co.uk/commentisfree/2012/sep/19/misleading-three-parent-babies-gene-therapy (Accessed on 6 March 2013).

47 For example: http://www.bbc.co.uk/blogs/theeditors/2008/12/changing_attitudes. html (Accessed on 6 March 2013).

48 For example: http://www.embo.org/news-a-media-centre/press-releases/ telomerase-gene-therapy-slows-ageing-improves-health-in-mice.html (Accessed on 6 March 2013).

49 David Ewing Duncan's *When I'm 164* has a very telling title.

50 Hans Ulrich Gumbrecht's *In 1926: Living at the Edge of Time* convincingly shows how the metaphysics of the everyday rely on both binary oppositions and experiencing their breakdown. Such a situation could be described as that of a culture caught in limbo, since it is possible to restore the stability of the oppositions.

51 Harold Bloom sees the strangeness of such works as the determining factor behind their canonical status, not only serving as sources of perpetual interpretation, but also as reflections of the lack of complete knowledge about the self and the universe, which is a human condition.

52 Andreas Huyssen (2003), Jeffrey Olick (2003) and Astrid Erll (2011) have written some of the best accounts of the 'memory boom'.

53 The study of autobiographical memories has given many insights to the structure of individual memory, for example, revealing a 'memory bump' around the formative years between the ages of 15 and 25, when the frequency of memories is particularly high.

54 See also Morris Berman (1981) on the relation between science and enchantment, and During (2002) on re-enchantment in general.

55 See also interview with Oxford philosopher Anders Sandberg: http://www.wired. com/wiredscience/2009/04/memoryedit/ (Accessed on 8 March 2013).

56 See also Richard Rorty's discussion of this in *Contingency, Irony and Solidarity* (1989).

57 See also Thomsen 2008.

58 In *Presents Past*, Huyssen writes extensively on the subject of a new culture, not least the hopes originating from Richard Wagner's *Gesamtkunstwerk* (Huyssen 2003, 43).

59 Thanks to Ane Martine Kjær Lønneker for pointing out this aspect of Virginia Woolf's work.

60 On evolution and enchantment, see also George Levine's *Darwin Loves You* (2008).

61 This is also a theme that Olaf Stapledon explores. See Part IV of this volume.

62 'To a solitary disciple' has been analyzed at length and with great insight in George Lakoff and Mark Turner's *More Than Cool Reason*.

63 Williams' parenthesis.

64 Guevara's status is remarkable, considering the violence he sanctioned, and his role in reforming the Cuban economy in a manner that would have brought the country to the brink of financial ruin, had it not been for substantial foreign aid, makes him at least controversial.

65 A cult-like regime of violence that stands in contrast to the 'boring everyday' is also at the centre of Chuck Palahniuk's *Fight Club*, which revolves around a secret network of fight clubs that could eventually spread, and dominate culture.

66 For example, by the Japanese Nobel laureate, Kenzaburo Oe.

67 In an article in *The Independent*, the London-based Chinese writer Xiaolu Guo defended Mo Yan's choice of writing from within the regime (Xiaolu Guo 2012).

68 In *Mao's Great Famine*, Frank Dikötter has written a thorough account of the many ways the Great Leap Forward produced misery, death and social unrest throughout China. See also Jang Yiseng's *Tombstone: The Great Chinese Famine, 1958–1962*.

69 As documented in Shuzhuo Li's 2007 report for the UN.

70 With great humor, Pamuk also describes his habit of cheering himself up by imagining whole rooms of people with severed heads or otherwise killed, in fantasies of being all-powerful, which he claims he had until his mid-forties (Pamuk 2005, 21).

71 Thanks to Aleksandar Hemon, Sara Tanderup, Johanne Helbo Bøndergaard and Kasper Green Krejberg for sharing their interpretations of the use of photography in W. G. Sebald, Alexander Kluge and Aleksandar Hemon.

72 In Robert A. Heinlein's many stories and novels, space travel plays a central role in the description of the future of humanity, whereas biology means less, although there is a significant interest in prolonging life. In the ingenious *Methuselah's Children*, the Howard lineage attains an average life span of more than 150 years, through selection and mating of individuals with long lives. As they reveal this to the public, they are disbelieved, and they flee the earth in an advanced spaceship that allows them to travel between distant destinations in a very short time. On two other planets they meet humanoid beings, one group of which can genetically change themselves by the force of their minds. When the Howards return to Earth, life extension has become common, and thanks to this and space travel, the solar system is becoming overpopulated.

73 Google ngrams demonstrate these are of recent date, as noted in the Introduction.

74 See: http://sf-encyclopedia.com/entry/posthuman (Accessed on 2 December 2012).

75 Although the world is full of very successful creatures that have not evolved much, such as the great white shark, which has remained virtually unchanged for millions of years.

76 Hilary S. Crew sees the function of the theme of cloning in science fiction, in her perspective on children and adolescents, as furthering reflection on what could be become a reality (Crew 2004, 218).

77 More on this aspect, in the chapter on Michel Houellebecq.

78 A different take on cloning appears in the novel by Swedish author and physician Per Olaf Jersild, *The Return of the Geniuses* (not translated into English). It is an ambitious story of humankind, and the ways people have been able to set new agendas. Going all the way back to the beginnings of humanity in Africa, taking its time to tell about life and conflict in humankind's earliest days, the novel includes Leonardo da Vinci, Charles Darwin and Sigmund Freud among its characters. At the end of the novel, Jersild describes a new society in which these geniuses have been brought back to life, thanks to cloning, but they live in what essentially seems like an unhappy asylum, rather than a playground for best minds ever (Jersild 1987, 394). Jersild's overarching point is that genius is possible at all times, but that it is also time-bound and dependent on context. In his lectures on Darwin, he suggests that, prior to the rise of agrarian societies 10,000 years ago, humans were perfectly adapted and 'fulfilled', and were so for 140,000 years or more (Jersild 1998, 111). Then, with rapid changes in the way of living, the complexities of societies, we were no longer so well-adapted, and our genetics have still not changed sufficiently to create a new sense of completeness and of being adapted to the world.

79 Thanks to Tore Rye Andersen for many helpful comments and references, in particular regarding the works of Pynchon and Gibson.

80 Also see Miguel Nicolelis's attempts to enable communication between brains: http://www.nicolelislab.net/?p=369 (Accessed on 6 March 2013).

81 Corey S. Powell has made a series of predictions about the future, ranging from the nearly certain end to available petroleum, to the highly improbable confirmation of the reality of telepathy. He posits that synthetic telepathy is more likely than unlikely to occur, noting that it would require implants, 'but such implants could soon become common anyway, as people merge their brains with computer data networks'. (Powell 2009, 22).

82 A search for 'immortal' on books.google.com/ngrams shows a steady decline over the past two centuries, but with a slight yet significant trend upward since 2000.

83 This is particularly the case when it comes to the risk of inherited diseases, for example women having their breasts removed in order to avoid cancer.

84 It might just be a coincidence, but at one point DeLillo had a photograph of
    Borges on his desk (Begley 1995).

85 Also published as *Atomised*.

86 Structurally, this solution is the same as the one George Orwell used in *Nineteen
    Eighty-Four*, where there also is a shift from an action-filled and tense main
    section, to a historicizing, essayist mode, which in broad measure describes a
    longer historical development.

87 A recent prediction by Nobel laureate Sir John Gurdon estimates that there will be
    50 to 60 years before human cloning will happen. Source: http://www.telegraph.
    co.uk/science/science-news/9753647/Human-cloning-within–50-years.html
    (Accessed on 14 March 2013).

88 An odd title with little relation to the French original, *Extension de la domaine de
    la lutte*.

89 One of the most memorable scenes, given how much Houellebecq has played
    with an alter ego throughout his novel, is the meeting between Jed and Michel
    Houellebecq, and the very nice atmosphere the self-mocking Houellebecq creates,
    serving good coffee as his strolls around in his corduroy pants.

90 The letter W is also an important intertextual reference to Perec's *W, Or the
    Memory of a Childhood*, which deals with the loss of his parents during the Second
    World War, and his subsequent attempts to understand himself, as well as the logic
    of concentration camps.

91 'Family resemblance', in the sense that Ludwig Wittgenstein used the term to
    designate a group defined by overlapping similarities, but without one common
    denominator.

92 Valerie Solanas's *S.C.U.M. Manifesto* includes a fascinating reflection on why
    humans are still mortal. She claims that ways to do away with death could easily be
    found, because 'the problems with aging and diseases could be solved within a few
    years, if an all-out, massive scientific assault were made on the problem'. (Solanas
    1971, 35), but that the male fear of his own emptiness keeps death around: 'The
    male likes death-it excites him sexually and, already dead inside, he wants to die'.
    (Solanas 1971, 36)

93 The complexity and analog structures of the brain still leave open to question
    whether an upload and recreations of consciousness would be possible, as Miguel
    Nocelelis asserts. Source: http://www.technologyreview.com/view/511421/
    the-brain-is-not-computable (Accessed on 1 March 1 2013).

94 See also Gillian Beer (2000), on the connections between Darwin's theory and
    literary narratives.

95 Nevertheless, one has to take into account the rapidity with which a technology
    can enter the world and produce promising new visions. A few years ago, there
    was no public discourse about self-driving cars. Google's self-driving car and a

number of similar projects have suddenly changed the perspective on what driving may be like in the future. This also produces a positive vision of a technology that would enable many people to get around, who would otherwise be limited by their disabilities, free up time for others, and dramatically reduce the number of traffic fatalities, perhaps even to the extent that human driving could become illegal. It is significant that the self-driving car does not alter the idea of what a human is, which is why it is something that actually generates enthusiasm. It could be a step toward dreams of a future where robots do practically all the work, and humans engage in all kinds of encounters and explorations of human existence. However, even such a premise could quickly develop into something troubling.

96   'Now, after three billion years, the Darwinian interlude is over. It was an interlude between two periods of horizontal gene transfer. The epoch of Darwinian evolution based on competition between species ended about 10,000 years ago, when a single species, Homo sapiens, began to dominate and reorganize the biosphere. Since that time, cultural evolution has replaced biological evolution as the main driving force of change. Cultural evolution is not Darwinian. Cultures spread by horizontal transfer of ideas more than by genetic inheritance. Cultural evolution is running a thousand times faster than Darwinian evolution, taking us into a new era of cultural interdependence which we call globalization. And now, as Homo sapiens domesticates the new biotechnology, we are reviving the ancient pre-Darwinian practice of horizontal gene transfer, moving genes easily from microbes to plants and animals, blurring the boundaries between species. We are moving rapidly into the post-Darwinian era, when species other than our own will no longer exist, and the rules of Open Source sharing will be extended from the exchange of software to the exchange of genes. Then the evolution of life will once again be communal, as it was in the good old days before separate species and intellectual property were invented'. (Dyson 2008, 6)

97   As Dorrit Cohn has shown in great detail in *Transparent Minds*.

Bibliography

Achebe, Chinua (1975). *Morning Yet on Creation Day*. Garden City: Anchor Press.

—(1994). *Things Fall Apart*. London: Heinemann.

—(2009). *The Education of a British-Protected Child*. New York: Alfred A. Knopf.

Alexander, Victoria N. (2006). 'The Whole Creature: Complexity, Biosemiotics and the Evolution of Culture'. *Configurations* 14:1–2.

Almog, Oz (2000). *The Sabra: The Creation of the New Jew*. Berkeley: University of California Press.

Almond, Ian (2003). 'Islam, Melancholy, and Sad, Concrete Minarets: The Futility of Narratives in Orhan Pamuk's *The Black Book*'. *New Literary History* 34:1.

Alt, Herschel and Edith Alt (1964). *The New Soviet Man: His Upbringing and Character Development*. New York: Bookman.

Ankerberg, John and John Weldon (1996). *Encyclopedia of New Age Beliefs*. Eugene: Harvest House Publishers.

Appiah, Kwame Anthony (2005). *The Ethics of Identity*. Princeton: Princeton University Press.

Armstrong, Nancy and Warren Montag (2009). 'The Future of the Human: An Introduction'. *Differences: A Journal of Feminist and Cultural Studies* 20:2–3.

Atwood, Margaret (2003). *Oryx and Crake*. New York: Nan A. Talese.

—(2008). *The Year of the Flood*. New York: Nan A. Talese.

—(2013). *MaddAddam*. London: Bloomsbury.

Badmington, Neil (2010). 'Posthumanism'. In *The Routledge Companion to Literature and Science*, (eds) Bruce Clarke and Manuela Rossini. London and New York: Routledge.

Bak, Per (1997). *How Nature Works: The Science of Self-Organized Criticality*. Oxford: Oxford University Press.

Balzac, Honoré de (2009). *Père Goriot*. Oxford: Oxford University Press.

Barnes, Julian (1990). *History of the World in 10½ Chapters*. London: Picador.

—(2008). *Nothing to be Frightened of*. London: Jonathan Cape.

Bataille, Georges (1933). 'Louis-Ferdinand Céline: Voyage au bout de la nuit'. In *70 critiques de* Voyage au bout de la nuit *1932–1935,* (ed.) André Derval. Paris: Imec.

Beer, Gillian (2000). *Darwin's Plots: Evolutionary Narrative in Darwin, George Eliot and Nineteenth-Century Fiction*. Cambridge: Cambridge University Press.

Begley, Adam (1993). 'Don DeLillo interview'. *The Paris Review* 128.

Bell, David (2007). *Cyberculture Theorists: Manuel Castells and Donna Haraway*. London: Routledge.

Bellos, David. (1993). *Georges Perec: A Life in Words: A Biography*. Boston: D. R. Godine.

Benesch, Klaus (2002). *Romantic Cyborgs: Authorship and Technology in the American Renaissance*. University of Massachusetts Press.

Bennett, Jane (2012). 'Systems and Things: A Response to Graham Harman and Timothy Morton'. *New Literary History* 43.

Bergerac, Cyrano de (1962). *Voyages to the Moon and the Sun*. New York: Orion.

Berman, Morris (1981). *The Reenchantment of the World*. Ithaca: Cornell University Press.

Biro, Matthew (2009). *The Dada Cyborg: Visions of the New Human in Weimar Berlin*. Minneapolis: University of Minnesota Press.

Blair, J. G., and McCormack, J. H. (2006). *Western civilization with Chinese comparisons*. Shanghai: Fudan.

Blazer, Dan G. (2009). 'The Myth, History, and Science of Aging'. In *The America Psychiatric Publishing Textbook Geriatric Psychiatry,* (eds) Dan G. Blazer et al. Arlington: American Psychiatric Publishing.

Bloom, Harold (1994). *The Western Canon: The Books and School of the Ages*. New York: Harcourt Brace.

Bohn, Annette and Dorthe Berntsen (2007). 'Pleasantness bias in flashbulb memories: Positive and negative flashbulb memories of the fall of the Berlin Wall among East and West Germans'. *Memory and Cognition* 35:3.

—(2008). 'Life Story Development in Childhood: The Development of Life Story Abilities and the Acquisition of Cultural Life Scripts from Late Middle Childhood to Adolescence'. *Developmental Psychology* 44.

Borch, Christian (2011). *Niklas Luhmann*. London: Routledge.

Borges, Jorge Luis (1999). *Collected Fictions*. New York: Viking.

Bostrom, Nick (2008). 'Why I Want to be a Posthuman When I Grow Up'. In *Medical Enhancement and Posthumanity,* (eds) B. Gordijn and R. Chadwick. New York: Springer.

—(2009). 'The Future of Humanity'. In *New Waves in Philosophy of Technology,* (eds) Jan-Kyrre Berg Olsen et al. Houndsmill: Palgrave Macmillan.

Bould, Mark and Sherryl Vint, (eds) (2011). *The Routledge Concise History of Science Fiction*. London: Routledge.

Bourdieu, Pierre (1990). *In Other Words: Essays Towards a Reflexive Sociology*. Stanford: Stanford University Press.

Bowen, Donna Lee (1997). 'Islam, Abortion and the 1994 Cairo Population Conference'. *International Journal of Middle Eastern Studies* 29:2.

Breton, André (1972). *Manifestoes of Surrealism*. Ann Arbor: University of Michigan Press.

Brockman, John, (ed.) (ed.) (2003). *The New Humanists: Science at the Edge*. New York: Barnes & Noble.

Brooks, Rodney A. (2002). *Flesh and Machines: How Robots Will Change Us*. New York: Pantheon.

Buchanan, Allen E. (2011a). *Better than human: The promise and perils of enhancing ourselves*. New York: Oxford University Press.

—(2011b). *Beyond humanity? The ethics of biomedical enhancement*. Oxford: Oxford University Press.

Burroughs, William S. (2002). *Junkie*. London: Penguin.

Butler, Octavia (2000). *Lilith's Brood*. New York: Grand Central Publishing.

Butler, Samuel (1949). *Erewhon: Or over the Range*. London: Jonathan Cape.

Caesar, Ed (2010). 'A writer like no other'. *Sunday Times* 20 February 2010.

Carman, Taylor (2012). 'Introduction'. In *Phenomenology of Perception*. London: Routledge.

Carroll, David (1980). *Chinua Achebe* (2nd edion). New York: Palgrave Macmillan.

Carroll, Joseph (2004). *Literary Darwinism: Literature and the Human Animal*. New York: Routledge.

Castells, Manuel (1996). *The Rise of the Network Society*. Malden: Blackwell.

Castree, Noel and Catherine Nash (2006). 'Posthuman geographies'. *Social & Cultural Geography* 7:4.

Céline, Louis-Ferdinand (1964). 'The Art of Fiction'. *The Paris Review* 31.

—(1971). *Death on the Installment Plan*. New York: New Directions.

—(2006). *Journey to the end of the Night*. New York: New Directions.

Chambers, Iain (2001). *Culture after Humanism: History, Culture, Subjectivity*. London: Routledge.

Chan, Sarah and John Harris (2011). 'Post-What? (And Why Does It Matter?', In *The Posthuman Condition*, (eds) Kasper Lippert-Rasmussen et al. Aarhus: Aarhus University Press.

Chan, Shelley W. (2011). *A Subversive Voice in China: The Fictional World of Mo Yan*. Amherst: Cambria.

Cheng, Yinghong (2008). *Creating the 'New Man': From Enlightenment Ideals to Socialist Realities*. Honolulu: University of Hawaii Press.

Clark, Andy (2003). *Natural-born Cyborgs: Minds, Technologies, and the Future of Human Intelligence*. Oxford: Oxford University Press.

—(2008). Supersizing the Mind: Embodiment, Action, and Cognitive Extension. London: Oxford University Press.

Clarke, Arthur C. (2002). *The Collected Stories of Arthur C. Clarke*. New York: Orb Books.

Clarke, Bruce (2008). *Posthuman Metamorphosis: Narrative and Systems*. New York: Fordham University Press.

Codrescu, Andrei (2009). *The Posthuman Dada Guide: Tzara & Lenin play chess*. Princeton: Princeton University Press.

Cohn, Dorrit (1978). *Transparent Minds: Narrative Modes for Presenting Consciousness in Fiction*. Princeton: Princeton University Press.

Colebrook, Claire (2011). 'The Context of Humanism'. *New Literary History* 42:4.

Cowart, David (2003). *Don DeLillo: The Physics of Language*. Athens: University of Georgia Press.

—(2012). 'The Lady Vanishes: Don DeLillo's *Point Omega*'. *Contemporary Literature* 53:1.

Damrosch, David (2007). 'Scriptworlds: Writing Systems and the Formation of World Literature'. *Modern Language Quarterly* 68:2.

Darwin, Charles (1985). *The Origin of Species*. London: Penguin.

Dawkins, Richard (2009a). *The Greatest Show on Earth: The Evidence for Evolution*. New York: Free Press.

—(2009b). 'Breaking the Species Barrier'. In *This Will Change Everything*, (ed.) (ed.) John Brockman. New York: Harper Perennial.

—(2011). *The Magic of Reality: How We Know What's Really True*. New York: Free Press.

De Grey, Aubrey (2007). *Ending Aging: The Rejuvenation Breakthroughs That Could Reverse Human Aging in Our Lifetime*. New York: St. Martin's Press.

DeLillo, Don (1976). *Ratner's Star*. New York: Alfred A. Knopf.

—(1982). *The Names*. New York: Alfred A. Knopf.

—(1985). *White Noise*. New York: Alfred A. Knopf.

—(1997). *Underworld*. New York: Scribner.

—(2001). *The Body Artist*. New York: Scribner.

—(2003). *Cosmopolis*. New York: Scribner.

—(2010). *Point Omega*. New York: Scribner.

Diamond, Jared (1998). *Guns, Germs, and Steel: The Fates of Human Societies*. New York: Norton.

Dick, Philip K. (1999). *Do Androids Dream of Electric Sheep?* London: Millennium.

Dikötter, Frank (2010). *Mao's Great Famine: The History of China's Most Devastating Catastrophe, 1958–1962*. New York: Walker & co.

Dinello, Daniel (2005). *Technophobia! Science Fiction Visions of Posthuman Technology*. Austin: University of Texas Press.

Donald, Merlin (1991). *Origins of the Modern Mind: Three Stages in the Evolution of Culture and Cognition*. Cambridge: Harvard University Press.

—(2001). *A Mind So Rare: The Evolution of Human Consciousness*. Cambridge: Harvard University Press.

Dostoyevsky, Fyodor (1992). *Notes from the Underground*. New York: Bantam Books.

Duncan, David Ewing (2012). *When I'm 164: The New Science of Radical Life Extension, and What Happens If It Succeeds*. Amazon Digital Services.

During, Simon (2002). *Modern Enchantments: The Cultural Power of Secular Magic*. Cambridge: Harvard University Press.

Dyson, Freeman (2008). 'Untitled'. In *Life: What a Concept!*, (ed.) John Brockman. Avaialble at: www.edge.org (Accessed on 20 January 2013).

—(2009). 'Radiotelepathy: Direct Communication from Brain to Brain'. In *This Will Change Everything*, (ed.) John Brockman. New York: Harper Perennial.

Engdahl, Horace, (ed.) (2002). *Witness Literature*. New Jersey: World Scientific.

Enriquez, Juan and Steve Gullans (2010). *Homo Evolutis: Please Meet the Next Human Species*. Kindle.

Erll, Astrid (2011). *Memory in Culture.* Houndsmills: Palgrave Macmillan.

Evans, Arthur B. et al., (eds) (2010). *The Wesleyan Anthology of Science Fiction.* Middletown: Wesleyan University Press.

Fleming, Ian (2002). *Dr No.* New York: Penguin Books.

Foer, Jonathan Safran (2009). *Eating Animals.* New York: Little, Brown.

Foucault, Michel (1984). *The Foucault Reader.* New York: Pantheon.

—(1994). *The Order of Things: An Archaeology of the Human Sciences.* New York: Vintage Books.

Froula, Christine (2005). *Virginia Woolf and the Bloomsbury Avant-Garde: War – Civilization – Modernity.* New York: Columbia University Press.

Fukuyama, Francis (1992). *The End of History and the Last Man.* New York: The Free Press.

— (2002). *Our Posthuman Future: Consequences of the Biotechnology Revolution.* New York: Farrar, Straus and Giroux.

—(2010). 'Nietzsche: A Philosophy in Context'. *The New York Times* 7 May.

—(2012). 'Agency or Inevitabllity: Will Human Beings Control Their Technological Future?' In *The Posthuman Condition*, (eds) Kasper Lippert-Rasmussen et al. Aarhus: Aarhus University Press.

Gao Xingjian (2002). *One Man's Bible.* New York: HarperCollins.

García, José Manuel (2008). 'The New Man in Cuba: Culture and Identity in the Revolution (review)'. *Arizona Journal of Hispanic Cultural Studies* vol. 12.

Geoghegan, Vincent (2005). 'Olaf Stapledon: Utopia and Worship'. *Utopian Studies* 16:3.

Gibson, William (1984). *Neuromancer.* New York: Ace.

—(2003). *Pattern Recognition.* New York: G. P. Putnam's Sons.

Gikandi, Simon (1987). *Reading the African Novel.* Portsmouth: Heinemann.

—(1991). *Reading Chinua Achebe: Language and Ideology in Fiction.* Portsmouth: Heinemann.

Goss, Theodora and John Paul Riquelme (2007). 'From Superhuman to Posthuman: The Gothic Technological Imaginary in Mary Shelley's *Frankenstein* and Octavia Butler's *Xenogenesis*'. *Modern Fiction Studies* 53:3.

Graham, Elaine (2002). *Representations of the Post/Human: Monsters, Aliens, and Others in Popular Culture.* New Brunswick: Rutgers University Press.

Gray, Chris Hables (1995). *The Cyborg Handbook.* New York: Routledge.

—(2012). 'Cyborging the Posthuman: Participatory Evolution'. In *The Posthuman Condition*, (eds) Lippert-Rasmussen, K. et al. Aarhus: Aarhus University Press.

Gray, Rosemary (2013). 'When Chaos Is the God of an Era: Rediscovering an Axis Mundi in Ben Okri's *Starbook* (2007)'. *Research in African Literatures* 44:1.

Greenblatt, Stephen (1980). *Renaissance Self-Fashioning.* Chicago: University of Chicago Press.

Guevara, Ernesto Che (2009). *Socialism and Man in Cuba.* New York: Pathfinder.

Gumbrecht, Hans Ulrich (1997). *In 1926: Living at the Edge of Time.* Cambridge: Harvard University Press.

—(2004). *Production of Presence: What Meaning Cannot Convey.* Stanford: Stanford University Press.

—(2006). *In Praise of Athletic Beauty.* Cambridge: Harvard University Press.

Gumbrecht, Hans Ulrich et al.. (2011). *What is Life? The Intellectual Pertinence of Erwin Schrödinger.* Stanford: Stanford University Press.

Habermas, Jürgen (2003). *The Future of Human Nature.* Cambridge: Polity.

Halberstam, Jürgen (1995). 'Introduction: Posthuman Bodies'. In *Posthuman Bodies,* (eds) Jürgen Halberstam et al.. Bloomington: Indiana University Press.

Halbwachs, Maurice (1992). *On Collective Memory.* Chicago: University of Chicago Press.

Hall, John R. (2004). *Gone from the Promised Land: Jonestown in American Cultural History.* New Brunswick: Transaction.

Halter, Peter (1994). *The Revolution in the Visual Arts and the Poetry of William Carlos Williams.* Cambridge: Cambridge University Press.

Hamilton, Edmond (2010). 'The Man Who Evolved'. In *The Wesleyan Anthology of Science Fiction,* (eds) Arthur B. Evans et al.. Middletown: Wesleyan University Press.

Hammond, Ray (2012). *The World in 2030.* http://www.rayhammond.com/The%20 World%20In%202030.html. (Accessed on 16 December 2012).

Hanlon, Michael (2012). 'Three-parent IVF is a chance to create a generation free from mitochondrial diseases'. *The Daily Telegraph* 17 September 2012.

Haraway, Donna (2004). *The Haraway Reader.* New York, Routledge.

—(2006). 'Encounters with Companion Species: Entangling Dogs, Baboons, Philosophers, and Biologists'. *Configurations* 14:1.

—(2007). *When Species Meet.* Minneapolis: University of Minnesota Press.

Harris, John (2011). 'Moral Enhancement and Freedom'. *Bioethics* 25:2.

Harris, Judith Rich (2006). 'Untitled'. In *What I Believe but Cannot Prove,* (ed.) John Brockman. New York: Harper Perennial.

Hassan, Ihab (1971). 'POSTmodernISM'. *New Literary History* 3:1.

—(1977). 'Prometheus as Performer: Toward a Posthumanist Culture?' In *Performance in postmodern culture,* (eds) Michel Benamou and Charles Caramello. Madison: Coda.

Hayles, N. Katherine (1999). *How We Became Posthuman: Virtual Bodies in Cybernetics, Literature, and Informatics.* Chicago: University of Chicago Press.

—(2002). 'Flesh and Metal: Reconfiguring the Mindbody in Virtual Environments'. *Configurations* 10.

—(2010) '*How We Became Posthuman:* Ten Years On. An Interview N. Katherine Hayles'. *Paragraph* 33:3.

Heinlein, Robert A. (1958). *Methuselah's Children.* New York: New American Library.

Hellbeck, Jochen (2006). *Revolution on my Mind: Writing a Diary under Stalin.* Cambridge: Harvard University Press.

Herbrechter, Stephan and Ivan Callus (2008). 'What is a posthumanist reading?'. *Angelaki* 13:1.

—(2009). *Cy-Borges: Memories of the Posthuman in the Work of Jorge Luis Borges.* Lewisburg: Bucknell University Press.

Hessler, Peter (2009). 'Chinese Barbizon: Painting the Outside World'. *The New Yorker* 26 October.

Hewitt, Nicholas (1999). *The Life of Céline: A Critical Biography.* Oxford: Blackwell.

Hillis, W. Daniel (2009). 'A Forebrain for the World Mind'. In *This Will Change Everything,* (ed.) John Brockman. New York: Harper Perennial.

Hollinger, Veronica (2009). 'Postmodernism and Cyborg Theory'. In *The Routledge Companion to Science Fiction,* (eds) Mark Bould et al. London: Routledge.

Hoogheem, Andrew (2012). 'Secular Apocalypses: Darwinian Criticism and Atwoodian Floods'. *Mosaic* 5:2.

Houellebecq, Michel (2003). *The Elementary Particles.* New York: Alfred A. Knopf.

—(2003) 'Why I want to be cloned'. *The Guardian* 1 January.

—(2004). *Platform.* New York: Vintage.

—(2005). *The Possibility of an Island.* New York: Alfred A. Knopf.

—(2012). *The Map and the Territory.* New York, Alfred A. Knopf.

Huang, Alexander C. Y. (2009). 'Mo Yan as Humorist'. *World Literature Today* 83:4.

Huxley, Aldous (1936). *Crome Yellow.* London: Penguin.

—(2005). *Brave New World and Brave New World Revisited.* London: Harper Perennial.

Huyssen, Andreas (2003). *Presents Past: Urban Palimpsests and the Politics of Memory.* Stanford: Stanford University Press.

—(2004). 'Urban Experience and the Modernist Dream of a New Language'. In *A New History German Literature,* (eds) David E. Wellbery et al. Cambridge: Harvard University Press.

Ishiguro, Kazuo (1989). *The Remains of the Day.* London: Faber and Faber.

—(2005). *Never Let Me Go.* New York: Alfred A. Knopf.

Jacobsen, Jens Peter (1993). *Lyrik og prosa.* Holstebro: Borgen.

Jameson, Fredric (2005). *Archaeologies of the Future: The Desire Called Utopia and other Science Fictions.* New York: Verso.

Jang Yiseng (2012). *Tombstone: The Great Chinese Famine, 1958–1962.* New York: Farrar, Straus, and Giroux.

Jenkins, Gareth (2011). 'Culture and multiculturalism'. *International Socialism* 131.

Jensen, Johannes V. (1992). *The Fall of the King.* Seattle: Mermaid Press.

Jersild, P. C. (1987). *Geniernas Återkomst.* Stockholm: Bonniers.

—(1998). *Darwins ufuldendte.* Copenhagen: Samleren.

Joas, Hans and Wolfgang Knöbl (2009). *Social Theory: Twenty Introductory Lectures.* Cambridge: Cambridge University Press.

Joy, Eileen A. and Craig Dionne (2010). 'Editor's Introduction'. *Postmedieval* 1:1–2.

Joyce, James (1996). *Dubliners.* New York: Viking.

Judt, Tony (2005). *Postwar: A History of Europe since 1945.* New York: Penguin.

—(2010). 'Edge People'. *The New York Review of Books* 25 March.

Jünger, Ernst (2004). *Storm of Steel.* New York: Penguin.

Kant, Immanuel (1991). *Kant: Political Writings*. Cambridge: Cambridge University Press.

Kass, Leon (2002). *Life, Liberty and the Defense of Dignity: The Challenge for Bioethics*. San Francisco: Encounter Books.

Krause, Marcus and Nicolas Pethes (2007). *Mr. Münsterberg und Dr Hyde: Zur Filmgeschichte des Menschensexperiments*. Bielefeld: Transcript.

Kurzweil, Ray (1999). *The Age of Spiritual Machines: When Computers Exceed Human Intelligence*. New York: Viking.

—(2005). *The Singularity Is Near: When Humans Transcend Biology*. New York: Viking.

—(2012). *How to Create a Mind: The Secret of Human Thought Revealed*. New York: Viking.

Lakoff, George and Mark Turner (1989). *More Than Cool Reason: A Field Guide to Poetic Metaphor*. Chicago: University of Chicago Press.

Lander, Eric S. (2011). 'Initial impact of the sequencing of the human genome'. *Nature* 470.

Landy, Joshua and Michael Saler, (eds) (2009). *The Re-Enchantment of the World: Secular Magic in a Rational Age*. Stanford: Stanford University Press.

Latour, Bruno (1993). *We Have Never Been Modern*. Cambridge: Harvard University Press.

LeClair, Thomas (1987). *In the Loop: Don DeLillo and the Systems Novel*. Urbana: University of Illinois Press.

—(2005). 'An Interview with Don DeLillo'. In *Conversations with Don DeLillo*, (ed.) Thomas DePietro. Jackson: University of Misssisippi Press.

Lenoir, Timothy (2002). 'Makeover: Writing the Body into the Posthuman Technoscape'. *Configurations* 10:2.

Lévi-Strauss, Claude (1993). 'L.-F. Céline: Voyage au bout de la nuit'. In *70 critiques de Voyage au bout de la nuit: 1932–1935*, (ed.) André Derval. Paris: IMEC.

Levine, G. L. (2006*). Darwin loves you: Natural selection and the re-enchantment of the world*. Princeton: Princeton University Press.

Lewis, Pericles (2010). *Religious Experience and the Modernist Novel*. Cambridge: Cambridge University Press.

Lightman, Alan (1993). *Einstein's Dreams*. New York: Pantheon.

Locke, Alain (1997). *The New Negro*. New York: Simon & Schuster.

Love, Jean O. (1979). 'Orlando and Its Genesis: Venturing and Experimenting in Art, Love, and Sex'. I: *Virginia Woolf: Revaluations and Continuity*, (ed.) Ralph Freedman. Berkeley: University of California Press.

Lu Xun (2009). *The Real Story of Ah-Q and other Tales of China: The Complete Fiction of Lu Xun*. London: Penguin Books.

Luhmann, Niklas (1990). *Essays on Self-Reference*. New York: Columbia University Press.

—(1995). *Social Systems*. Stanford: Stanford University Press.

—(1997). *Die Gesellschaft der Gesellschaft*. Frankfurt am Main: Suhrkamp.

Lukács, Georg (1971). *The Theory of the Novel: A Historico-Philosophical Essay on the Forms of Great Epic Literature*. London: Merlin Press.

Mao Zedong (1996). 'Talks at the Yan'an conference on literature and art'. In *Modern Chinese Literary Thought*, (ed.) Kirk A. Denton. Stanford: Stanford University Press.

Marinetti, Filippo Tommaso (1998). 'The Founding and Manifesto of Futurism 1909'. In *Modernism: An Anthology of Sources and Documents*, (eds) Vassiliki Kolocotroni et al. Edinburgh: Edinburgh University Press.

McLuhan, Marshall (1994) *Understanding Media: The Extensions of Man*. Cambridge: MIT Press.

—(2011) 'Pattern Recognition. Probes and Idea'. At http://www.mcluhanstudies.com/index.php?option=com_content&view=article&catid=98&id=489 (Accessed on 9 March 2013).

Mehlman, Maxwell (2009). *The Price of Perfection*. Baltimore: Johns Hopkins University Press.

—(2012). 'How Close Are We to Being Able to Achieve the Transhumanist Vision?' In *The Posthuman Condition*, (eds) Kasper Lippert-Rasmussen et al. Aarhus: Aarhus University Press.

Mendelsohn, Daniel (2010). 'The Wizard'. *The New York Review of Books* 25 March.

Metzner, Elke and Roman Lesmeister (2001). 'Der neue Mensch'. *Analytische Psychologie* 32:2.

Miccoli, Anthony (2010). *Posthuman Suffering and the Technological Embrace*. Lanham: Lexington.

Mo Yan (1993). *Red Sorghum*. New York: Viking.

—(2000). *The Republic of Wine: A Novel*. New York: Arcade.

—(2001). *Shifu, You'll Do Anything For A Laugh*. New York: Arcade.

—(2006). *The Garlic Ballads*. London: Methuen.

—(2008). *Life and Death are Wearing Me Out*. New York: Arcade.

Moeller, Hans-Georg (2006). *Luhmann Explained: From Souls to Systems*. Chicago: Open Court.

Moretti, Franco (1988). *Signs Taken for Wonders* 2nd edition. London: Verso.

—(1996) *Modern Epic: The World-System from Goethe to García Márquez*. London: Verso.

—(2006). 'Evolution, World-Systems, Weltliteratur'. *Studying Transcultural Literary History*, (ed.) Gunilla Lindberg-Wada. Berlin: Walter de Gruyter.

Mousley, Andy (2010). 'Limits, Limitlessness and the Politics of the (Post)human'. *Postmedieval* 1:1–2.

—(ed.) (2011). *Towards a New Literary Humanism*. London: Palgrave Macmillan.

Musil, Robert (1994). *The Man without Qualities* vol. I. New York: Vintage Books.

Naremore, James (1973). *The World Without a Self: Virginia Woolf and the Novel*. New Haven: Yale University Press.

Nietzsche, Friedrich (1968). *The Will to Power*. New York: Vintage Books.

—(2006). *Thus Spoke Zarathustra*. Cambridge: Cambridge University Press.

Ogede, Ode (2007). *Achebe's Things Fall Apart*. London: Continuum.

Okri, Ben (1991). *The Famished Road*. London: Jonathan Cape.

—(2007). *Starbook: A magical tale of love and regeneration*. London: Rider.

Olick, Jeffrey (2003). *States of Memory: Continuities, Conflicts, and Transformations in National Introspection*. Durham: Duke University Press.

Olick, Jeffrey K. et al. (eds) (2011) *The Collective Memory Reader*. Oxford: Oxford University Press.

Orwell, George (1987). *Nineteen Eighty-Four*. London: Penguin.

Padura, Leonardo (2005). *Havana Red*. London: Bitter Lemon Press.

Palahniuk, Chuck (1996). *Fight Club*. New York: Norton.

Palencia-Roth, Michael (1985). 'Cannibalism and the New Man of Latin America in the 15th-and 16th-century European Imagination'. *The Comparative Civilizations Review* 12.

Pamuk, Orhan (1997). *The New Life*. New York: Farrar, Straus, and Giroux.

—(2004). *Snow*. New York: Vintage Books.

—(2005). *Istanbul: Memories and the City*. New York: Knopf.

—(2006). *The Black Book*. New York: Vintage Books.

—(2007). *Other Colors: Essays and a story*. New York: Alfred A. Knopf.

—(2011). *The Naïve and the Sentimental Novelist*. New York: Vintage Books.

Papastergiadis, Nikos (2000). *The Turbulence of Migration*. Cambridge: Polity.

Perec, Georges (1988). *W, or, The Memory of Childhood*. Boston: D. R. Godine.

—(1992). *Life: A User's Manual*. Boston: D. R. Godine.

Persson, Ingmar and Julian Savulescu (2008). 'The Perils of Cognitive Enhancement and the Urgent Imperative to Enhance the Moral Character of Humanity'. *Journal of Applied Philosophy* 25:3.

Pethes, Nicolas (2005). 'Terminal Men. Biotechnical Experimentation and the Reshaping of 'the Human' in Medical Thrillers'. *New Literary History* 36:2.

—(2007). *Zöglinge der Natur. Der literarische Menschenversuch des 18. Jahrhunderts*. Göttingen: Wallstein.

Pethes, Nicolas et al., (eds) (2008). *Menschenversuche. Eine Anthologie 1750–2000*. Frankfurt am Main: Suhrkamp.

Pinker, Steven (2002). *The Blank Slate: The Modern Denial of Human Nature*. New York: Viking.

—(2011). *The Better Angels of Our Nature: Why Violence has Declined*. New York: Viking.

Pordzik, Ralph (2012). 'The Posthuman Future of Man: Anthropocentrism and the Other of Technology in Anglo-American Science Fiction'. *Utopian Studies* 23:1.

Powell, Corey S. (2009). 'Slippery Expectations'. In *This Will Change Everything*, (ed.) John Brockman. New York: Harper Perennial.

Powers, Richard (2009). 'Foreword'. In Don DeLillo: *White Noise*. New York: Penguin.

Proust, Marcel (1998). *In Search of Lost Time: The Guermantes Way*. New York: Modern Library.

Pynchon, Thomas (1973). *Gravity's Rainbow.* New York: Viking.

—(1984). 'Is it O.K. to be a luddite?' *New York Times* 28 October.

Resnik, David B. (2000). 'The Moral Significance of the Therapy-Enhancement Distinction in Human Genetics'. *Cambridge Quarterly of Healthcare Ethics* 9.

Richardson, John (2008). *Nietzsche's New Darwinism.* Oxford: Oxford University Press.

Rilke, Rainer Maria (1983). *The Notebooks of Malte Laurids Brigge.* New York: Random House.

Risse, Thomas and Stephen C. Ropp, (1999). 'International human rights norms and domestic change: conclusions'. In *The Power of Human Rights: International Norms and Domestic Change,* (eds) Thomas Risse et al.. Cambridge: Cambridge University Press.

Robinson, Marilyn (2010). *Absence of Mind: The Dispelling of Inwardness from the Modern Myth of the Self.* New Haven: Yale University Press.

Rorty, Richard (1989). *Contingency, Irony, and Solidarity.* Cambridge: Cambridge University Press.

Rose, Nikolas (2007). *Politics of Life Itself: Biomedicine, Power, and Subjectivity in the Twenty-First Century.* Princeton: Princeton University Press.

Rushdie, Salman (1991). *Imaginary Homelands.* London: Granta.

Saler, Michael (2012). *As if: Modern Enchantment and the Literary Pre-History of Virtual Reality.* Oxford: Oxford University Press.

Salewski, Michael (1986). *Zeitgeist und Zeitmaschine. Science Fiction und Geschichte.* München: Deutscher Taschenbuch Verlag.

Sandberg, Anders and Nick Bostrom (2006). 'Converging Cognitive Enhancements'. In *Annals New York Academy of Sciences.*

Sandel, Michael J. (2007). *The Case against Perfection: Ethics in the Age of Genetic Engineering.* Cambridge: Belknap Press.

Santesso, Z. Esra Mirze (2011). 'Vision and Representation: Photography in Orhan Pamuk's Istanbul: Memories and the City'. *The Comparatist* 35: May 2011.

Saramago, José (2008). *Death with Interruptions.* Orlando: Harcourt.

Savulescu, Julian (2009). 'The Human Prejudice and the Moral Status of Enhanced Being: What Do We Owe the Gods?' In *Human Enhancement,* (eds) Julian Savulescu and Nick Bostrom. Oxford: Oxford University Press.

—(2012). 'Enhancing Equality'. *The Posthuman Condition,* (eds) Kasper Lippert-Rasmussen et al. Aarhus: Aarhus Univeristy Press.

Schaller, Al (2009). 'Pursuit of the 'New Man' in Edmundo Desnoes' *Memories of Underdevelopment'.* Hispanófila 155.

Scheider, Joseph (2005). *Donna Haraway: Live Theory.* London: Continuum.

Schmitt, Carl (2003). *The Nomos of the Earth in the International Law of the Jus Publicum Europaeum.* New York: Telos Press.

Schuster, Joshua (2007). 'William Carlos Williams, *Spring and All*, and the Anthropological Imaginary'. *Journal of Modern Literature* 30:3.

Schwartz, Paul (1988). *Georges Perec: Traces of his Passage.* Birmingham: Summa Publications.

Seed, David, (ed.) (2005). *A Companion to Science Fiction*. Malden: Blackwell.

Seel, Martin (2009). *Theorien*. Frankfurt am Main: S. Fischer Verlag.

Serra, Ana (2007). *The 'New Man' in Cuba: Culture and Identity in the Revolution*. Gainesville: University Press of Florida.

Shakespeare, William (1996). *Complete Works of William Shakespeare*. Oxford: Wordsworth.

Shelley, Mary (1965). *The Last Man*. Lincoln: University of Nebraska Press.

—(2000). *Frankenstein*. Boston: Bedford/St. Martin's.

Shuzhuo Li (2007). *Imbalanced Sex Ratio at Birth and Comprehensive Intervention in China*. 4th Asia Pacific Conference on Reproductive and Sexual Health and Rights, 29–31 October. Hyderabad, India.

Simpson, David (2009). *Post-Human*. Bloomington: iUniverse.

Smith, Rachel Greenwald (2009). 'Ecology Beyond Ecology: Life After the Accident in Octavia Butler's Xenogenesis Trilogy'. *Modern Fiction Studies* 55:3.

Snyder, Katherine V. (2011). ''Time to go': The Post-Apocalyptic and the Post-Traumatic in Margaret Atwood's *Oryx and Crake*'. *Studies in the Novel* 43:4.

Solanas, Valerie (1971). *S.C.U.M. Manifesto*. London: Olympia Press.

Solomon, Don (2007). 'Interview with N. Katherine Hayles: Preparing the Humanities for the Post Human'. http://onthehuman.org/archive/more/interview-with-n-katherine-hayles/ (Accessed on 6 March 2013).

Spengler, Oswald (1966). *The Decline of the West*. New York: Alfred A. Knopf.

Stapledon, Olaf (1930). *Last and First Men: A Story of the Near and Far Future*. London: Methuen.

—(1937). *Starmaker*. London: Methuen.

Stevenson, Robert Louis (2008). *Strange Case of Dr Jekyll and Mr Hyde and Other Tales*. Oxford: Oxford University Press.

Stock, Gregory (2002). *Redesigning Humans: Our Inevitable Genetic Future*. Boston: Houghton Mifflin.

Stringer, Chris (2012). *Lone Survivors: How We Came to be the Only Humans on Earth*. New York: Henry Holt.

Sturgeon, Theodore (1953). *More Than Human*. New York: Farrar, Straus and Young.

Sturrock, John (1990). *Louis-Ferdinand Céline: Journey to the End of the Night*. Cambridge: Cambridge University Press.

Swift, Jonathan (2011). *Gulliver's Travels*. USA: Simon & Brown.

Tally, Robert T. (2011). *Kurt Vonnegut and the American Novel: A Postmodern Iconography*. London: Continuum.

Tanner, Tony (2000). *The American Mystery: American Literature from Emerson to DeLillo*. Cambridge: Cambridge University Press.

Theweleit, Klaus (2010). 'Menschliche Drohnen'. *Der Spiegel* 9.

Thomsen, Mads Rosendahl (2008). *Mapping World Literature: International Canonization and Transnational Literatures*. London: Continuum.

—(2010). 'Subversive Foundations: Renaissance Classics and the Imported Canon'. In *Foundational Texts of World Literature,* (ed.) Dominique Jullien. New York: Peter Lang.

—(2012). 'Three Ways of Changes: The New Human in Literature'. In *The Posthuman Condition,* (eds) Kasper Lippert-Rasmussen et al. Aarhus: Aarhus University Press.

Todorov, Tzvetan (2002). *The Imperfect Garden: The Legacy of Humanism*. Princeton: Princeton University Press.

Trotsky, Leon (1960). *Literature and Revolution*. Ann Arbour: University of Michigan Press.

Turney, Jon (1998). *Frankenstein's Footsteps: Science, Genetics and Popular Culture*. New Haven: Yale University Press.

Ungaretti, Giuseppe (1994). *Vita d'un uomo: Tutte le poesie*. Milano: Mondadori.

Vance, Ashlee (2010). 'Merely Human? That's So Yesterday'. *The New York Times* 12 June.

Vint, Sherryl (2007). *Bodies of Tomorrow: Technology, Subjectivity, Science Fiction*. Toronto: University of Toronto Press.

—(2008). 'Embodied texts, embodied subjects: an overview of N. Katherine Hayles'. *Science Fiction Film and Television* 1:1.

—(2009). 'Simians, subjectivity and sociality: 2001: A Space Odyssey and two versions of Planet of the Apes'. *Science Fiction Film and Television* 2:2.

Vonnegut, Kurt (1969). *Slaughterhouse-Five; or, The Children's Crusade, a Duty-Dance with Death*. New York: Delacorte Press.

—(1985). *Galápagos*. New York: Delacorte Press.

Wade, Nicholas (2006). *Before the Dawn: Recovering the Lost History of our Ancestors*. New York: Penguin.

Wallace, Jeff (2005). *D.H. Lawrence, Science and the Posthuman*. Houndmills: Palgrave.

Waters, Brent (2006). *From Human to Posthuman: Christian Theology and Technology in a Postmodern World*. Aldershot: Ashgate.

Watson, Peter (2001). *The Modern Mind: An Intellectual History of the 20th century*. New York: Perennial.

Wehm, M. Darusha (2007). *Beautiful Red*. Self-published.

Weisman, Alan (2007). *The World without Us*. New York: Thomas Dunne Books.

Wells, H. G. (1965) *The Time Machine*. London: Heinemann.

—(1970). *The Complete Short Stories of H. G. Wells*. London: E. Benn.

—(2005). *A Modern Utopia*. London: Penguin.

Wells, Spencer (2002). *The Journey of Man: A Genetic Odyssey*. Princeton: Princeton University Press.

—(2006). *Deep Ancestry: Inside the Genographic Project*. Washington: National Geographic.

—(2010). *Pandora's Seed: Why the Hunter-Gatherer Holds the Key to our Survival*. New York: Random House.

Whitehead, Anne (2011). 'Writing with Care: Kazuo Ishiguro's *Never Let Me Go*'. *Contemporary Literature* 52:1.

Whitworth, Michael H. (2005). *Virginia Woolf.* Oxford: Oxford University Press.

Wiener, Norbert (1954). *The Human Use of Human Beings: Cybernetics and Society.* Garden City: Doubleday.

Wilde, Oscar (2001). *The Soul of Man under Socialism and Selected Critical Prose.* London: Penguin.

—(2007). *The Collected Works of Oscar Wilde.* London: Wordsworths Edition.

Williams, Raymond (1976). *Keywords.* London: Fontana.

Williams, William Carlos (1986). *The Collected Poems of William Carlos Williams,* vol. 1. New York: New Directions.

—(1988). *The Collected Poems of William Carlos Williams,* vol. 2. New York: New Directions.

Wittgenstein, Ludwig (1997). *Philosophical Investigations.* Oxford: Blackwell.

Wolfe, Cary (2003). *Animal Rites: American Culture, the Discourse of the Species, and Posthumanist Theory.* Chicago, IL: University of Chicago Press.

—(2010). *What is Posthumanism?.* Minneapolis: University of Minnesota Press.

Woolf, Virginia (1964). *Mrs Dalloway.* London: Penguin.

—(1966a). *Collected Essays* vol. 1. London: Hogarth Press.

—(1966b). *Collected Essays* vol. 2. London: Hogarth Press.

—(1980). *The Diary* vol. 3. London: Hogarth Press.

—(1990). *Orlando.* New York: Harcourt Brace.

—(1992). *Jacob's Room.* London: Penguin.

—(1993). *The Waves.* Oxford: Blackwell.

—(2002). *Moments of Being.* London: Pimlico.

Wren, Robert M. (1981). *Achebe's World: The Historical and Cultural Context of the Novels of Chinua Achebe.* Harlow: Longman.

Xiaolu Guo (2012). 'Great art behind an iron curtain: Are all Chinese novelists 'state writers'. *The Independent* 15 December.

Yang Jisheng (2012). *Tombstone: The Great Chinese Famine 1958–1962.* New York: Farrar, Straus and Giroux.

Youngquist, Paul (2011). 'The Mothership Connection'. *Cultural Critique* 77.

Zimmerman, Michael E. (2008). 'The Singularity: A Crucial Phase in Divine Self-Actualization?' *Cosmos and History: The Journal of Natural and Social Philosophy* 4:1–2.

Žižek, Slavoj (2010). *Living in the End Times.* London: Verso.

Zürcher, Erik J. (2004). *Turkey: A Modern History.* London: Tauris.

Index